PELICAN BOOK A759

KT-140-091

A History of
English Architecture

Peter Kidson was born at York in 1925. He was educated at Cambridge, reading History and Moral Sciences, and the Courtauld Institute of Art, where he wrote his doctorate thesis on Early Medieval Architecture. Dr Kidson is now Conway Librarian at the Courtauld Institute. In 1959 he published *Sculpture at Chartres*.

Peter Murray is a lecturer at the Courtauld Institute and also does part-time teaching at Birkbeck College. Born in London in 1920, he studied at the Slade School before the war and afterwards at the Courtauld Institute, where he took his degree in 1947. He held the post of Witt Librarian there for thirteen years. In collaboration with his wife, Dr Murray wrote *The Penguin Dictionary of Art and Artists* and *The Art of the Renaissance*. He has also published *The Architecture of the Italian Renaissance* (1963) and other books and articles.

Paul Thompson was born in 1935 and educated at Oxford, where he wrote a thesis on London working-class politics. He is now a lecturer in Social History at the University of Essex. His interest in architecture is centred on periods of controversy – such as the aesthetic conflicts of the Victorians and the functional conflicts of today. He has written a biography of William Morris and articles on the architecture of William Butterfield; he organizes conferences for the Victorian Society. He has also published a Young Fabian pamphlet, *Architecture: Art or Social Service?* He is married, with one son.

PETER KIDSON, PETER MURRAY,
AND PAUL THOMPSON

A History of English Architecture

Revised edition for Penguin Books
179 illustrations

PENGUIN BOOKS

Penguin Books Ltd, Harmondsworth, Middlesex, England
Penguin Books Pty Ltd, Ringwood, Victoria, Australia

First published by Harrap 1962. Published in Pelican Books 1965
Copyright © Peter Kidson and Peter Murray, 1962. Copyright © Paul Thompson, 1965

Made and printed by Brightype litho in Great Britain at Taylor Garnett Evans & Co Ltd,
Watford, Herts
Set in Monotype Times

Parts I and II of this book were originally published under the present title by Harrap.
Part III has been specially written for the Pelican edition to replace Chapter 7 of that book.
The overall number of illustrations has been increased by fifty per cent; there is a new,
illustrated Glossary.

Contents

Part III

BY PAUL THOMPSON

List of Illustrations

1

Acknowledgements

Peter Kidson and Peter Murray wish to thank Dr Margaret Whinney, who read one whole section of the book in typescript, and who made a large number of improvements, which are most gratefully acknowledged. They further wish to thank Miss J. Allday, Miss M. Mount, Mr G. McIntosh, and Mr H. Murray, who read the proofs.

Paul Thompson would like to acknowledge the helpful criticisms he received from Professor Nikolaus Pevsner, Royston Lambert, and Thea Thompson.

Plates 68 and 70 in this book are reproduced by gracious permission of Her Majesty the Queen. Permission to reproduce other illustrations has been given by the following: T. & R. Annan & Sons, Ltd, 147, 157, 161; *Architects' Journal*, 163, 174; *Architectural Design*, 172, 176; Architectural Press, 106 (detail from drawing by R. B. Brook-Greaves and W. Godfrey Allen); *Architectural Review*, 141, 142, 146, 169, 178; the Governor and Company of the Bank of England, 133; Barber Institute of Fine Arts and Dr K. Downes, 135; J. Bony, 16; Brecht-Einzig, 173; Brentford and Chiswick Public Libraries, 118; Brighton Corporation, 139; British Transport Commission, Historical Relics Section, 143; Sir John Burnet, Tait, & Partners, 167; Central Electricity Generating Board, 171; Central Press Photos, Ltd, 69; Country Life, Ltd, 78, 88, 119, 120, 124, 125, 128, 130, 156, 165; Courtauld Institute of Art, 3, 4, 12 (by Thomas Britton), 17 (by Thomas Britton), 19, 21, 27, 31, 32, 36, 37, 41 (by John Britton), 42, 43 (by John Britton), 46, 49, 51, 52, 56, 59, 65, 72, 91, 95, 96, 97, 99, 100, 101, 102, 105 (aquatint by T. Malton), 108, 109, 113, 123, 129, 131 (by John Britton), 134, 137; F. H. Crossley, 6, 11, 18, 22, 24, 25, 34, 38, 39, 45, 47, 48, 50; Fox Photos, Ltd, 145; the *Guardian*, 177; Her Majesty's Stationery Office (Crown Copyright), 73, 84, 86, 107, 117; A. F. Kersting, 28, 44, 53, 60, 62, 111, 115, 121, 122, 150; L.C.C. Photograph Library, 149; National Buildings Record, 5, 7, 9, 13, 14, 20, 23, 30, 35, 55, 57, 61, 63, 66, 70, 77, 104, 116, 132, 133, 136, 151, 152, 158, 164; National Coal Board, 168; Nottingham City Corporation, 75; Nottinghamshire County Council, 179; Professor Nikolaus Pevsner, 148, 159, 160, 162; Photo Precision, Ltd, 80, 98; Pitkin Pictorials Ltd, 114; Pyroc, 170;

Note to the Reader

It should be pointed out that in many cases a single date has been assigned to a building with an obscure and often complicated history of construction. This date is not intended to do more than indicate when the design was likely to have been made. In the case of some of the later houses a date is actually found on the building itself, and this is often the only date we possess for its construction.

Numbers in square brackets in the text refer to the illustrations.

Part I

PETER KIDSON

1 The Anglo-Saxon Period

For the purpose of this book architecture in England is the architecture of the English people. No doubt if one wished to be really thorough it could be argued that there has been something which deserved to be called architecture of a sort in England at least as far back as Stonehenge, for the great circles of upright stones joined overhead by horizontal lintels use a constructional technique well known in Mycenaean Greece. Or, if Stonehenge seems too isolated and remote, one could still very well begin with the buildings of Roman Britain. At Bath, St Albans, Colchester, along Hadrian's Wall, and elsewhere there is still abundant evidence of building activity which, though modest by the standard of Roman achievements elsewhere in Europe, certainly reveals a higher level of competence than anything to be found in the country for centuries afterwards.

All the same, there are good reasons for beginning with the Anglo-Saxon invaders who settled in England during the fifth and sixth centuries. Not only were they to form the nucleus of the permanent population of the country, which means that they can provide the necessary element of continuity that gives meaning to any study of changing and developing forms, but from a strictly architectural point of view there is the added convenience that they made what virtually amounts to a fresh start. Whatever their reactions may have been to Romano-British buildings, they were certainly indifferent to them as an architectural inheritance. It is true that here and there Roman cities such as York, Lincoln, Canterbury, and London appear to have survived in some form or other to become the local capitals of Anglo-Saxon kingdoms; but in terms of actual buildings this does not mean very much. During the early stages of the occupation the amount of sheer destruction must have been considerable, and nearly all those vestiges of the comparatively highly organized way of life in Roman

Britain which were not destroyed outright seem to have been treated by the newcomers with the disdain of incomprehension. Buildings such as baths, temples, basilicas, and theatres lay wholly beyond the range of their experience. Moreover, the pattern of settlement changed over the entire country. Many Roman towns and nearly all the Roman country villas were totally abandoned; so that from the Anglo-Saxon point of view perhaps the most important aspect of Roman buildings was the facility with which they could be exploited for building material.

It is now almost impossible to say with any accuracy how much use there was for buildings other than dwelling-houses in Anglo-Saxon society. They were certainly among the least civilized of the Teutonic peoples who partitioned among themselves the Western provinces of the Roman Empire; and if one had to commit oneself to an opinion it would perhaps be prudent to stress their backwardness, and the simplicity of their way of life, rather than their sophistication. Yet we know from *Beowulf* and Bede that their chieftains held court with their retainers in great communal halls, and more than once Bede alludes to pagan temples which were destroyed by Christian proselytes in the zeal of conversion. Their skill in purely decorative work is known to have been formidable. So it would be unwise to dismiss their capacity for construction out of hand. The communal halls in particular must be accounted the ultimate ancestors of the great dwelling houses of later times. But the one important thing that needs to be said about the earliest Anglo-Saxon buildings is that once they aspired beyond the level of mud, wattle, and thatch they must have been made of wood, not stone. By origin, and perhaps by inclination, the English were forest-dwellers, and the handling of wood came as easily to them as brick, stone, and concrete did to the more civilized peoples of the Mediterranean. Timber was their natural building material; masonry was something which they had to learn about from abroad. Even when they acquired proficiency in masonry, timber continued to be used on a large scale, and throughout the Middle Ages the virtuosity of English woodwork was one of the most remarkable and distinctive features of English architecture.

Building in stone came to England with the first Christian missionaries, led by St Augustine, who arrived from Rome at the end of the sixth century. The provision of church buildings adequate to serve the needs of the cult was an obvious, if not always an immediate, aim of the Christian bishops and clergy. It is true that in the early stages of the Conversion many congregations were compelled to assemble in the open around great crosses, which were set up in public places because the means were not available for the building of churches; and it is also true that in many cases where churches were built they were of wood. But the desire for permanent buildings, and even more the desire for imposing buildings, proved a constant inducement for church designers to master and exploit the technique of masonry construction. The Conversion therefore deserves to be regarded as the most decisive event in the creation of what we can recognize as English architecture. From the beginnings of Christianity (about 600) until the Reformation in the sixteenth century – i.e. for a period of more than 900 years – church-building continued to offer by far the most numerous and lavish opportunities for the exercise of architectural talents. No doubt the volume of building for secular purposes was always large and became steadily larger, especially towards the end of this period; but it was set consistently at a lower pitch of ingenuity and skill. The view that English architecture before the Reformation was fundamentally an ecclesiastical architecture cannot seriously be disputed. After the Reformation this was no longer so. That is why this book divides there, and why the first half of it is so overwhelmingly concerned with churches.

Anglo-Saxon architecture falls very definitely into two periods. The first of these extends from the Conversion to the Danish invasions of the ninth century. The second may perhaps be said to have begun with the efforts made by King Alfred to restore English society, at the end of the ninth century, although it hardly got under way before the middle of the tenth. The impetus with which it began had virtually spent itself before the Conquest. For neither period have we anything like enough evidence for a fair assessment. The great buildings such as cathedrals and abbeys, which set the pace and showed what could be done, have all been rebuilt many times. Occasionally we have descriptions of important buildings by people who saw them; but these accounts are so notoriously vague that they seldom add anything more than confusion to our ignorance. Apart from these, there is Brixworth Church, Northamptonshire, the one really substantial and impressive Anglo-Saxon building that has come down to us. But for the rest all we have to go on are a few mutilated fragments, ruins, and excavated foundations which, although of absorbing antiquarian interest in so far as some of them can be identified with buildings mentioned in surviving texts, and because their similarities prove that there were definite types of church-design in vogue at certain times, hardly deserve to be taken very seriously as architecture. No one could infer the splendours of Gothic cathedrals from the modest parish churches which were contemporary with them; and, in the same way, although the parallel is not exact, it would be unwise for us to judge Anglo-Saxon architecture merely by what is left of it for us to see.

According to Bede, when St Augustine arrived in England there were at least two Roman churches in the vicinity of Canterbury that were still capable of being put into a state of repair. One of these, St Martin's, was already being used as a private chapel by the Christian Queen of Kent. The other stood inside the city, and when it had been patched up it became the first cathedral of Canterbury (602). Quite a number of Christian churches must have existed in Britain during Roman times. Three British bishops, including those of York and London, attended a Council of the Church at Arles, in 314. These must have had churches of some kind. The foundations of another have actually come to light among the ruins of the Roman city of Silchester. It is doubtful whether many of these Romano-British churches were in a fit state to influence their Anglo-Saxon successors, but the case of Canterbury provides at least two exceptions. We have a description of the cathedral by a certain Edmer the Singer, who had seen it before it was burnt down in 1067. Edmer says that it was 'arranged in some parts in imitation of the church of the blessed Prince of the Apostles, Peter', i.e. old St Peter's, at Rome. It would be a mistake to read too much into medieval statements of this kind, for similarities between buildings were not always, or even often, thought of in terms of appearances. In this instance we know that what really impressed Edmer was the fact that the cathedral of Canterbury possessed a 'confessio', or crypt, similar to that of old St Peter's. In other respects the analogy may not have been very close. We have no means of telling how much restoration was carried out by Augustine, or how much of what Edmer saw was the work of later archbishops. But there is no reason to doubt Bede's word that it was originally a Roman building, or Edmer's that it had an apse at the east end and a nave flanked with side aisles, like the earliest Christian churches of Rome itself. The fact that it was taken over by a body of Roman missionaries, sent direct from Rome where they had been familiar with the early Roman churches, seems to suggest that, so far as he was able, Augustine wished to reproduce in England the traditional type of Roman church-building along with all the other aspects of Roman Christianity.

But this was not the only church with which Augustine was concerned. Bede also tells us that he persuaded Ethelbert, the King of Kent, to build another near the monastery which he had founded outside the city walls. It was dedicated to SS Peter and Paul, and it became the church of the Benedictine Abbey of St Augustine. Unlike the cathedral, this seems to have been an entirely new building, and although only the lower parts of the walls can still be seen, it is clear that it must have been a much less grandiose affair, and of quite a different design. Instead of the usual arrangement of nave and aisles, it consisted of a series of compartments, or chambers, of varying sizes, with a large one in the centre, and the rest grouped round it, and opening from it. With one exception, all the other early churches in Kent about which anything is known conformed to this type of plan in preference to that of the cathedral. Two others were at Canterbury; another formed the first cathedral at Rochester; another was at Lyminge, also in Kent; and most impressive, as well as the latest of the group, was Reculver [1] on the Kentish coast (c. 669). The only differences are to be found in the number and arrangement of the subsidiary rooms.

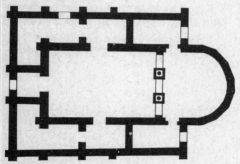

1. Reculver Church, plan

The most important questions that can be asked about this Kentish group of churches are: Who built them? How was the design arrived at? The mere fact that the competence of the masonry was of a high order rules out the possibility that Augustine used local Kentish workmen. Nor is it likely that he brought masons with him all the way from Italy. The case of SS Peter and Paul suggests the most plausible explanation. When churches were needed they were provided by the King of Kent himself. He made available the sites on which they were built, and, according to Teutonic custom, he retained a proprietary interest in the fabric of the church. The men who actually did the work would have been recruited by him; and there can be little doubt that he borrowed their services from his kinsmen in the Frankish royal family just across the Channel. It is a great pity that nothing is known of the typical church buildings of northern France in those times, and scholars have been forced to look farther afield for illuminating comparisons. It has always been urged that the polygonal-apse form, which appears in Kent instead of the more familiar semicircular variety, was derived directly from Ravenna, in Italy. This may have been the case, although polygonal apses of a slightly different form were certainly known north and west of the Alps as well – for instance, at Saint-Maurice-d'Agaune, in Switzerland, and Saint-Bertrand-de-Comminges, in the South of France. But the crucial matter, and the one most urgently in need of a satisfactory explanation, is the use of the subsidiary chambers, or 'porticus', as they are called.

The earliest porticus seem to have made their appearance in the eastern Mediterranean to serve the special needs of the clergy and the cult. Something of the kind was known in Italy in the fifth century, for we hear of chambers flanking the nave of a church built at Nola soon after 400, and again at Como at the end of the fifth century. Saint-Bertrand-de-Comminges also had them. At Nola they were reserved for private devotions, and as memorials for the dead. In this connexion it is worth noting that in SS Peter and Paul, at Canterbury, two porticus were used as burial-chambers, one on the north side for the early archbishops of Canterbury, and the other on the south for the Kentish royal family. Others were apparently used as porches.

But to know the uses to which they were put offers only a partial explanation. Certain purely architectural exigencies were also involved. One way of describing churches of the kind found in Kent is to say that the porticus have taken the place of side aisles. Another way of putting the same point would be to say that as far as possible they were built without columns and arches. The column, with its carefully turned and tapered shaft, sometimes fluted, sometimes smooth, surmounted by a well-carved capital, and standing on a moulded base, is a most evocative symbol, not only of the balanced calm and dignity of Roman architecture, but also of the precision and craftsmanship which made that architecture possible. Except in the monumental structures, which were made of concrete, rows of columns were a traditional feature of Roman public buildings; and the earliest churches which were built after Christianity was officially recognized were all raised upon such rows, which served to divide the aisles from the nave as well as to support the upper parts of the nave. When the Roman Empire in the West went into decline, one of the symptoms of its decadence was the gradual disappearance of the skill which in earlier times had produced these columns, and they tended to become scarce. One solution to this difficulty was to use again old columns from buildings that were no longer required, such as pagan temples. But this was a restricted and uncertain source of supply, especially in the more remote and less developed parts of the Empire; and in the end the inevitable result was that buildings had to be designed without columns. Sometimes masons felt competent to put piers of masonry in their place; but more often than not they were content with walls unbroken except for occasional doors and windows. Where churches were involved, this meant either abandoning side aisles altogether, or else turning them into self-contained compartments which were, in effect, porticus. All these ideas were tried in all parts of western Europe including Italy itself, and it would probably be a mistake to attempt to associate any one solution with a particular region. Instead, it would be better to think of all western European architecture during the centuries which we call the Dark Ages as being in varying degrees a debased survival of Roman provincial styles. Occasionally, where conditions were propitious, a building might be produced which approximated in form and even quality to the archetypes in Rome. But at the other extreme a crude rusticity prevailed, in which architecture was little more than the making of walls.

In such a hierarchy the Kentish group of churches must have occupied a lowly place. Yet even here we find traces of an awareness of the finer points of architecture. At Lyminge and Reculver, at Bradwell, in Essex, and at Brixworth, we know that pairs of columns were used to carry a triple arcade between the nave and the chancel or apse. Those from Reculver can still be seen in the crypt of Canterbury Cathedral, together with fragments of a great stone cross which stood between them. In their original setting columns and cross must have made an imposing sight, in sharp contrast to the bare walls which converged upon them.

The extent to which Canterbury Cathedral was distinguished from the Kentish group of churches is something that cannot now be

2. Escomb Church, plan

determined. It is reasonable to suppose that it was put in order by the same workmen who built SS Peter and Paul, but we cannot say whether it had columns or piers, or whether it had an upper storey. It seems to have had porticus as well as side aisles, but the mere fact that it had aisles puts it further up the scale than the little churches with only porticus.

When we turn to the other group of early Anglo-Saxon churches which were built in the north of England towards the end of the seventh century these distinctions can be handled with more precision. In the last third of the seventh century, and at the beginning of the eighth, Northumbria witnessed a remarkable efflorescence in literature and the arts. The early history of Christianity in the north was hardly affected by Augustine's mission. In 625 Paulinus left Canterbury on his spectacular journey to the King of Northumbria, which resulted in the building of a temporary wooden church at York, in 627, and its replacement by a permanent building a few years later. This was still unfinished when the pagan reaction of 632 put an end to further progress for a time. Paulinus is also known to have used a church at Lincoln, which may or may not have been a survival from Roman times. The pagan reaction in Northumbria lasted only two years, but as a result the whole course of Christian expansion in the north was deflected into a new channel. The new Christian king, Oswald, had imbibed his religion not from Paulinus but from Irish monks at Iona; and as soon as he was in power he gave his support and protection to an Irish mission from Iona, led by St Aidan. This operated from Lindisfarne, and for the next twenty years or so the Irish applied themselves to the work of conversion with a zeal that made the activities of the southern church seem tepid by comparison. But so far as architecture was concerned, their influence was retrogressive. The extreme asceticism, which the Irish prized as the highest religious virtue, was satisfied with very small, crude, and simple buildings. The church at Lindisfarne was of wood and only roughly thatched. Sometimes they used dry-stone walling, but even when this was handled

20

with the virtuosity which we can still admire in the Oratory of Gallerus, in County Kerry, Ireland, the scale remained of necessity small. The result is that English architecture, unlike the decorative arts, owes hardly anything to Irish influence. The long and extremely narrow nave of Escomb Church, in County Durham [2], may perhaps owe its shape to an earlier Irish building; but at Bradwell Church [3], which is known to have been built by the Irish-trained St Cedd, there are no recognizable Irish features. On the contrary, it was built in the corner of an old Roman fort, and has to be accounted an outlier of the Kentish group.

3. Bradwell Church

The impact of Roman Christianity in the north was therefore delayed until after the Synod of Whitby, in 663, which settled outstanding differences between the Irish and the Roman missions in favour of the latter. Soon afterwards, the arrival from Rome of a new Archbishop of Canterbury, Theodore of Tarsus, infused new life into the English Church; but although Canterbury remained undisputed as the ecclesiastical capital, all the great achievements took place in Northumbria, where the political centre of gravity lay. Caedmon's verses and Bede's *Historia ecclesiastica gentis anglorum* were the great literary landmarks of this age; the crosses at Ruthwell, in Dumfriesshire, Bewcastle, in Cumberland, and elsewhere testify to the vigour of its sculpture; and the Lindisfarne Gospels preserve a wonderful repertoire of its decorative art. Its architecture was no less interesting. Here the evidence allows us to divide the buildings very clearly into two main groups. On the one hand were the comparatively ambitious churches that were built by Bishop Wilfrid of York. According to Wilfrid's biographer, he built a church at Hexham, Northumberland, which had aisles, and columns between the nave and aisles, and galleries over the aisles. The description is not profuse, but it is clear from these facts alone that it was fairly closely modelled on the galleried churches of Rome itself, which had been built during the previous century. Wilfrid's crypt at Hexham still survives, along with other fragments of foundation walls, and it confirms the Roman affiliation. Wilfrid knew Rome well. He went there several times in connexion with lawsuits that arose out of the numerous ecclesiastical appointments which he held. He was precisely the kind of churchman whose conception of clerical dignity found expression in fine buildings, and, not satisfied with his church at Hexham, he provided two more, at Ripon and York. The crypt at Ripon survives to suggest that the whole church was similar to Hexham. About York nothing whatever is known, although when Archbishop Albert rebuilt his cathedral round about 770 'it was supported on columns and arches, and surrounded by porticus; it had a great number of upper apartments with separate roofs, and had as many as thirty altars'; all of which suggests that whether or not Wilfrid's York had aisles and galleries the tradition which he introduced, and patronized so lavishly elsewhere, lasted for a long time after his death. Wilfrid is also known to have built a centrally planned church at Hexham, which again implies a source of inspiration close to Roman works of this kind.

Over against Wilfrid's group can be set the much less ambitious churches of Benedict Biscop, a contemporary and colleague of Wilfrid, who founded monasteries at Jarrow and Monkwearmouth, in County Durham. According to Bede, Benedict brought over to England masons from Gaul who were to build a monastery 'after the manner of the Romans'. Presumably the reference is to one of his own monasteries, but the remark is confusing because fragments of churches at both places have survived, and it is clear that neither was the least bit Roman in the sense that Wilfrid's were. Bede may have meant no more than that the churches were built of re-used Roman masonry from the near-by Roman Wall, and that the only place where masons were to be found capable of handling such material was southern Gaul, which still preserved something of its old classical character. Certainly if we are to judge their work by what is left at Monkwearmouth and Jarrow they deserved their reputation, for the masonry is of a high quality. But their skill does not seem to have extended further. The windows at Jarrow [4] and the door in the north side of the related church at Escomb are almost pathetically primitive; while the crudely turned balusters in the porch at Monkwearmouth are very little better.

4. Jarrow Church, detail of Saxon masonry

In plan, these surviving Northumbrian churches were simpler than those of the Kentish group. They made little use of the porticus, although the nave at Jarrow (which was once a separate church) had a row of four down each side. The others, however, were long, high, and narrow buildings, with small flat-ended chancels projecting eastward from the naves. In spite of their simplicity, or perhaps because of it, buildings of this kind seem to have been erected well into the eighth century, for the type appears in Germany, where English missionaries were active at that time. The first church at Paderborn, Westphalia (777), is a case in point.

In the absence of Wilfrid's churches it would be unfair to judge Northumbrian architecture by those of Benedict Biscop, which probably represent the least enterprising level of contemporary Gallic work. Much more impressive in every way is Brixworth [5], the only surviving early Anglo-Saxon church which gives us some idea of what could be produced on a more ambitious plane. Brixworth was founded about 670 by monks from Peterborough, and there is no reason to suppose that it was particularly outstanding among the churches of its time. Yet the scale is unexpectedly monumental. It consisted of a nave of four great arches which have since been walled up but which

5. Brixworth Church

originally opened into porticus arranged like those in the larger church at Jarrow. Beyond this was a chancel, and beyond that a polygonal apse. Between the nave and the chancel was a triple arcade, all trace of which has been removed. The really important thing about Brixworth, by comparison with the other surviving Anglo-Saxon churches, is the fact that the masons were prepared to use arches systematically, and on a large scale. Columns were either not available or, more probably, the designer preferred to rest his arches on great rectangular masses of masonry. Sir Alfred Clapham considered that this masonry was sufficiently defective to be regarded as the work of native Anglo-Saxons; but if this was the case, then paradoxically the enterprise must be rated even more ambitious.

In the third region of England, the West Country, the origins of Christianity were traced in Glastonbury legends to a time long before the coming of the Saxons. But the conversion of the invaders only began in earnest during the second half of the seventh century. Of the first important ecclesiastical figures, one, Agilbert, the first bishop of Dorchester on Thames, was a Frank by birth; while the other, Wine, the first bishop of Winchester, received his education across the Channel. No doubt their notions of church architecture were likewise derived from Gaul.

The nearest counterpart in Wessex to Wilfrid in the north was St Aldhelm, who founded churches at Malmesbury in Wiltshire, Sherborne in Dorset, and Bradford-on-Avon, Wiltshire. At Bradford a Saxon church still remains, but in the form that it has come down to us it hardly represents the style of Aldhelm's time. The earliest church in Wessex of which we have archaeological information is that built by King Ine, c. 700, at Glastonbury, Somerset. This was of the porticus type. We know that Aldhelm received his education at Canterbury, and this sort of link could easily account for the appearance of the Kentish type in the west. Another church, however, dating from c. 680, the first monastic church at Abingdon, in Berkshire, seems to have been much more original in form. We know of it only from a later description, but this states unambiguously that it was 'round at both ends', which almost certainly means that it had two apses. If this was the case, then it anticipated the famous example of this arrangement at Fulda, in Hessen, by more than a century.

It is a great pity that we cannot follow the fortunes of this first English architecture in stone, once it was established. In particular we cannot say for certain when the first symptoms of insularity began to show. The period of two hundred years between the middle of the eighth century and the great monastic revival of the second half of the tenth century is the most obscure in the whole history of English architecture. The lead which had already passed from Kent to Northumbria no doubt passed later, along with the political supremacy, to Mercia and Wessex. Brixworth remains to show that Mercian architecture had an auspicious beginning; but of the first Midland cathedrals and abbeys, such as Worcester, Lichfield, Peterborough, or Ely, nothing remains that will afford us any notion of their scale and form. The great age of Mercian prosperity came at the end of the eighth century when its king, Offa, was recognized as overlord throughout England. At this time, across the Channel, Charlemagne was bringing the kingdom of the Franks to the zenith of its power, and relations between the two countries, both in learning and commerce, were close enough for us to speculate on the possibility that Offa tried to emulate the building activities of his great contemporary. The so-called Carolingian Revival was a crucial epoch in the development of European architecture, and many historians have detected references to Carolingian works in later Anglo-Saxon buildings. The time of Offa is when we should expect this new wave of Continental influences to begin, but if anything of the kind happened then all traces have been thoroughly effaced. The key building was Offa's own abbey at St Albans, but we know nothing whatever about its appearance. The only positive clues are to be found in the field of decorative sculpture. In the church at Breedon-on-the-Hill, in Leicestershire, there are to be seen built into the present walls an angel and friezes which are distinctly Carolingian in type, and which seem to date from this period. But although evidence of this kind suggests that Carolingian art began to exercise its influence in England during, or soon after, the reign of Offa, and although we can infer from records and surviving traces that certain Carolingian architectural ideas were belatedly used in England during the tenth and eleventh centuries, it is necessary to resist the temptation to bracket later Anglo-Saxon architecture wholeheartedly with that of the Carolingian Empire or its immediate successors. There is no evidence of any building in England that could ever have been seriously mistaken for a Carolingian construction. On the contrary, as we shall see, everything suggests that later Anglo-Saxon architecture fell farther and farther behind the most ambitious Continental works, and that it developed idiosyncrasies which imply separation from, rather than contact with, Europe. This insularity was by far its most important characteristic, and it is this which distinguishes later from earlier Anglo-Saxon architecture.

The Danish invasions of the ninth century destroyed the precocious cultural life of Northumbria, and played havoc with organized religion throughout the country. Monastic communities living under strict rule virtually disappeared. It was not until Dunstan became Abbot of Glastonbury, in 943 or 944, that a serious and permanent improvement in the quality of English religious life took place. Once started, however, Dunstan's reform movement acquired considerable momentum. Abingdon was revived in 954 by one of his disciples, Ethelwold, who later became Bishop of Winchester. Dunstan himself became Archbishop of Canterbury in 960, and another follower, Oswald, was made Bishop of Worcester in 961. Although they were bishops, the primary aim of these men was to restore monastic life according to the full rigour of the Rule of St Benedict, and it is through the foundation of a veritable spate of new monasteries, or the restoration of old ones more or less moribund, that they left their mark on the history of English architecture. More than thirty monasteries and at least six nunneries came into being between the middle of the tenth century and the beginning of the eleventh. Each of the leaders was responsible for a group of these foundations. Thus Malmesbury, Bath, and Westminster owed their revival to Dunstan. Ethelwold brought monks from Abingdon to Winchester, and refounded both Ely and Peterborough. Oswald's chief foundation was at Ramsey, in Huntingdonshire, but the main field of his activities was in the West Country, where houses were established by him at Pershore and Evesham, in Worcestershire, and at Winchcombe, and probably Deerhurst, in Gloucestershire. He also introduced monks at Worcester; and later, when he was made Archbishop of York, his attention turned to the north as well.

This monastic reform movement was directly inspired by similar movements on the Continent. All the leaders spent periods at European monasteries such as Ghent and Saint-Benoît-sur-Loire, so they were familiar with architecture there. One would have expected the new English monasteries to have been modelled on appropriate Continental examples. Perhaps they were; but so little on either side of the Channel has survived that the extent and precise nature of such relations cannot be investigated. On the whole, however, the main wave of activity in England came rather too early to benefit from the enterprising architectural experiments which were conducted under the

general influence of the European reform movements towards the end of the tenth century. So far as we can tell, this new English monastic architecture tended to be conservative. Some of the features known to have appeared in its church designs undoubtedly came from the Carolingian tradition. For instance, at Durham, c. 999, and at Ramsey, we hear of churches that had towers at either end; and in one case – Canterbury Cathedral – a western choir seems to have been added to the original building during this period. Both of these ideas imply the Carolingian notion of a 'double-ended' church. But if this means anything at all in the tenth and eleventh centuries it is symptomatic of insularity rather than of new Continental inspiration. In two cases where we can study late Saxon churches of cathedral or monastic rank – North Elmham, in Norfolk, and Deerhurst – we are confronted by architectural remains of an extremely modest, not to say retarded, character. Admittedly neither foundation commanded great resources. All the same, when we find that neither was built with side aisles it is clear that we are not dealing with the Carolingian notion of a great church, but with the sort of thing represented by the lesser buildings of the early Anglo-Saxon period. It is not just the absence of columns or piers that gives this impression. In plan both were frankly archaic. Deerhurst still adhered to the porticus type, while North Elmham went back still farther to the Early Christian T transept and simple apse. It is true that some German churches of the same period shared these characteristics of North Elmham, but there the scale and articulation were infinitely more developed. The bare walls of Deerhurst, which seem to have been built not long before the Conquest, suggest an almost total incapacity to think of masonry in any other terms except flat surfaces; and if anything was done to make them interesting to look at it must have been by means of painted decoration. This brings us back to that contrast between the strictly architectural conceptions and the embellishment of Anglo-Saxon buildings which was mentioned earlier.

All the evidence suggests that the Anglo-Saxons were far more interested in decorating their buildings than in giving them imposing structural forms. The best-known instance of their taste for surface ornament is undoubtedly the early eleventh-century tower at Earls Barton, Northamptonshire, which is plastered with little strips and arches. At Earls Barton [6] the effect is harmless if bizarre. But in a work like the crypt at Repton, Derbyshire [7], we find it assuming a slightly more disturbing aspect. At Repton there are columns which

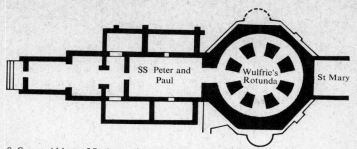

8. Saxon Abbey of St Augustine, Canterbury, plan showing Wulfric's Rotunda

have been roughly but deliberately shaped to give the impression that they were made of an elastic instead of a rigid material. This is done by spiral thongs which are, as it were, wound round the shafts to produce a series of slight bulges. The motive on which this pattern was based came ultimately from Roman sources, and no doubt it was intended to simulate the twisted columns which stood around St Peter's shrine at Rome. But at Rome the columns were purely decorative, whereas here they have a definite structural function to perform. The incongruity of handling a supporting member as if it were no more than an element in the decoration of a building tells us a great deal about the attitude of the Anglo-Saxons towards architecture at this time. It was not so much a case of their being out of touch with Europe as of their not caring. Where money was plentiful it was spent, not on masonry, but on precious objects such as gold and silver reliquaries, crosses and plate, rich vestments and sumptuous books, as were showered upon the abbey of Peterborough by its last Anglo-Saxon abbot, Leofric.

Even before the Norman Conquest there were signs that this insularity was coming to an end. At Sompting, in Sussex, Norman capitals and a German type of tower-spire made their appearance in a late Saxon church. Two much more important building operations during the reign of Edward the Confessor must have convinced a lot of Englishmen that what was happening across the Channel deserved their attention. One was the rotunda which was started at St Augustine, Canterbury [8], soon after the return of its abbot from the Council of Reims, in 1049. This was clearly inspired by the rotunda of Saint-Bénigne, at Dijon. The other was the Confessor's own church of Westminster Abbey. Although it has completely disappeared, we know that it was modelled on the abbey of Jumièges, in Normandy, which was then the most up-to-date building in the Duchy. The Confessor's taste for all things Norman is notorious; but in this case we may be certain that he had good reason for his preference. The implied criticism of the native tradition is highly significant. There is something highly symbolic in the fact that the last Saxon king should have built what was in effect the first Norman church in England.

2 Norman Church Architecture

After the Norman Conquest of 1066 the lack of evidence in the shape of surviving monuments, which drastically curtails our ability to make a just assessment of Saxon architecture and tends to reduce nearly all our statements about it to the level of tentative guesses, is no longer quite such a serious problem. From this point onward we are in a position to base our opinions on buildings of a kind which set the standards instead of following them at a considerable distance – that is, the great cathedrals and abbey-churches. Many of the Norman buildings in this category are still standing, even though they are seldom to be found in their original form. It would be idle to pretend that we know all we should like to know about these greater Norman churches. As we shall see, there are several problems outstanding which are simply due to the fact that some of them have disappeared without a trace. But the handicaps are no longer crippling.

A problem of another kind arises from the fact that whereas we know what many of these greater Norman churches looked like, we do not in the case of their Saxon counterparts. This means that we have to try and measure the significance of the change from Saxon to Norman without being able to make a true comparison between the beginning and end of the process. As the Normans themselves were chiefly responsible for the effacement of the larger Saxon churches, it seems fairly safe to say that, whatever else may be involved in the change, the Normans had such a poor opinion of the buildings they found in England when they arrived that they set about replacing them with buildings of a quality to which they were accustomed as soon as possible. This tends to give the impression that Norman architecture in England was transplanted bodily from Normandy, and that it involved a total repudiation of everything the Saxons had achieved. But although there may be a good deal of truth in this view, it needs to be hedged around by numerous qualifications.

The contempt which the Normans felt for English church buildings was only a part of their wider contempt for almost everything connected with the religious life of the country. This attitude was not merely an expression of their natural arrogance. There is no doubt that by the middle of the eleventh century the impetus and zeal imparted to the English church by Dunstan, Ethelwold, and Oswald a century before had virtually spent itself, except in parts of the West Country. On the other side of the Channel, however, for more than fifty years before the Conquest, the Normans had been in the throes of a reform movement which had completely transformed the religious life of their Duchy. A similar movement was active farther north, in what was then called Lower Lorraine, and is now called Belgium. Even before the Conquest, Edward the Confessor had recognized the merits of this reformed Continental clergy by importing men from Normandy and Lower Lorraine to fill high offices in the English Church. After the Conquest William the Conqueror found the majority of the native-born English clergy not merely unimpressive, but in many cases far too deeply involved with the displaced Saxon aristocracy for them to be entirely trustworthy. So it is hardly surprising that as soon as he was firmly established on the throne he started to do systematically what Edward had attempted spasmodically, i.e. to fill all important ecclesiastical vacancies in England with reliable and well-qualified Continental churchmen. Drastic action such as the deposition of Archbishop Stigand of Canterbury was exceptional. The transformation was effected slowly and patiently as the vacancies occurred. By the end of William's reign, however, there were only four native-born English churchmen left in high places: Bishop Wulfstan, of Worcester, and three abbots.

The connexions between this transformation of the English clergy and the introduction of Norman architecture into the country are close and obvious. The lofty conception of the Church as an institution, which inspired the reformers of the eleventh century, required for its visible image increasingly majestic church buildings. As we have seen from the donations which Abbot Leofric made to Peterborough, Saxon churches were not lacking in material splendours, but we can only infer from the consistent attitude of the Norman clergy that the buildings themselves fell far short of the magnificence of their contents. It was almost certainly the 'provincial' character of Saxon architecture, not the specific manifestations of Saxon taste, which the Normans despised. In fact, there were already symptoms in the time of Edward the Confessor (see page 31) that some English patrons were aware of the discrepancy between the standards of architecture current in England and on the Continent; and their efforts to have copies made in England of interesting Continental designs suggest that even if there had been no Norman Conquest an attempt would have been made in the second half of the eleventh century to rebuild at least some English cathedrals and abbeys in conformity with the more ambitious standards in vogue across the Channel. Without the Conquest, however, it is doubtful whether the transition to the Continental idea of what a great church should look like would have been effected so quickly, so thoroughly, or with so few concessions to insular waywardness. From the point of view of the development of English architecture in the Middle Ages, the supremely important thing about the Conquest is that it brought to an end a long period when England had been to all intents and purposes a backwater. By establishing contacts with some of the main currents of Continental architecture at a critical period, it secured the conditions for what amounted to another fresh start.

While it is true that in almost every case the appointment of a Norman bishop or abbot was followed sooner or later by the rebuilding of his church, the circumstances varied from place to place. The first two Norman archbishops, Lanfranc and Thomas of Bayeux, reached their respective cathedrals at Canterbury and York in 1070 to find them in ruins. When Paul of Caen came to St Albans in 1077, material for rebuilding was already being collected by his Saxon predecessors from the Roman ruins at Verulamium. It was a fire in 1087 that gave Bishop Maurice the opportunity to rebuild St Paul's, in London, and another fire, in 1116, was responsible for the reconstruction of Peterborough. The number of Saxon buildings which were deliberately pulled down to make way for larger Norman structures was perhaps not very great, although some of the most imposing monuments of the new style resulted from such actions – for instance, Winchester, Bury St Edmunds, in Suffolk, and Durham. Even the Saxon Bishop Wulfstan of Worcester felt constrained to follow the fashion set by his Norman colleagues, although he at least wept over the passing of Oswald's church. Then, of course, there were many new foundations such as the Conqueror's own abbey at Battle, in Sussex; and re-foundations such as Gloucester; and a whole series of new cathedrals had to be built because several Saxon village bishoprics were transferred to towns after 1072. This was how Lincoln, Chichester, Norwich, and Old Sarum acquired their cathedrals, and Bath Abbey was rebuilt with the intention of replacing Wells. A similar explanation accounts for the abbey of Tewkesbury.

It is clear from all this that the Norman building campaign was spread over a long period, and the individual works were undertaken spasmodically. Except for Canterbury and the abbey at Battle, there seems to have been a time-lag of several years after the Conquest before the movement got under way. Lincoln was begun about 1073; but it was not until the late 1070s and the 1080s that there came the full spate of what might be called the first generation of English Norman buildings: churches like St Albans, Winchester, Ely, and Worcester. Then in the 1090s we encounter the earliest of another series which form a second generation. Durham Cathedral and the abbey at Tewkesbury are the outstanding works of this period. There was a certain amount of overlapping between these two groups; but it is very important to distinguish them from one another, and also to realize that both were patronized by the new Norman clergy. It must be emphasized that this clergy, while passionately interested in having great and splendid churches, was not exclusively attached to one particular style of great church. As we shall see, it is only among churches of the first generation that we find evidence of really close affinities with buildings in Normandy, and even among these there are certain differences which suggest that other Continental influences were at work in England as well as those which were specifically Norman. The connexions with Normandy, which are implied in the name we use to distinguish English architecture during the century which followed the Conquest, tend to conceal the fact that Norman architecture in England was always Norman architecture with a difference, and that as time went on the differences became greater and greater. When we come to buildings of the second generation it is much less misleading to use a term like 'Anglo-Norman', in so far as this carries with it the implication that Norman architecture in England began to acquire distinctly insular characteristics from about 1090 onwards; although even this is perhaps not entirely straightforward, because it might convey too strongly the impression that there was a revival of Anglo-Saxon influences at that time. It would certainly be wrong to make any very sweeping claims of that sort. All that we can say is that some of these second-generation Norman buildings make use of specific Anglo-Saxon ideas. What is more important, they tend to make their effects in ways which seem to anticipate the remarkably consistent outlook of our later medieval architects. Their 'Englishness' is something that is more apparent if we look forward than if we look back. But again it is dangerous to be too dogmatic, precisely because we do not know what the best Saxon buildings were like just before the Conquest. The inordinate love of decoration which is so characteristic of later Anglo-Norman buildings, and which contrasts so strongly with the austerity of the first-generation works, may very well have been a symptom of the resurgence of Anglo-Saxon taste. But however we interpret these facts, the important thing to have in mind when we attempt to understand Norman architecture in England is that it was not a static style, complete and perfect when it arrived, but something which showed a remarkable capacity for developing new forms. If one compares the choir of St Albans (*c.* 1080) with Oxford Cathedral (*c.* 1160), the extent of this metamorphosis seems almost sensational. Yet both are called Norman. It should be abundantly clear from this comparison that if the term has any meaning at all it cannot be confined merely to what these two buildings have in common. St Albans and Oxford represent extremes of primitive simplicity and ultimate sophistication, and if there is any case for using the same word to describe them it must be shown that they belong to a common tradition with a long series of legitimate intermediaries and exhibit a recognizable process of change.

In a book of this kind discussion of all the buildings which contributed their distinctive nuances to the evolution of Norman architecture would be out of place. It will be more to the point to examine in detail a few of the salient works which form landmarks between St Albans and Oxford. But first, because it is impossible to explain many of the features of Norman churches in England without alluding to Normandy, it is necessary to start with an example of the kind of great church being built in Normandy just before the Conquest.

The abbey-church of Saint-Étienne, at Caen, was founded by William the Conqueror himself between 1064 and 1066, and was finished by 1077. Of the original building, only the lower part of the west front, the nave, and transepts are still standing, and even the vaulted roof of the nave was an addition of the early part of the twelfth century. In its original state only the side aisles were vaulted; the nave was covered with a wooden roof. This seems to have been the usual arrangement in Norman churches until well into the twelfth century, although we know of some cases where the walls of the nave were

joined overhead by a series of transverse, or 'diaphragm', arches.

When all these things have been taken into account the architectural interest of what is left of the eleventh-century work centres in
the walls of the nave [9]. When we compare these walls with even the
most ambitious of our surviving Saxon examples we are at once struck
by the very much greater degree of articulation in the Norman work.
Nothing could be further from the bare surfaces of a church like
Deerhurst. At Caen we are confronted not so much by a surface as by
an organized system of arches raised in tiers one above the other. The
three sections of the elevation are almost equal in height. The main
arcade, which opens into the side aisles, and the arcade above, which
opens into the galleries, each consist of large single arches. The
clerestory openings form a triple-arch unit, or at least they did so
before the vaults were introduced. Between each vertical section of the
wall is a semicircular wall-shaft, and these, in conjunction with the
well-defined horizontal divisions, break up the wall into a network of
rectangular compartments – an effect which must have been considerably more pronounced when the clerestory was wholly visible.
Although so much of these walls has been cut away to form the arches,
it is not difficult to realize that their basic dimensions would define an
extremely sturdy block of masonry. It is perhaps in the clerestory that
the thickness of them is most easily grasped. At that level the wall is
visible in two planes. On the inside the surface is broken up by the
triple-arch unit; while the outer plane is represented by the clerestory
windows. Between the two is a continuous passage cut through the
residual masonry. The lower sections of the wall were obviously
designed to carry this broad clerestory, but there the bulk is all concentrated in the piers. It follows as a matter of course from this thick-
wall construction that pier design was bound to assume considerable
importance. The same is true of the arches between the piers. Basically,
we may think of the core of the pier as being formed by the residue of
wall left when the arches have been cut away, and the simplest kind
of pier would therefore be square or rectangular in section. Such piers
can actually be found in the most primitive Romanesque churches,
but in the course of the eleventh century the practice of embellishing
the core with subsidiary forms became fairly general. Definite rules
governed these accretions, and they are beautifully illustrated at Caen.
The dominant idea was that every arch, or visible part of every arch,
should be supported by its own supporting member. This usually took
the form of a half-column, complete with base and capital. The nave

at Caen shows us how this principle was applied to a thick wall. The great arches of the main arcade and the gallery all have contiguous subsidiary arches to offset their width. These are carried on half-columns, and so are the exposed parts of the main arch. The effect of all these half-columns, together with the wall-shaft on the side facing into the nave, is to produce a characteristic congestion of forms around the exposed parts of the piers. This congestion reaches its climax in the capitals of the half-columns which are carved in crude imitation of classical acanthus capitals. The arches themselves are left comparatively plain, although the exposed part of the main arch has a simple roll moulding.

It is necessary to describe this Norman thick-wall technique in some detail because it was by far the most important contribution which the Normans made to architecture in England. More than any other factor, it separates post-Conquest from pre-Conquest buildings – at least among those known to us. So completely was it adopted in England that it persisted in use long after it had been abandoned on the Continent, and we can still find traces of it in purely Gothic buildings of the thirteenth and even fourteenth centuries. The form in which it is found in England is not always identical with that of Saint-Étienne, at Caen. A very common variation is the arrangement known as the alternating system, where, instead of the piers forming a uniform series, two different kinds of pier alternate with one another. This type of elevation had already been introduced into England before the Conquest if, as we think, it was copied from the Norman abbey of Jumièges, in the Confessor's church at Westminster.

Neither Saint-Étienne at Caen nor any other Norman cathedral or abbey built before the Conquest preserves its original choir in anything more than plan. This is a pity for several reasons, but in particular, because one choir would have told us much more than any of the surviving naves as to the precise point which the Normans had reached – if they had reached any point at all – in the matter of vaulting wide spans. Two types of choir-plan are known: one in which the side aisles are continuous right round the apse, forming what is called an ambulatory, and sometimes, though not always, having chapels opening from it; and the other in which the side aisles terminate in chapels flanking the choir, and other chapels open from the eastern walls of the transepts. The former of these dispositions seems to have been regarded as the more ambitious; but the latter probably maintained its importance during the eleventh century because it could be more easily and safely adapted to receive a choir vault. It is known that in some cases the walls between the choir and the side aisles consisted of solid masonry, which would be perfect supports for a barrel vault, and not easy to explain otherwise. Be this as it may, it is certain that when vaults were introduced into Norman churches in England it was in choirs of the kind just described that they appeared first. It was natural that the choir, which was the focus of all the liturgical activity of these great churches, and which housed the relics and altars which were their *raison d'être*, should be distinguished from the rest of the building by having this more imposing form of roof. So far as we know, nearly every Norman building of the first generation in England conformed in the plan of its east end to one or other of these types; but it is highly significant that among works of the second generation both become increasingly rare.

Outside, the outlines of Norman churches were dominated by towers. The most important of these was usually placed over the crossing, but it was accompanied in the more important buildings by a pair of towers at the west end of the nave, rising out of the west front. This arrangement can still be seen at Caen, although in a modified form. Like other Norman ideas, it was brought over to England and, although very few of the original towers can still be seen, Norman ancestry can be detected in the grouping of several Gothic cathedral towers. But again it is important to realize that there were Norman towers in England which were not inspired by prototypes in Normandy.

When we turn to England – once we have recognized things like the Norman elevation, the thick wall, the two kinds of choir plan, and the characteristic distribution of towers – what is apt to strike us most forcibly is a general increase in size. Naves in particular were made very much longer – even twice as long; although choirs also were extended. In fact, the dimensions of Norman cathedrals and abbeys in England place them in the very largest class of medieval churches. The responsibility for this increase rests with the Norman clergy and their demand for great churches. Although by itself a change of scale does not constitute a change of style, in this particular case we can see how it entailed many of the detailed changes which mark the movement of Norman architecture in England away from the standards of Caen. At Caen the average thickness of the nave walls was about four feet nine inches; at Canterbury and Lincoln it was the same; but at St Albans it was over seven feet, and at Durham [10], Peterborough, and

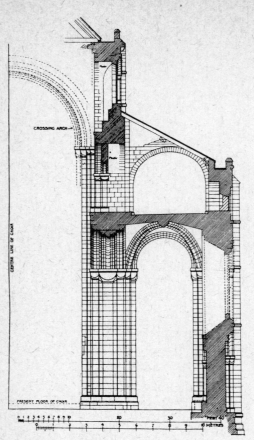

CROSSING ARCH

CENTRE LINE OF CHOIR

PRESENT FLOOR OF CHOIR

10. Durham Cathedral, half cross-section of the choir

Norwich even more. It should be readily apparent that as the walls got thicker so the articulation of the piers and arches became a more and more complicated problem. Perhaps the best way to approach the question of the historical development of Norman architecture in England is to start with a series of buildings such as Winchester, Ely, Norwich, and Peterborough, all of which are descended from the Caen type of elevation, and see how the appearance of their walls was gradually transformed by the increased articulation of their piers and arches.

42

Although Winchester is perhaps the English building which stands closest to Caen, at least among those which survive, there are special reasons for considering St Albans first. The St Albans walls [11] have different proportions, and they give the impression of being much more primitive than those of Caen. This is no doubt due to their greater bulk, and to the absence in the recesses of the piers of the half-columns and capitals which were so conspicuous at Caen. And instead of semicircular wall-shafts there are broad, flat buttresses. The removal of the original fillings of the gallery openings also contributes to the effect of simplicity. Comparison with Caen is not quite fair, because

11. St Albans
Cathedral,
nave

St Albans was built very largely of Roman brick, which is a material that cannot be made to take complicated forms. The austerity was therefore not entirely a matter of choice. Be that as it may, the result is that the nave walls of St Albans present us with the Norman thick wall in its most elementary form, with the barest minimum of articulation. It would hardly be too drastic to describe them as crude masses of masonry with three rows of holes cut into them. This, so to speak, is the raw material which was to be worked with ever-increasing sophistication in the course of the next hundred years.

Much closer in general effect to Caen is the architecture of the transept arms of the cathedral of Winchester [12]. These are all that is left of the great work begun in 1079 by Bishop Walkelin. The division into three more or less equal storeys, the division into bays by means of wall-shafts, the thick wall with its clerestory wall-passage, and the use of secondary arches to articulate the piers – all this follows the prescription of Caen and other Norman churches. Two features call for special comment, however. One is the division of the gallery opening by the introduction of a central shaft. This gives the middle section of the wall an added degree of complexity which is appropriate to its position between the main arcade and the clerestory. The other is the distinctive form of capital employed for all the small shafts and half-shafts. It is known as a cushion capital, and it is a form hardly known in Normandy. How it came to play such an important part in the decoration of English churches is one of the besetting problems of this field of study, and one to which it will be necessary to return later. Winchester also preserves intact its Norman crypt.

The cathedral of Ely was begun by Walkelin's brother, Simeon, in the 1080s. Its original choir has disappeared, but there is a definite similarity between the transepts of the two buildings. At Ely, however, we encounter a version of the alternating system, and when we come to the nave [13] which was designed and perhaps largely carried out in the first third of the twelfth century we are confronted by a characteristic development – namely, the use of two subordinate arches in the opening of the main arcade and the gallery, so that now three arches are visible in each opening; what is more, each now has its own roll-moulding. The alternating system is not obtrusive, but it is interesting to see that where the cylindrical piers are used the principle of every arch having its own support breaks down. Capitals are left projecting into space unsupported. On the other hand, the orthodox compound piers have correspondingly enriched profiles. But in spite

12. Winchester Cathedral, north transept

13. Ely Cathedral, nave

of these anomalies, the nave walls at Ely represent perhaps the most satisfying stage in the transformation of the Caen type of elevation in England. Conceived on a more monumental scale, and far more richly articulated than any of their possible Norman prototypes, they have a weight and orderliness appropriate to their function as walls. At the same time they seem to achieve some of the decorative effects of abstract sculpture.

In later designs of the Ely type, of which Norwich (begun in 1096) and Peterborough (begun in 1118) are the most outstanding, the development of the plastic possibilities of the great interior walls is taken even further. If anything, the walls are even thicker than at Ely, and the enrichment is more profuse. At both Norwich and Peterborough we find arches covered with chevrons and billet-mouldings; and at Peterborough there are areas of diaper pattern in the gallery arcades. It is hardly surprising to find that the breakdowns in the logical handling of the supports now became numerous and blatant. At Norwich the arcades and gallery arches have immense depth, but they are almost wholly unarticulated. Instead, we find them carried by as many as three shafts side by side – an arrangement which recalls the groups of shafts in the Anglo-Saxon church at Great Paxton, Huntingdonshire. Again there are capitals which have no shafts to support them. This is particularly disturbing in the side aisles at Peterborough, which have ribbed vaults. The ribs seem to stop short, as though suspended in space. These two features – increased decoration and increased dislocation of the Norman conception of structural logic – are symptomatic of the change from the first to the second generation of Norman buildings. Norwich and Peterborough are really 'overlap' buildings. If they derive from the first-generation type they were already responding to new tendencies which had their origins in the second. But before we turn to consider these new tendencies in their more radical forms this is perhaps the place to pause and mention one of the greatest of the Norman buildings that have disappeared – an abbey of Bury St Edmunds – and to say what has been said on the question of early Norman crypts.

From what we know of it from written sources and its fragmentary remains, the nave of Bury belonged to the second quarter of the twelfth century, and was probably akin to the Ely–Norwich–Peterborough group. But perhaps the most interesting thing about Bury was its crypt, which, together with the choir, was built much earlier, i.e. in the time of Baldwin, who was abbot from 1065 to 1097. This means that it could well have been the earliest of the Norman crypts in England. It is usual to explain these crypts as variations on the precedent of the eleventh-century crypt in the cathedral of Rouen; but the similarities are not very close. One important difference is that the English crypts make extensive and sometimes exclusive use of cushion capitals, a form which was hardly known in Normandy. The ultimate source of spacious crypts was Italy, but they were also common in the Rhineland in the eleventh century. Cushion capitals were also familiar there and, if crypts and cushion capitals came together, the Rhineland would be the obvious centre from which they reached England. It is intriguing to learn that before he came to England Abbot Baldwin had been in charge of the Alsatian priory of Leberau, where he must have known some of the Rhenish crypts. It has always been hoped that Bury would shed light on these matters, but unfortunately recent excavations have proved inconclusive. The important thing, however, is that Normandy was not the only available source from which Norman architecture in England could draw its ideas.

The building which more than any other marks the transition from first- to second-generation Norman buildings in England is the cathedral of Durham. The rebuilding of Aldhun's Saxon cathedral seems to have been envisaged from the moment it was decided by the Lotharingian Bishop Walcher to introduce a community of monks in place of the old Congregation of St Cuthbert, but the actual church was not begun until 1093, by Bishop William de Carilef. The choir was finished by 1104, and the nave by 1133. The reputation which Durham enjoys of being the most splendid of our Norman buildings is wholly justified. When we compare the walls of its nave [14] with those of Winchester or even Ely we are at once aware of a boldness and imaginative power in the dispositions of the masonry, which betoken a complete emancipation from the restraints inherited from Normandy. The proportions of the elevation have been drastically transformed. The main arcade now occupies a much larger part of the whole, and dominates the interior. The gallery has been reduced practically to the status of a triforium, while the clerestory seems almost to have disappeared among the ribs of the vaults. At the same time the old unity of the wall has been seriously impaired. For one thing, the wall-shafts now project dramatically into the nave, and really disrupt the even flow of the horizontal lines. Then again the walls seem to taper upwards in the manner of a tree-trunk or a lighthouse. All their bulk is concentrated in the arcade, in the compound

14. Durham Cathedral, nave

piers, and even more so in the cylinders, whose enormous girth is aggressively proclaimed by the eye-catching patterns with which they are incised. By comparison, the forms of the middle section seem almost slight, while the clerestory – partly because of the vaults – gives the impression of being more void than solid. This tapering is particularly evident in the choir, for which it is known a ribbed vault was intended from the outset. So we may think of these walls, as it were, bracing themselves to bear the weight and thrust of the vaults. Between the choir on the one hand and the nave and transepts on the other there are slight but significant differences which seem to imply that the decision to vault the rest of the church was an afterthought. In the choir the wall-shafts which support the diagonal ribs rest on the ledge left by the 'contraction' of the triforium; in other words, the supports are themselves directly supported by the main arcade. In the nave, however, the diagonal ribs are corbelled out of the triforium wall and have no supports of any kind. This change is symptomatic of the growing indifference of the Durham masons to things like the logical handling of supports. But either way the impression of an intimate and organic relation between walls and vaults is inescapable. Monumental though they are, the walls of Durham are no longer detached and self-contained monoliths like those of Ely. They seem to grow together overhead, and a new and impressive shape is thereby imposed upon the interior.

These famous vaults of Durham are clearly the clue to the understanding of the whole design. So much has been written about them from what might be called the technical angle that it will do no harm to approach them for once from the point of view of their contribution to the visual effect of the building. Nevertheless it would be wrong to underestimate their importance as a feat of engineering. The task of roofing a church in stone was one of the constant preoccupations of European architects throughout the eleventh century. The simplest form of stone-roof, and the earliest to be used, is the kind known as a barrel vault [15a]. This is nothing more than a half-cylinder. It is easy to see how such vaults, with their evenly distributed weight, need more or less continuous supporting walls. This is the kind that may have been used in those early Norman choirs which had solid walls between them and their flanking aisles. It is perhaps worth mentioning that some of the earliest Norman churches in England had these solid choir walls – e.g. Canterbury and St Albans – although of course nothing is known for certain as to how they were roofed.

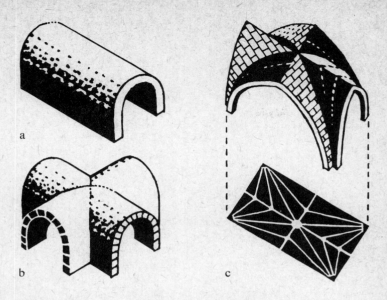

15. Types of vaulting: a. Barrel vault; b. groined vault; c. ribbed vault

A more advanced form of vault is that which is called a groined vault [15b]. Essentially this consists of two barrel vaults intersecting at right angles. Where the two intersect, characteristic ridges appear in the surface, becoming more and more pronounced towards the corners. This form of vault had been systematically used in Continental churches for many centuries in side aisles and ambulatories, where the structural risks involved were slight and a rough-and-ready finish did not matter. But it was a long time before masons had the courage to use a vault of this kind for a major span. One of the things which may have deterred them is the fact that a groined vault is only really suitable for a more or less square space. As soon as it is applied to a definite rectangle complications begin to appear. It can be done, but the construction of the centring and the cutting of blocks of stone to form the surface of the vault would call for a knowledge of geometry well beyond the capacity of most eleventh-century masons, at least in the north of Europe.

The ribbed vault [15c] was the solution which finally proved most satisfactory. In appearance a ribbed vault is similar to a groined vault, with the addition of a rib along the edge formed by the intersection of the compartments. But whereas in a true groined vault the groins are in effect by-products of the intersecting half-cylinders, and in their simplest form have an elliptical profile, in a ribbed vault the ribs are the starting-point, and their profiles are always arcs of circles. The intervening surfaces of the vault are no longer parts of a complicated set of geometrical relations, but present a series of separate and localized problems that can be disposed of without undue difficulty. From the point of view of the people who invented the ribbed vault these geometrical simplifications were perhaps the aspects which recommended it most strongly. But of course its possibilities extended far beyond considerations of this sort, and eventually the ribbed vault became one of the constituent elements of Gothic architecture.

In several respects Durham anticipates early Gothic buildings. Not only is it vaulted throughout with ribbed vaults, but in the nave some of the transverse arches are pointed; while under the roof of the nave triforium can be seen arches abutting on to the upper walls of the nave which in function, if not in appearance, foreshadow the Gothic flying buttress. In spite of all this, however, it would be a paradox to call Durham a Gothic building. The massive strength of its walls is alone sufficient to dispose of any such idea. Although we habitually associate ribbed vaulting with Gothic buildings, it is not difficult to see how the practice could have developed naturally within the Norman tradition; and if the similarities mean anything it is not that Durham is Gothic, but that Gothic has its roots in Norman Romanesque. All this gives us special reason to deplore the series of historical accidents which have robbed us of the stages leading up to Durham, and so left that building in a position of splendid isolation. One fairly certain predecessor seems to have been the choir of the Norman cathedral of Lincoln, begun somewhere about 1073.

Although the vaults of Durham are its most celebrated feature, it is rather disconcerting to find that their immediate influence on English architecture was well nigh negligible. This is all the more surprising because the theme of ribbed vaulting was at once taken up seriously in Normandy, and transmitted from there to the adjacent parts of France; but in England, apart from an isolated case, such as the vaulting of the nave of Lincoln in the 1140s, it was not until well into the second half of the twelfth century that it became at all common. Perhaps there were vaults directly inspired by Durham which failed to stay up (like the vaults of the choir of Durham itself), but even if this were so it is still tantamount to saying that English architects were easily discouraged, and that their main interests lay elsewhere.

This brings us to other aspects of Durham. By comparison with the vaults, the success of the new decorative techniques which seem to have made their appearance at Durham was immediate and widespread. Apart from the incised patterns on the great cylindrical piers of the main arcade, three other new elements contribute to the enrichment of the interior. First, there is the addition of a roll-moulding in the centre of the arcade arches. This imparts a characteristic V-profile to the arch, and, although in itself a comparatively modest addition, it has the effect at Durham of combining with other innovations to destroy the ordered sequence of arches within arches, and to substitute for it that of a freely designed arch moulding. In this respect the Durham arches stand at the head of a long and extremely rich tradition in English medieval architecture and mark a definite bifurcation between English and Continental ideas on this subject. Moreover, this is one of the features of Norman architecture for which definite Saxon antecedents can be found. Second, there is the use throughout the nave of the chevron ornament. Once it had been adopted at Durham, its use spread very rapidly throughout the country, and it became perhaps the most ubiquitous of all the later Norman decorative motives for the embellishment of doorways, windows, vault ribs, and chancel arches. The third of the new decorative ideas found at Durham is the inter-laced arcade along the aisle walls. The effect of this is undoubtedly to bring the outer walls of the church into line with the main walls of the nave, and to complete the general impression inside the building of what has been called an 'all-over linear pattern'. In this respect Durham anticipates one of the fundamental trends of later English medieval architecture, one which can be traced right down to the sixteenth century; although the linear quality of its later manifestations might make one hesitate to use the same word of a building like Durham, where so many of the forms assert their bulk rather than their surfaces.

The monastic movement in the north of England, which culminated in the rebuilding of Durham, was initiated by a group of monks from the abbey of Winchcombe. It is not easy for us to follow the development of Norman architecture in the west of England, but the situation there must have been more complicated than in any other part of the country. On the one hand, it was the only part of Saxon England in which the enthusiasm kindled during the tenth-century monastic revival had not diminished; and it is possible – although it could not now be proved – that its architecture in the eleventh century was more enterprising than elsewhere. Unfortunately, we know nothing whatever of the appearance of Winchcombe or any other Saxon monastery in the west, except Deerhurst, which was too small and poor to be representative, although it is interesting to find at Tewkesbury and Gloucester a type of apse which seems to reflect the influence of the arrangement at Deerhurst. Another factor which is possibly relevant is the presence of a number of Continental churchmen holding high ecclesiastical positions in the west during the eleventh century. The Diocese of Hereford seems to have been particularly exposed to Continental influences from a variety of sources. The priory of Chepstow in Monmouth, which was founded soon after 1071 and was a dependency of the Norman abbey of Cormeilles, shows signs of having been vaulted throughout, probably with groined vaults. At Hereford itself the Bishop's Chapel, now destroyed, seems to have reflected methods of construction used in Burgundy; while in the

16. Tewkesbury Abbey, north transept

cathedral itself, started *c.* 1110, the aisles of the choir terminated in towers – an arrangement that can be paralleled in German, or even Italian churches of this and earlier periods. With so many different factors involved it is a pity that we know so little of the circumstances in which this West Country school of architecture came into being, but by 1090, when both Tewkesbury [16] and Gloucester [17] had been started, the school was evidently capable of producing designs that were in some ways even more precocious than that of Durham.

If at Durham the orthodox Norman thick wall was freely adapted for the task of supporting a stone vault, in the naves of Tewkesbury and Gloucester it was virtually replaced by a continuous series of monumental drum piers which must have occupied in their original context nearly two thirds of the total elevation. Nothing known to us in earlier Norman or Saxon architecture prepares us for this drastic deviation. If antecedents are to be found it is as far away as Tournus, in Burgundy, or Como, in Italy, that we have to go to find drum piers

17. Gloucester Cathedral, nave

equally impressive. The possibilities inherent in such connexions are fascinating. Above the drum piers at Tewkesbury we find a series of very squat openings which give access to a passage in the thickness of the wall – which is none other than the old clerestory wall-passage detached from the clerestory, and turned into an independent feature of the elevation; followed above by a clerestory which is now no more than a series of small windows. The nave of Gloucester follows almost exactly the same pattern.

What we find at Tewkesbury and Gloucester is, in effect, a three-storey elevation which implies a completely new conception of a wall. The visual importance of the vertical members, which is strong enough at Durham, is now overwhelming. And when we proceed from the naves of these buildings to their respective choirs, which were earlier, and attempt to reconstruct their original state, we find the same idea used in a less dramatic, but perhaps even more suggestive, way. Both choirs were remodelled in the fourteenth century, but the surviving Norman masonry at both places is sufficient, if we put them together, as it were, to allow us to understand how their structural systems worked. By contrast with the very high aisles flanking the naves of Tewkesbury and Gloucester, the choir aisles and ambulatories are reduced to the status of low tunnels. At Gloucester enough survives of the upper parts of the Norman choir for us to see that these low choir aisles were surmounted by a true Norman gallery. The one at Gloucester has half-arches leaning against the choir walls in the manner of those of the nave of Durham and, whether or not the original choir was vaulted, it seems clear that these buttresses were built with the intention of supporting vaults. In effect, the aisle and gallery together in the choir correspond to the aisle alone in the nave. It follows from this that if the upper parts of the choir were treated in the same way as the upper parts of the nave the choir must have had a four-storey elevation. In the transept at Tewkesbury we can see that this was in fact the case.

It is well known that the four-storey elevation played an important part in the development of Gothic architecture in northern France; but, so far as we know, there are no surviving examples in that part of the world earlier than the choirs of Tewkesbury and Gloucester. It may of course be the case that the idea was invented in the English West Country but, in view of the fact of its wider use and much greater development in the Low Countries and northern France, one is tempted to postulate earlier instances there which have disappeared.

Here the Lotharingian clergy of the West Country come again to mind. Another feature of the choir at Tewkesbury seems to strengthen this point of view. Enough remains of the original piers for us to be able to infer that from the interior of the choir they would seem to rise without a break from the floor to the top of the gallery. In other words, they would have the same general appearance as the drum piers of the nave, only with arches joining them in the middle to form the floor of the gallery.

Although both Tewkesbury and Gloucester no longer show this arrangement, they were undoubtedly the buildings to which the credit should go for the innovation, at least so far as the West Country is concerned. The idea was evidently popular, for it was used again several times in the course of the twelfth century – for instance, in what is now Oxford Cathedral. Even later it appeared in a Gothic form in the abbey of Glastonbury. What beautiful and delicate architectural effects were made possible by means of this idea we can see perhaps best at the east end of the nave of Romsey Abbey. The term 'Giant Order' has been used to describe this device for making one arch span two sections of an elevation [18], and it rightly suggests that the ultimate origins of the idea are to be found in classical architecture.

18. Romsey Abbey, first bay of the nave

The immediate source, however, was Germany. There is a Roman building at Trier where the arrangement can still be seen, and in the eleventh century this building seems to have inspired the architects of the Rhenish cathedrals of Speyer and Mainz. The transept façades at Romsey have this feature more or less in its German form, but hardly anticipate the boldness and beautiful effects found in the Romsey nave bay. The whole idea clearly underwent some development either in England or *en route* to England, i.e. in Lower Lotharingia.

Tewkesbury and Gloucester form the starting-point for the most capricious and imaginative variations on the original Norman theme. But the most characteristic expressions of Anglo-Norman taste throughout the twelfth century are to be found in the field of decoration. We have met this tendency already in the nave of Durham; but the chief source from which it spread was probably Canterbury.

At Canterbury, the first thirty years of the twelfth century saw the building of a new and very much enlarged choir in place of the short eastern limb of Lanfranc's cathedral. According to William of Malmesbury, who saw it, there was nothing like it in all England 'either for the brilliance of its glass windows, the beauty of its marble pavement, or the many coloured pictures which led wondering eyes to the very summit of the ceiling'. This choir was not vaulted in stone like Durham, for it was destroyed by a fire in the roof in 1174, which left only the outer walls of the aisles and the crypt. Both were preserved when the Gothic choir was built after 1174, and in the crypt especially we can get some idea of the splendours which dazzled William of Malmesbury from the paintings in St Gabriel's Chapel and from the wonderful series of carved capitals [19].

19. Canterbury
Cathedral, crypt capital

20. Castle Acre Priory, west front

A distinctive feature of this new choir at Canterbury was the fact
that it opened into a second, or eastern, transept. This was almost
certainly derived from the plan of the great Burgundian abbey of
Cluny, whose third church was begun in 1088, and the idea may have
reached Canterbury through the mediation of the Cluniac priory of
St Pancras, at Lewes, which is known also to have had this second
transept. Cluniac churches were famous, and even notorious, for the
extravagance of their decoration, and the few fragments which survive
of Lewes Priory suggest that it conformed to the general practice of
the Order in this respect. The west front of Castle Acre Priory [20], in
Norfolk, gives a good idea of the kind of rich effects which the Cluniacs
admired.

Even more magnificent than either of these must have been the favourite foundation of King Henry I, at Reading, in Berkshire, which was colonized by Cluniac monks without being attached to the Order. The abbey at Reading was begun in 1121 and, although again we know what it was like only from a few fragments, it seems certain that it played a very important part in spreading the use of decorative sculpture as a form of architectural embellishment.

Yet another work of this period which has completely disappeared, but which probably vied in splendour with Canterbury and Reading, was the eastern extension of Old Sarum; and finally, although it belongs to the second half of the twelfth century, the new choir of York Minster ought perhaps to be added to this list. It was begun in *c*. 1154, evidently with the intention of making the appearance of the Minster match the pretensions of its archbishop to be the equal of Canterbury.

Although fragments are no substitute for the overwhelming effects of the total ensembles, we can still get some idea of the richness of the sculptural decoration of the twelfth century from doorways like those at Ely and Malmesbury; and, where the great works have disappeared, there are sometimes humble parish churches in the vicinity which

21. Kilpeck Church, south door

preserve less grandiose, but not less interesting, records of their carvers' art. Kilpeck, in Herefordshire [21], is perhaps the outstanding example.

Towards the end of the twelfth century the number of large-scale works in the Anglo-Norman style gradually declined. The church at the Hospital of St Cross, Winchester, begun soon after 1151 but often interrupted, has a lavish display of the chevron ornament which is combined with a number of new structural ideas from across the Channel. Elsewhere, however, buildings on a smaller scale gave the Anglo-Norman decorators untrammelled scope, and it is at Durham in the 1170s that we find what are perhaps their most extreme achievements in the galilee of the cathedral, and in the doorway of the Bishop's Hall in the castle. Work of this delicacy has a *fin de siècle* quality which prepares us for the imminent arrival of a new style.

In all this drift towards the rich, the subtle, and the complicated, there was one oddly discordant note. It was during this period that one of the most distinctive features of later English church architecture made its appearance. This was the straight – or flat – east end, which was preferred to both the earlier Norman round types. Undoubtedly this led to a simplification of plans; but there was a good deal of experiment before the final clarification was reached. Thus at Hereford Cathedral the central apse rose less than half way up the eastern wall, the upper part of which was flat. At Southwell Cathedral, in Nottinghamshire, the old three-apse plan was modified by the squaring of the central one; and at Chertsey Abbey (started 1110), in Surrey, the old semicircular ambulatory became rectangular, the radiating chapels acquiring a rectangular form and being placed side by side. This latter configuration was further developed at Romsey Abbey, Hampshire, and received what was to become its standard form at Old Sarum between 1125 and 1130. The square-ended chancel had already been adopted for other reasons by the Cistercian Order of monks, and when they arrived in England (see Chapter 3) they did much to ensure its continued use. The results of this simplification were most apparent from the outside. Although the external walls of English churches received their share of ornamental enrichment – for instance, the choir of Canterbury Cathedral – their actual silhouettes seldom seem to have been considered capable of yielding aesthetic effects. With the transformation of the east end the central tower could no longer serve as the climax of a carefully graduated hierarchy of ascending forms, and it became increasingly an object which rose in splendid isolation above the long horizontal roofs of nave and choir. The two-tower façade was certainly known in England; at Canterbury, Lincoln, Durham, and Southwell, for instance, it was combined with a massive central tower in the Continental Norman manner. But the inordinate extension of the naves in English churches required something more impressive than two small towers to give an adequate accent to their west end. Thus at Lincoln we find the two towers embedded in a massive block, and at Bury St Edmunds there was an elaborate complex involving corner turrets which turned the façade into a great screen – perhaps the first of what was to become a long series. At Ely the western emphasis was even greater. Here the western transept with corner turrets and a projecting porch verged upon a great monolithic tower. The idea of a single central tower at the west end may be regarded as an Anglo-Saxon survival, and it is possible that a similar great western tower was intended at first for the abbey of Tewkesbury. The other Anglo-Norman solutions also had their origins outside the Continental Norman tradition, and a search for them would lead us to the Low Countries, Germany, and even to St Mark's, Venice. Few of the towers which remain – e.g. those at St Albans, Norwich, and Tewkesbury – are now to be seen in the settings for which they were originally designed. All three have become the only external features of importance in their respective buildings.

At the beginning of the twelfth century no one in England would have considered building a great church in any other style than the Anglo-Norman. After the middle of the century, however, this was no longer so. Yet the style lingered on for nearly fifty years, and exercised a strong, if indirect, influence on English Gothic architecture of the thirteenth century. The situation between 1150 and 1200 was, in fact, extremely complicated. The essence of the matter was the rapid growth of the new reformed monastic orders during the middle years of the century – chief among them the Cistercians. With their arrival, ecclesiastical patronage bifurcated. The Cistercians were not satisfied with the Anglo-Norman style, and they insisted on a kind of architecture that was in keeping with their own astringent tastes. Henceforth the Anglo-Norman style tended to become more and more the architecture of what we might think of as the High Church party of the day. Its persistence was really due to the conservative outlook of its patrons. But the situation was confused still more by a third factor. This was the growing influence of French Gothic on both the Cistercian and the Anglo-Norman styles. On the whole, this Gothic aspect is perhaps the most important, so perhaps the best way of dealing with the whole problem is to make it serve as an introduction to the subject of Gothic architecture in England.

3 Gothic Church Architecture before Westminster

In the year 1114 or thereabouts a group of monks from the French abbey of Tiron was settled at St Dogmells, in the far west of Wales. Some ten years later another foundation, this time from Savigny-le-Vieux, was established at Tulket, in Lancashire. Later it moved to Furness, a name which is perhaps better known. The first of the Cistercians followed in 1128. The earliest of their houses in England was at Waverley, in Surrey. Tintern, Monmouthshire, was founded in 1131, and Rievaulx, in Yorkshire, the following year. After Rievaulx the movement assumed the dimensions of a torrent. Between 1128 and 1150 there were thirty-five Cistercian (and twelve Savignac) foundations. With these ought to be included the numerous priories of Augustinian canons which sprang up everywhere during the same period. All these movements were animated by a common desire to purify regular religious life from what was regarded as the contagion of worldliness; and renunciation and privation played a prominent part in their respective programmes. Eventually the Cistercians became by far the most important of these reformed orders. Not only were they the most numerous, but also the best organized. Under their patronage was conducted a very considerable proportion of all the building operations in the country during the middle years of the twelfth century, and to some extent the orders which shared their sympathies in religion followed their example in architecture. Inevitably their attitude on matters of architectural style was bound to have tremendous repercussions.

In the past a great deal of attention has been given to Cistercian architecture on account of the role which it is supposed to have played in the evolution of English Gothic. Because it is so emphatically the antithesis of everything Anglo-Norman, it has been felt that in some way it must belong with what eventually took the place of Anglo-

Norman, i.e. Gothic. Perhaps this was partly due to the pointed arches which were used systematically in Cistercian churches. But pointed arches alone do not make a Gothic church; and in general it seems to have been the case that so long as Cistercian architecture in England remained truly Cistercian it was not Gothic; and when it became Gothic it ceased to be distinctively Cistercian. The only exception is at the critical point where we find at least one building that was both Cistercian and Gothic; and it cannot be denied that the Cistercian Order functioned to some extent as a catalyst in the great process of change from Anglo-Norman to Gothic, especially in the north. But the situation was extremely involved, and requires very careful analysis.

The Cistercian movement began in Burgundy, and the only interest which its early leaders had in architecture was to ensure that the monastic buildings, and chief among them the abbey-church, were suitable to the way of life which was to be lived within them. The one thing on which they insisted was the exclusion of all superfluous ornament, which they regarded as distracting, and therefore as an abomination. Apart from this, they wanted buildings that were convenient to use, and simple to the point of severity. Accordingly they adopted the starkest form of contemporary Burgundian Romanesque, and when the need arose they devised a standard church-plan. The plan they took with them everywhere, and it became for many years an unmistakable and indispensable feature of every Cistercian church. But they were less insistent about the style. In countries like Germany and northern Italy, where the local versions of Romanesque were severe enough to meet with their approval, they were quite willing to compromise. In England, however, the situation was different. Here the established style was, from their point of view, hopelessly contaminated, and their attitude towards it was therefore much more critical. That is why we find so many purely Burgundian features in the earliest English Cistercian churches: relatively unarticulated piers, pointed arches, and barrel vaults over the chapels and aisles set at right angles to the main walls. Yet even so there was no question of importing the Burgundian style whole. We have only to compare the substantial remains of the nave of Fountains Abbey, Yorkshire (some time after 1135), with Fontenay (c. 1140), in France, which is the best preserved of the truly Burgundian Cistercian churches, to realize the extent of the variations which were tolerated in England. At Fontenay there is no clerestory, and the nave has a pointed barrel vault; at

22. Fountains Abbey, nave and aisle

Fountains [22], on the other hand, there is a clerestory, and the nave
had a flat wooden roof. Perhaps these ought to be regarded as concessions to the English climate rather than to English taste. But it is
difficult to explain the other deviation at Fountains – namely, the
central tower. This is quite remarkable, for towers were specifically
prohibited by Cistercian regulations, and we know that an architect
was sent from Clairvaux to Fountains to ensure that the buildings of
the new foundation should conform to Cistercian practice. But
although Master Geoffroi de Ainai came from France, most of his
masons were Yorkshiremen, and certain reminiscences of their
previous experience were bound to intrude. Central towers were
common among Anglo-Norman buildings. And in spite of the tower,
Fountains must have presented an appearance of formidable austerity;
there was never any question of contravening the spirit of the Order.

The concessions at Fountains are none the less significant. If the
slightly earlier nave at Rievaulx Abbey had survived it would have

been a little more severe and a little more Burgundian than Fountains. On the other hand, at Kirkstall Abbey, near Leeds (*c.* 1152), which was the next great Cistercian church in the north after Fountains, the relaxations and the infiltration of Anglo-Norman forms went a stage further. The simple square of cylindrical piers at Rievaulx and Fountains were abandoned in favour of a compound pier whose shape was generated from an eight-pointed star. The incipient mouldings on the arcades of Fountains were developed into a definite echelon profile; and there are several instances of the discreet use of Anglo-Norman ornament to be seen at Kirkstall. Even more important was the use of Anglo-Norman ribbed vaults instead of the Burgundian barrels for the choir and side aisles.

If Kirkstall shows Cistercian architecture in the process of being domesticated the development of the style was soon to be deflected in another direction altogether. The abbey of Roche [23], at Maltby,

23. Roche Abbey, south transept

Yorkshire, was founded in 1147, but the church is certainly later than Kirkstall, and its design ought to be assigned to about 1160. Two features distinguish Roche from all its Cistercian predecessors. One is the appearance of a third storey in the elevation between the main arcade and the clerestory. The other is the fact that the whole church was vaulted. In both these respects Roche drew its inspiration from France, not England. The vaults in particular, with their supporting wall-shafts running right down the walls, were conceived wholly in the French manner, and they make Roche the first English church which has any serious claim to be called Gothic.

To use this famous word for the first time in connexion with Roche is apt to suggest that it was an epoch-making building. Yet it is anything but revolutionary. To appreciate just how conservative the Gothic of Roche is, we should compare it with a really advanced French building such as the cathedral of Laon, which was begun at almost exactly the same time. At Laon the walls no longer seem massive or solid. They have been hoisted up, as it were, on long rows of slender columns; and wherever possible they have been perforated by rows of openings. Each aperture is framed by a pointed arch with a simple roll-moulding, supported by colonnettes or detached shafts; and the overall impression is not so much that of a wall as a seemingly endless system of arches, shafts, and spaces. This effect is intensified by the bundles of wall-shafts which carry the ribbed vaults. At first sight it is all rather bewildering; but the more one looks at Laon, the more evident does it become that everything has been thought out with the same kind of thorough-going logic as that which characterized the earliest Norman architecture. The visible system of forms symbolizes the structural system of the actual building. In fact, French Gothic, regarded from this point of view, can trace its ancestry back to Norman architecture no less convincingly than Anglo-Norman itself. The point of divergence began at the point where logic and decoration came into collision. As we have seen, the English readily sacrificed the logical clarity of their buildings as soon as they set out to explore new decorative possibilities. The one principle of Norman architecture which they never seriously questioned was that represented by the thick wall. They changed its proportions, turned it into cylindrical piers, cut away large parts of it; but always in the last analysis they were left with a residue that could only be described as thick. The French, on the other hand, assimilated the Norman logic with avidity. But at the same time they made a fundamental distinction between the logic as such and the thick-wall system within which it had been developed. The latter they rejected; and in its place they gradually evolved a new and revolutionary structural system, in which the diffused supporting strength of the thick wall was replaced by a much more rational and economical system of supports applied at the points of real stress. This allowed the non-essential parts of the wall to be handled with unprecedented freedom. The relations between solid forms and voids became much more complicated, and windows began to assume a new importance. There was certainly much more to Gothic than the invention of a new kind of structural engineering; but this was undoubtedly the essence of the new style during its formative period, and the extent to which it was understood and reproduced elsewhere is a sure index of the penetration of specifically French Gothic influences.

By this criterion the Gothic of Roche is extremely tentative. The solidity of the walls has certainly not diminished. Indeed, we can see at Roche the reappearance in a Cistercian context of the Anglo-Norman wall-passage; while the new intermediate section of the elevation, indicated by pairs of blind recesses hollowed out of the thickness of the wall, merely accentuates the massive effect. Apart from the wall-shafts, the vaults, and the third storey, very little has changed. When it comes to the point we call Roche Gothic only because, in a superficial way it reminds us of real Gothic works.

Nevertheless Roche is a remarkable building. It will not do to explain its Gothic features simply on the grounds that it belonged to the Cistercian Order. It is true that by 1160 the Cistercians had started to come to terms with the new style in France; but in England there was no uniform trend in this direction. It was only in the north that they took the lead in adopting Gothic. The explanation is perhaps to be found in the close commercial bonds that were developing between the sheep-farming Cistercians of northern England and the cloth-manufacturing towns of northern France which bought their wool. It was in these towns – Douai, Arras, Valenciennes, etc. – that the new architectural style developed most rapidly during the 1150s and 1160s. Roche probably took its inspiration from some Cistercian house in the vicinity.

The next great Cistercian abbey in the north of England, Byland, in Yorkshire, survives only in fragments. Yet there is enough for us to be able to reconstruct its elevation, and to infer that it must have been a work even more decisive than Roche in the formation of the first distinctly English school of Gothic architecture. In one important

respect Byland was less French than Roche. It was not vaulted. On
the other hand, there seem to have been a great many more arches and
shafts used in the design, and to the casual observer the effect must
have been far more reminiscent of buildings like Laon. Yet a closer
comparison would have disclosed a fundamental difference. To anyone who could understand it, Laon was an intricate system; but to the
uninitiated it might seem that Gothic was nothing more than the use
of shafts and arches in large numbers – a way of making the walls
interesting to look at. When Englishmen made the acquaintance of
Gothic this was in fact precisely how they saw it. True to their insular
bias they chose to regard it, not as an alternative system of construction, but as an alternative system of decoration. In a sense they completely missed the point of what the French were doing; but because of
this they created a totally different kind of Gothic of their own. It was
at Byland Abbey that this insular twist first became apparent. If
Roche was the first Gothic building in England, Byland was the first
English Gothic building. It was dedicated in 1177, and it must have
been under construction before Canterbury choir was started in 1175.
The new collegiate church at Ripon was probably slightly later than
Canterbury. Roger of Pont l'Evêque, whose chief concern as Archbishop of York was to keep abreast of Canterbury in all things, had
already provided his Minster at York with a choir commensurate with
the Anglo-Norman splendours of Canterbury. Now the new Gothic

24. Ripon Cathedral, restoration of original nave elevation

choir at Canterbury goaded his pride once more, and he resolved to rebuild Ripon, one of his subsidiary minsters, in the new style. But if the stimulus came from Canterbury, his masons came from Byland. Ripon is important because enough survives for us to form an impression of the Byland style; and also because it marks the point where this incipient Gothic of the north was emancipated from the exclusive patronage of the Cistercians. The Gothic of Ripon is purely an affair of applying arch mouldings and shafts to the openings in thick walls. This is clear enough in the transepts and choir which still survive. But it must have been even more obvious in the twelfth-century nave [24] which, for reasons not wholly clear, was built without side aisles. Enough of the original dispositions were left when side aisles were added in the fifteenth century for us to be able to imagine how it must have looked. On each side there were two wall-passages, one above the other. These opened on to the nave through rows of arches which were grouped into patterns. Two patterns appear in each row, and they were repeated alternately along the nave.

Nothing could illustrate more clearly the almost exclusive preoccupation of these northern masons with the articulation of walls; and it is a great pity that the nave of Ripon has gone the way of so many other large buildings in this style. Time has in fact dealt very severely with them. The only mature example which survives in anything like its original condition is the abbey-church at Hexham. There the choir and transepts [25] have escaped destruction, but only at the price of heavy restoration. Otherwise we have the romantic, often splendid, but melancholy ruins of Whitby Abbey, in Yorkshire, Tynemouth Priory, in Northumberland, and the Gothic choir of Rievaulx. Although they are picturesque, ruins are no substitute for complete buildings, save perhaps in so far as they serve as skeletons on which to conduct classes in architectural anatomy. At Whitby and Rievaulx, for instance, the ruined state of the structures allows us to see heavy masses of masonry which originally must have been concealed behind a purely ornamental screen of shafts and mouldings. Here, if anywhere, it is abundantly evident that early northern Gothic was only skin-deep; that the shafts and mouldings were no more than a veneer masking the depth of the wall perhaps more effectively than the old Anglo-Norman patterns, but not differing from them at all in purpose. Later, as in the choir of Rievaulx or the presbytery at Tynemouth (both early thirteenth century), stone vaults were introduced; but in the earlier stages of the style vaults were certainly not considered an essential feature of a Gothic building. To a Frenchman all this would have seemed little better than heresy; yet in the north of England it meant merely that the local masons were slow to cut the traces linking them with their Anglo-Norman past. For that reason alone it is perhaps more illuminating to approach English Gothic from the north than from any other direction.

Early Gothic in the south was more or less dominated by the new choir of Canterbury [26]. Already at St Cross and elsewhere there had

25. Hexham Abbey, north transept

26. Canterbury Cathedral, choir

been spasmodic signs of French influences penetrating across the Channel, but at Canterbury the authorities went a stage further and summoned a Frenchman, William, who came originally from Sens, but who evidently had been working in the region of the most advanced Gothic buildings – the vicinity of Arras and Valenciennes. Had their patrons wished them to do so, English masons might very well have learnt to build a purely French Gothic church at Canterbury. But the monks insisted that whatever could be salvaged from the old Anglo-Norman choir should be incorporated into the new building. In effect this meant retaining most of the early twelfth-century plan, which, from William's point of view, was not a very suitable starting-point for an up-to-date Gothic design. At the same time adequate provision had to be made for the rising cult of St Thomas à Becket. In this respect the disaster of 1174 could hardly have occurred at a more propitious moment. To accommodate Becket's shrine it was decided to extend the church still farther towards the east. This made the plan even more rambling and irregular, and still less amenable to William's style. It is not surprising, therefore, to find that in the event his design for the new choir of Canterbury was a good deal less revolutionary than it might have been if he had been given a free hand.

Even so, Canterbury is more French than any other English building before Westminster Abbey. Here we find walls raised on rows of columns in the French manner; and in the first part of the choir at least there are circular and octagonal columns alternating with one another, and corresponding to the double-bay system of the sexpartite ribbed vaults overhead. And there are wall-shafts systematically relating the ribs of the vaults to the columns of the main arcades. The walls above these columns are not thick walls in the technical Anglo-Norman sense at all. Although the traditional wall-passage appears at clerestory level, this is not a true indication of the thickness of the wall, for the clerestory is built out over special arches which rest, not on the main columns, but on the haunches of the transverse arches across the side aisles. No doubt this represents a compromise between Gothic and Anglo-Norman practice. But the point from which the compromise starts is very much farther in the Gothic direction than was the case in the north.

Canterbury was conceived first and foremost as a splendid approach to Becket's shrine. As the work proceeded eastward, so the level of the floor rose, and the richness of the decoration steadily increased, until the climax was reached in the Trinity Chapel where the shrine was to be housed. After the second transept we find some of the stone columns of the main arcades festooned with supporting shafts of dark marble. Then the columns are doubled, as in some French churches; and finally when we come to the Trinity Chapel the columns themselves are made of richly coloured and highly polished marble. These surround the apse and, together with the marble-shafted upper storeys, the tiled floor, and the stained-glass windows, they must have formed a setting of unprecedented brilliance for the shrine.

In all this Canterbury probably owed as much to the memory of its Anglo-Norman predecessor as to the contemporary Gothic buildings known to William of Sens; and, as one might have expected, it was the decorative display rather than the original structural features which made the deeper impression on English masons and their patrons. Even when something new appeared – like the marble shafts, which seem to have come from Valenciennes – the extent to which they were used at Canterbury was far more lavish than in Continental Gothic, and it already anticipates the extraordinary vogue which Purbeck marble enjoyed in England during the thirteenth century.

More indirectly, however, the importance of Canterbury was not that it represented this or that kind of Gothic, but that it was Gothic and not Anglo-Norman. It marks the point at which the higher English clergy abandoned their conservative attachment to the older style and set out to bring themselves up to date. Perhaps it was not entirely a coincidence that this should happen almost immediately after the Cistercians had come to terms with Gothic on their own account. At any rate, from this time onward it is no longer possible to think of the differences in English church architecture as manifestations of high- and low-church policies. Canterbury being a metropolitan church, its example was sufficient to establish Gothic of whatever kind once and for all as the fashionable style for great churches; and when every one went over to Gothic the only significant differences left were those between regional schools.

The immediate influence of Canterbury is evident in the columns of the retrochoir at Chichester Cathedral, which was remodelled after 1187; and one may suspect that the Gothic elements which appear so curiously mixed with pure Anglo-Norman survivals in the round nave of the City Temple church (dedicated 1185), in London, came from the same source. But to see what English masons could do with themes from Canterbury when they were freed from all restraints, one must turn to Lincoln. First, however, the West Country school of early Gothic remains to be discussed.

The origins of Gothic in the West Country are more obscure than in the north or the south-east. The role of the Cistercians, so far as we are now in a position to judge, seems to have been less crucial than in the north. The earlier parts of Abbey Dore (1170s), in Herefordshire, represent a later stage than Roche. Already in the nave of Malmesbury (*c*. 1165) some Anglo-Norman masons had gone over to pointed arches for their main arcades. The same thing happened in the two bays at the west end of the nave of Worcester Cathedral, which seem to have replaced a part of Wulfstan's church that was damaged by the fall of a western tower. They belong to the 1170s and, perhaps more than any other design of this period, they merit the description 'transitional'. Here wall-shafts and ribbed vaults appeared side by side with Anglo-Norman ornament and in conjunction with Anglo-Norman thick walls. The handling of the piers is particularly interesting, for the wall-shafts and the shafts in the angles of the set-backs together produce a diamond shape with a rippling profile that foreshadows in a rudimentary way the purely Gothic piers at Wells.

In 1184 the abbey-church at Glastonbury was destroyed by fire. At once all the abbey's considerable resources of relics and legend were geared to the task of raising money; and with help from the King, the celebrated Chapel of St Mary, or *vetusta ecclesia* as it was called, was rebuilt in well-nigh record time. This chapel itself had been something of a relic, and in its new form it was lavishly decorated. Much of the ornament was Anglo-Norman, and in many ways it can be regarded as the last important Anglo-Norman work to be started in England. But it is a complicated building, and there are several concessions to the new taste. The capitals have early Gothic leaf-forms, and it was completed with a ribbed vault. In the abbey-church itself, which was started only shortly after the chapel, the Gothic idiom was much more prominent. The only considerable fragments that remain belonged to the transept walls; but they are sufficient for us to see that the elevation was a transcription of the Romsey–Oxford type of Anglo-Norman, with a considerable admixture of Worcester influence, especially in the clerestory. We find at Glastonbury clusters of shafts with a very distinctive form. They are arranged in threes, and their capitals are in effect bunches of curly leaves. With or without the capitals, this motive appears in many West Country and Midland churches of the period, and suggests that there was a definite school with common pattern-books.

The church with the closest links to Glastonbury in this respect is the cathedral of Wells. The two buildings must have been nearly contemporary. Work on Wells was certainly in progress during the 1180s, and the latest views seem to imply that Wells was slightly earlier than Glastonbury, although of the two it makes the more definite break with the past. Here in fact West Country Gothic assumes a precocious maturity. Although it is later than Canterbury, it shows singularly little Canterbury influence; and although there is perhaps a vague indebtedness to the Cistercians, it is far more advanced than contemporary work in the north. The design underwent a slight but significant change as it passed from choir to transept and from transept to nave. This is most readily apprehended in the treatment of the triforium and the vertical divisions between the bays. In the choir and transepts the triforium section of each bay consists of a double-arch unit. The wall-shafts which separate the bays are not taken down to the ground as at Worcester and Glastonbury; or to the capitals of the piers of the main arcade as at Canterbury. They reach only to corbels where the main arcade and triforium meet. These vertical divisions in the choir are by no means conspicuous; but even so in the nave [27] they are attenuated still further. Here a third arch is introduced into the triforium, and this has the effect of 'squeezing out' the wall-shafts and merging the discrete sections of the triforium into a band of contiguous arches.

This tendency at Wells to stress the horizontal divisions of the building at the expense of the vertical was to become very characteristic of English Gothic in the thirteenth century; and it is one of the things which distinguishes English Gothic of this period from all Continental versions of the style. Whatever else English masons may have been trying to do, there was no question of their buildings soaring heavenward. This was even more apparent from the outside. The silhouettes of early English Gothic churches were uniformly long and low, with occasional squat towers. The taller towers and spires which now adorn them all belong to a later age. When they were built only the external features which really disturbed their outlines were the high-pitched gables of their numerous façades. With a sure instinct, the English realized that their particular kind of Gothic was most effective when it was allowed to form long, receding vistas. In the nave of Wells the effect of recession is particularly vivid, and this is due as much to the conceptions of the walls as a series of self-contained horizontal strata, as to its actual length. Below the triforium the piers and arches of the main arcade make an even more emphatic and clearly defined zone of patterning. Their profiles and mouldings and, above all, their foliage capitals, to which the not very appropriate designation 'stiff-leafed' is usually applied, leave us in no doubt at all that this was the aspect of Gothic design which exercised the deepest fascination for English masons. Even when we realize that the piers are simple crosses of masonry with groups of triple shafts placed against each face and in each angle they remain visually bewildering. It goes without saying that such richness and profusion of form was only possible because the whole wall was conceived on Anglo-Norman proportions. There is the traditional wall-passage at clerestory level, and the external buttressing of the main vaults is still concealed under the aisle roof. The vaults and clerestory, which constitute the third horizontal section of the nave, have sometimes been criticized on the grounds that there the patterning is weaker, i.e. less dense than in the lower parts. The fact may be admitted, but it is not necessarily a defect. To see Wells in this way is to see it in the light of Lincoln. But it is at least arguable that the Wells designers thinned out their patterning deliberately with the intention of suggesting that the lighter parts of the building were at the top.

The work at Wells culminated in the great west front. This seems to have been started about 1220, by which time two other important cathedral façades in the Gothic style had been designed in England – those of Lincoln and Peterborough. At Lincoln a flat screen-façade had been built around the old Norman west front, and its ancestry clearly goes back to Bury St Edmunds. The Peterborough design was far more original and impressive, comprising three enormous portals which occupy the whole façade. This is the only instance in England where we find deep portals like those of the French High Gothic cathedrals, but it was very much a case of beating the French at their own game, and it does not seem to have provoked the sort of admiration which leads to imitation. Although the Wells façade was intended to accommodate a vast array of figure sculpture devoted to eschatological themes such as the French deployed in their cathedral portals, its design followed the example of Lincoln rather than Peterborough, at least in the fundamental respect of being a screen. This projects beyond the church to north and south to embrace the roots of the fourteenth-century towers. The actual portals are insignificant, the main public entrance to the cathedral being through a splendidly

decorated porch on the north side of the nave. This was not the only difference between Wells and French Gothic cathedrals. The French figures were always crowded together in rows; at Wells they are dispersed over the whole façade, and even spread round the corners of the towers to their eastern sides. Moreover, while the French statues tended to come right away from the walls to which they were attached, so that they could be seen in the round, at Wells they were set back into niches in the buttresses, where they could be seen only from the front, and then not easily. In fact, everything about this façade is as wilfully insular as the architecture behind it.

And so to Lincoln [28]. From Canterbury and from Wells streams of Gothic ideas converged on Lincoln, and mingled there with others that were wholly new, to produce what is by common consent the masterpiece of the style. An earthquake in 1185, which broke the back of the Anglo-Norman church, provided the opportunity for a complete rebuilding; and the resources of patronage were equal to the most extravagant demands that could be made upon them. So apart from the re-use of the old Norman west front, hardly anything at Lincoln Cathedral can be blamed on the exigencies of economy or compromise. We can sense that it was built as a *tour de force*, and it is no accident that of all the churches of its period it is the one that seems to embody most completely the English ideal of what a great Gothic cathedral should look like.

Work began in 1192. The original apse, a singular arrangement with almost triangular sides, has gone, and the earliest surviving parts are the eastern transepts and the choir, called St Hugh's Choir after the bishop who built it, to distinguish it from the later eastward extension which is known as the Angel Choir. The idea of a church with two transepts suggests at once a link between Lincoln and Canterbury, and many of the details of St Hugh's Choir owe their inspiration, if not their exact form, to the Gothic work at Canterbury. There are also structural similarities. But it is characteristic of Lincoln that the enrichment should be taken to a far greater pitch of sophistication. Purbeck marble now appears everywhere. The piers of the main arcade in the choir, which are variations on the Canterbury theme of shaft-supported piers, each have their own peculiar design. And the arcades along the aisle walls replace the simple arches or intersecting arches which sufficed in Anglo-Norman times by two rows, each with its distinctive arch-form, and one superimposed on the other in what can only be described as a kind of architectural counterpoint. It is in

28. Lincoln Cathedral, nave

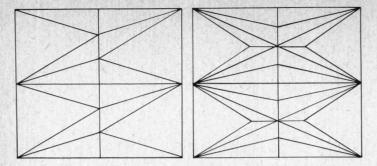

29. Lincoln Cathedral, vault systems: a. In St Hugh's Choir; b. In the nave

keeping with this trend that the capitals should follow the stiff-leafed type of Wells rather than the more formal convention at Canterbury.

But the most important contribution of Lincoln to English Gothic was in the field of vaulting. The vaults in St Hugh's Choir [29a] are famous for their bizarre asymmetry, and they are not at all easy to understand. Both transepts have orthodox sexpartite vaults, and it has been suggested that the choir vaults were intended to produce something like the visual effect of a sexpartite vault without having to find room for an intermediate transverse rib. One can see well enough what the intention behind this curious formation was, by comparing the clerestories of the eastern transepts and St Hugh's Choir. In the transepts where there are ordinary sexpartite vaults there is room for only two lancets, and these are heavily obscured by the converging ribs. In the choir the intermediate transverse rib has, as it were, been shifted to one side; and this makes room for a third lancet. Moreover, the other two admit a great deal more light. Another advantage of such a vault is that it could be placed over a crossing as well as an ordinary bay. At Canterbury there was an anomaly between the choir and the crossing which arose from the necessities of sexpartite vaulting, and which was avoided at Lincoln. This explanation may contain part of the truth, but it is not entirely convincing, because the Lincoln vaults do not really resemble sexpartite vaults at all, except at a great distance when they are heavily foreshortened. They differ from sexpartite vaults in two ways. One is the presence of what is called a ridge rib, which runs right along the crest of the vaults, and joins all the key stones together to provide another and very effective longitudinal accent. This idea had already been used on a small scale at Ripon. The other is the provision of two key stones instead of one for the ribs in each bay. This was not entirely unprecedented, for some such arrangement can be seen in the nave of Durham. It is true that at Durham the vaulting compartments were related to a double-bay system, and treated like two bays in one. But at least in respect of the two centres the parallel between Lincoln and Durham is exact, and at this point it becomes pertinent to wonder what form the ribbed vaults took in twelfth-century Lincoln.

Together these differences are crucial. The essence of a sexpartite vault is that it spreads like a canopy over its bay or double bay. The ribs, converging on a single and isolated centre, bind the space below into a unified and clearly defined spatial compartment. This effect is entirely due to the converging ribs, and as soon as they cease to converge it is lost. This is precisely what happens at Lincoln. There the pattern made by the vaults is clearly based on the notion of divergence rather than convergence. The ribs spread out in groups from points along the walls towards the ridge rib. The importance of this change can hardly be overestimated. It implies a totally new conception of the function of vaulting, one that is visual and decorative rather than structural. Lincoln marks the point where the English discovered that they could do with ribbed vaults what they had already done with other Gothic elements – namely, transform them into devices for pattern-making. To this end they were prepared to dispense with the hitherto unquestioned assumption that vaults should be related to the bay system. The diverging ribs of St Hugh's Choir, in fact, cover parts of adjacent bays.

What makes it almost certain that the designers of St Hugh's Choir were thinking along these lines is the fact that in the nave, only a few years later, a much more mature and ambitious system of diverging ribs was carried out with complete assurance [29b]. There are two differences between the vaults of the choir and those of the nave: one is that the latter are perfectly symmetrical; and the other is that they contain more ribs. These facts have a common explanation. Within each bay of the nave there are now three centres instead of two. This means that the number of ribs in each diverging group has increased from four to five (in fact, there are seven, but two of these do not reach the ridge rib). It needs only a little thought to realize that for any vault to be both continuous and symmetrical there must be an odd number of centres; and it is a standing wonder that this never occurred to the designers of St Hugh's Choir. But it must be remembered that they were feeling their way towards something entirely new, and were probably not clear as to what they really wished to achieve when they began. The idea of two centres may have been given to them as a fixed starting-point, and they only emancipated themselves from this restriction when they reached the nave.

The result of all this was a vault pattern which is as interesting to look at as the rest of the building below; and for the first time we can say that all the exposed surfaces have been accorded equal emphasis. In a sense this is an extension of the Wells principle; but it also involves to some extent a repudiation of Wells, and with it the first signs of a revision of English thinking on the subject of the thick wall. This point can easily be spoilt by being overstated. The walls at Lincoln are still thick enough to carry wall-passages at clerestory level, and the mouldings of the arcade arches are as florid as ever. But there is a definite shift of emphasis. The main arcade at Lincoln is not so massive as at Wells, and it is far less obtrusive. This is because the span of the arches has been increased. The Lincoln arcades are wider than any others in England, except those of the nave of York, which are much later. As a result of this we can look right through them to the aisle walls beyond, and these are allowed to participate directly in the overall effect. Quite apart from making the interior lighter and more spacious, it means that we tend to see it in terms of its peripheral surfaces. Piers and columns which are surrounded by space are inevitably apprehended as solid volumes. This was frankly admitted and deliberately exploited in Norman times; and although the early Gothic masons cased their piers with rippling profiles, these scarcely concealed their bulk. At Wells we feel that they were making a virtue of necessity. But at Lincoln the trend is reversed, and although it is too early as yet to speak of linear, as opposed to plastic, patterns, there is undeniably something about Lincoln which foreshadows the later development of English Gothic.

Yet there is no question of external – i.e. French – influences. We realize this if we compare Lincoln nave with the elevation of the inner choir aisle at Le Mans, which is almost exactly contemporary (c. 1218) and has almost exactly the same basic design, but which seems almost poverty-stricken when it is set against the profusion of English decorative forms. The change at Lincoln is wholly a change within the context of English taste and English presuppositions, and it is perhaps typical of English waywardness that though Lincoln was frequently copied in this or that particular, the further implications of its design were not explored until much later in the thirteenth century.

In spite of its importance, the nave of Lincoln was neither the end nor the climax of the first Gothic building period there. It is in the chapter house [30] that we find the most perfect expression of the aesthetic point of view which developed as the work progressed. In plan this is a centralized figure with ten sides. Centrally planned chapter houses were adopted in the West Country during the twelfth century as an alternative to the more usual rectangular form. The earliest seems to have been at Worcester, which still survives. Two more are known at the Cistercian abbeys of Margam, Glamorganshire, and Abbey Dore; and another was planned at Wells, although it was not built until much later. Perhaps it was from Wells that the idea reached Lincoln. The centralized plan was well suited to the special needs of the Lincoln style. The walls are all shafts, arcades, and lancet windows; and the roof offers an unprecedented display of purely decorative rib vaulting. The whole building was really designed around a central column which branches out into a lovely cone of no less than twenty ribs. These correspond to smaller groups of ribs which start from the corners of the building. The cone of ribs was the final achievement of the series of vaulting experiments at Lincoln, and its success was immediate and lasting. The idea haunted the imaginations of English masons almost down to the end of the Middle Ages.

Most of the buildings which followed Lincoln inevitably seem something of an anti-climax by comparison. In the new choir at Worcester (begun in 1224) the triforium has an enlarged but diluted version of the contrapuntal arcades of St Hugh's Choir. There is also a ridge rib, and the pier design perhaps owes something to Lincoln. But the Worcester piers have a bulk that seems more akin to Wells than Lincoln. The arch mouldings are the most extravagant in the whole repertoire of English Gothic. On the other hand, the vaults, in spite of the ridge rib, are treated with a restraint that again makes us think of Wells. The same mixture of influences can be seen in the early parts of Lichfield Cathedral, which were more or less contemporary with Worcester.

It is significant that in the only two cases where systematic attempts were made to go one better than Lincoln, one – the new choir of Ely (*c.* 1238) – is little more than a copy of the Lincoln nave; while the other – the transept at York (*c.* 1230) – overreached itself, and fell victim to the necessities of compromise. It is clear that before the rebuilding of Westminster Abbey Lincoln represented a limit beyond which no one could see any way of advancing further. The other

northern minster, Beverley, in Yorkshire, which was rebuilt at about the same time as the York transept, was more modest. Several of the Lincoln decorative techniques were used, notably the contrapuntal arcades, which, as at Worcester, were transferred to the triforium. But the northern masons remained curiously shy of vaulting in the Lincoln manner. At Beverley they were content with simple quadripartite vaults; and at York there were no vaults at all. At one time vaults seem to have been projected, but either the designers baulked at the technical problems involved, or they simply did not leave themselves sufficient room. As a result of this infirmity of purpose the York transept only succeeded in becoming a rather more splendid version of those at Byland and Hexham.

Two other buildings in the north call for special mention. These are the eastern transepts at Fountains Abbey and Durham Cathedral, both of which are known as Transepts of the Nine Altars. The type may be thought of as a special version of the double-transept plan in which there is no extension beyond the eastern transept. The origin of this modification is obscure. Fountains is the earlier of the two, and there the primary consideration seems to have been liturgical. But at Durham there were severely practical reasons. The nature of the site precluded any considerable building to the east of the Norman apse; and when Bishop Poore decided to repair and extend the choir of his cathedral just before his death in 1237 (work did not begin until 1242) the choice of this particular form was virtually forced upon him and his successors. In spite of the fame of these two buildings it must be admitted that the aisle-less transept hardly offers much scope for architectural invention, and in almost every other country apart from England it would have been abandoned as an intractable problem. At Durham the full repertory of marble shafts and wall-arcading was brought to bear, and the building is saved by the sheer weight of ornament with which it is encrusted. At Fountains it is more difficult to judge, for there we see the Nine Altars roofless, and denuded of its marble shafts. One suspects that time and decay have endowed it with a more potent magic than the men who built it. The incredibly slender cores of the free-standing piers which formerly rose sheer from floor to roof, and which now stand out against the sky, contrive to evoke the vision of an ethereal Gothic which never existed in England save in Romantic imaginations.

Bishop Poore, who was responsible for the decision to build the Nine Altars at Durham, was already an experienced patron of cathedral

Gothic before his preferment to Durham. In 1220, as Bishop of Salisbury, he had decided to abandon his episcopal church inside the cramped fortress of Old Sarum in favour of an entirely new site by the river Avon a few miles away. Opportunities of this kind, which gave designers almost unrestricted freedom, were becoming very rare in England, and one might have expected that the occasion would have been graced by a magisterial affirmation of the current style. The result was rather less than this, but it remains interesting as the one serious effort that was made before the rebuilding of Westminster Abbey to escape from the tyranny of Lincoln. One would hesitate to say that Salisbury offers a genuine alternative to Lincoln; but the similarities and debts to Lincoln are less obvious than in any other important church of the early thirteenth century.

In plan Salisbury Cathedral conforms to the double-transept type, with a single-storeyed lady chapel projecting eastward from the ambulatory between two subsidiary chapels. All these features tend to make the outline of the building complicated, and there are many façades and gables, especially at the east end, which gave the exterior the little interest it had before the tower and spire were added in the

31. Salisbury Cathedral, from the north-east

32. Salisbury Cathedral, Lady Chapel

fourteenth century [31]. But all the changes of direction are made through right angles, and in each panel of wall the articulation comprises a group or series of groups of lancet windows. Together these introduce an element of order, simplicity, and even monotony into the design. Inside, the lancets are equally prominent, not because they are larger or more numerous than in other churches, but simply because everything else has been handled with unusual restraint so that there is nothing to compete with them. The main piers are far less elaborate than at Lincoln. The aisles are high, and simple quadripartite vaults reappear. Wall-arcading under the aisle windows is conspicuous by its absence. It is almost as though Lincoln did not exist. The only part of the building where we find a rich display of marble-shafting is in the triforium. Elsewhere, although there is marble to be seen, it is used with extraordinary discrimination.

It is clear that the Salisbury masons were trying to do something quite different from their colleagues at Lincoln. The question is: what? The stress on the windows suggests that they were much more interested in lighting effects than in surface patterning of the Lincoln kind. Today light comes flooding in through the lancets, and Salisbury is perhaps the brightest church of its period. But it must be remembered that originally these windows would be filled with stained glass, and in the first half of the thirteenth century stained glass tended to be dark-toned and brilliant in the intensity of its colour. Salisbury would have been particularly well suited for the presentation of a display of such glass; and the chromatic effects still evident in the alternating horizontal bands of dark and light material in the nave seem to imply that colour was the primary consideration, as it had been at Canterbury. The Lady Chapel [32] probably reveals the kind of architecture which the masons of Salisbury had in mind more truly than any other part of the building. Although it was designed with two rows of supports for the vault, which turn it into a sort of miniature hall-church, these supports are so attenuated that we hardly notice they are there at all. They are no more than free-standing marble shafts, and they leave an almost uninterrupted view of the surrounding lancets. The damage and drastic restorations that Salisbury has suffered in the course of its history have robbed it of almost all its original character, and it is now a deceptively difficult building to appreciate. Even so, the shift of emphasis to the windows is symptomatic of one of the most important developments in English Gothic, that started at Westminster Abbey; and it is well known that Westminster was indebted to Salisbury more than to any of its other English predecessors.

At Salisbury the idea of a church designed wholly or mainly as a frame for its windows was no more than hinted at. Even if the intention had been there the means were not yet to hand. Simple lancets are hardly capable of sustaining our interest by themselves, and we can sense a growing dissatisfaction with their limitations in the attempts that became steadily more impressive as the thirteenth century un-

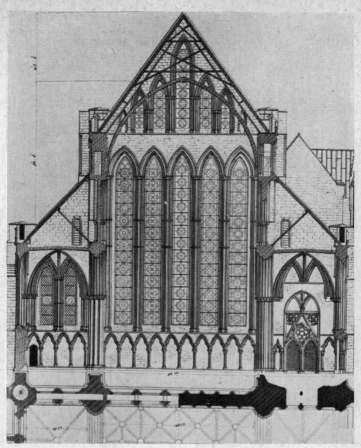

33. York Minster, north transept elevation, showing the Five Sisters Window

folded, to combine them into larger patterns occupying whole façades. Perhaps the most imposing of these are the groups of five at Lichfield and York [33], which treat the whole wall of their respective transepts as a unit, and make no concessions to the divisions of the elevation. With these groups of lancets the great traceried windows of the next generation do not seem far away. By 1240 England was ripe for the introduction of tracery; and even without Westminster it would have made its appearance more or less when it did. The west window of Binham Priory, in Norfolk, for instance, may even pre-date Westminster by a few years. Westminster, however, was undoubtedly the building which put tracery 'on the map' in England. And in many other ways as well it cut right across the native Gothic tradition. It marks the beginning of another of those momentous periods when Englishmen turned aside from their insular preoccupations and took a long look at what was happening in the main stream of Continental architecture. As on other occasions, they were immensely stimulated by what they saw. The whole question of how they wanted their churches to look was re-opened, and when the upheaval eventually subsided an entirely different Gothic style was established. It is not true to say that the late Gothic style in England was created at Westminster; but the early Gothic period certainly came to an end there.

4   From Westminster to Gloucester

The first move in the rebuilding of Westminster Abbey was made in 1220, when Henry III laid the foundation stone of a new lady chapel. Just what was projected in 1220 remains obscure; but it seems to have involved the transformation of the east end of the Norman abbey, which was round, by squaring off the presbytery and adding chapels on the eastern side. The problem seems to have been roughly similar to that at Chichester in 1187, and the solution was also essentially the same. How far they got with this enterprise is not known, although the Lady Chapel was being roofed in 1234, and some work 'on the church' was in progress at the same time. But it was certainly never finished, for in 1245 the King took over the whole financial burden, and promptly began to rebuild the abbey anew to his own liking.

This royal intervention at Westminster marks the emergence of the king and court as the most important source of architectural patronage in the country; and although there were lapses and intervals when little was done, this remained the case down to the time of Henry VIII. In two ways the patronage of the court differed from that of the earlier bishops and abbots. On the whole, these had been content to use local talent; and although occasionally, as at Canterbury, they were prepared to call in foreigners, they were undoubtedly responsible for the insular and regional character of early English Gothic. The king, on the other hand, could and did procure the services of the best masons from all over the country. We find names like Richard Canterbury, Roger Luton, John of Gloucester, and John of Beverley on his payroll. Moreover, his territorial, ecclesiastical, and dynastic connexions with Europe put him in a peculiar position of advantage when it came to knowing about the contemporary state of art on the Continent. Other names, such as Richard of Paris, John Norman, Henry of Reyns, Peter of Rome, and Peter of Spain, show just how far afield he was prepared to look for artists. It is clear that royal patronage created the conditions in which a national style of Gothic could be formed; and at the same time ensured that it should be, if not exactly cosmopolitan, at least a Gothic strongly flavoured with Continental ideas.

The man placed in charge of the work at its inception was Henry of Reyns. A great controversy has raged around the nationality of this man. Protagonists of the Englishness or the Frenchness of Westminster have claimed him with equal vehemence for their respective causes. It is true that if we try hard enough Reyns can be found in England; but for the Middle Ages the Reyns *par excellence* was Reims, in France. There are certainly echoes of Reims Cathedral at Westminster. This was only to be expected, for Reims was the coronation church of the French kings, and Westminster was its equivalent in England. But Reims was not the only source of the French influences at Westminster. Amiens is often mentioned; and another no less important was the abbey of Saint-Denis, near Paris, which was another counterpart of Westminster in so far as it enjoyed the special and intimate protection of the French kings. Finally, there was the Sainte-Chapelle, which was being built for the palace of Saint-Louis in Paris at the very moment that Westminster was started. On the whole it seems necessary to postulate the presence at Westminster of someone who had a long, close, and up-to-date knowledge of French architecture; and we can admit that Master Henry was a Frenchman without prejudice to the English contribution to the building.

King Henry's interest in Westminster did not spring from a desire to emulate any or all of the French buildings which it resembles in part, but from his personal devotion to St Edward the Confessor. In a very literal sense his plan for the abbey [34] centres on the Confessor's shrine. The very point where the head of the saint was to be placed is the apex of a right-angled triangle of which the hypotenuse is the base-line of the transept; and from this point the whole system of radiating chapels is generated. Master Henry made very skilful use of the restricted space at his disposal. He adopted the latest French scheme for a five-sided apse which is in effect five sides of an octagon. This allowed him to get half a chapel on either side behind, i.e. to the west of his starting-point. (There is a slight modification apparently due to the necessity of incorporating the already completed Lady Chapel into the design. This took the place of the axial chapel, and it entailed reducing the sides of the octagon by a small amount. This has left the two outermost sides of the apse canted inward.) Another desideratum

94

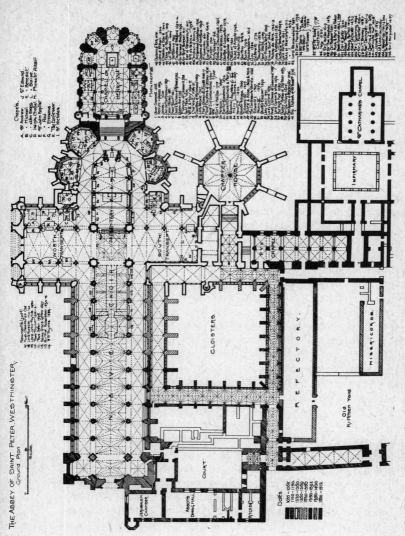

34. Westminster Abbey, ground plan

was a broad and spacious transept with two aisles. The transept of the Norman abbey had only an eastern aisle. The new western aisle had of necessity to be placed on the western side of the base-line, and this results in the curious compromise on the south side where the western aisle is, as it were, superimposed on the eastern arm of the cloister.

On this plan was raised the closest approximation that was ever made in England to a French High Gothic chevet. Although Westminster can hardly compare in absolute height with cathedrals like Amiens or Beauvais, it remained higher than any other English medieval church, and it tends to look higher than it is because it is relatively narrow. As a whole the elevation has the characteristic French dispositions: a comparatively narrow triforium with a high arcade and a high clerestory on either side. There is no question of a wall-passage, and the stability of the upper storey is ensured by means of flying buttresses. All the windows in the chevet are filled with tracery.

The traceried window may be thought of as a much more versatile alternative to the idea of increasing window space by grouping lancets together. Instead, the lancet itself is enlarged, its shape altered, and thin strips of stone inserted to form a pattern. The essential point is that the stonework is never thick enough to suggest that it is part of the wall. In order that the pattern made by the tracery should register, it was necessary that it should stand out against the surrounding glass; and it was about this time that the deep-toned glass of the early thirteenth century began to give way to the much lighter-toned 'grisaille'. This was used in the chapter-house windows at Westminster. In the choir at Westminster the patterns of the tracery derived mainly from Reims; although in the triforium there are triangular windows that came from Amiens or Notre-Dame, Paris; the chapter-house windows also repeat a design from Amiens. At the time, *c*. 1245, these were already out of date in France. The transepts at Westminster, however, have two enormous rose windows [35] in which the tracery followed the latest Paris fashion. Windows of this kind had been invented only a few years before at the abbey of Saint-Denis, near Paris; and those at Westminster were among the first imitations. Even more up to date were the angels on the transept walls, just below the rose windows. These are Westminster's clearest obligation to the Sainte-Chapelle.

When all these debts to France have been acknowledged what is left to form the English contribution? The answer is more than might have been expected. The main columns of polished marble are clearly in the Salisbury–Canterbury tradition, and lead us to suppose that

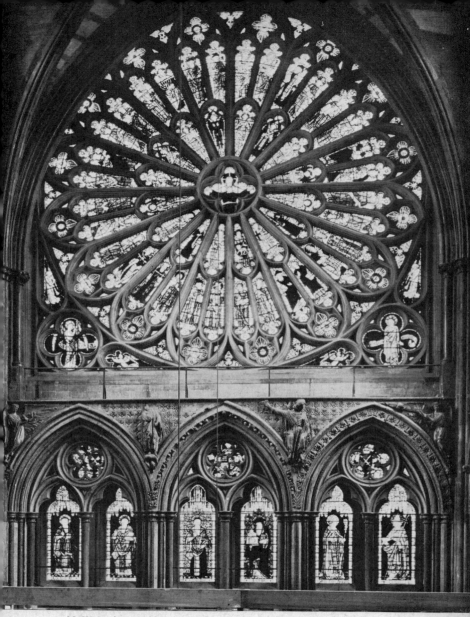

35. Westminster Abbey, south transept, rose window

colour played an important part in the decoration of the abbey. Around the transept walls there is a zone of carving in relief which was inspired from Worcester. And in the roof a ridge rib makes a solitary concession to Lincoln. But over and above these specific features there is a general richness of form and texture which in its way is as English as anything at Lincoln. The triforium, for instance, is far richer than its prototype at Amiens. Another case in point is the diaper pattern which is liberally applied to the upper surfaces of the choir and transepts, and which recalls to mind the Anglo-Norman use of such patterns. The same is true outside. The main façade of the abbey was on the north transept, facing the Palace of Westminster. Its inspiration seems to have been the west front of Amiens without the towers; but even when allowances have been made for the several restorations it must have been a very free transcription. In the process all the French features except the rose window were drastically altered, and none more so than the portals. These were reduced in size, and tracery patterns took the place of figure sculpture. The result was a compromise of the worst kind, and it is not surprising that as an essay in façade composition it was quietly forgotten.

The hostility of the English to deep sculptured portals was matched only by their allergy to flying buttresses. There are flying buttresses at Westminster, but it is only on the cloister side of the nave that we find bank upon bank of them, as in France. Around the chevet in particular they are almost completely obscured by the upper storeys of the radiating chapels – a feature without parallel in France, but which occurred occasionally in Anglo-Norman churches, e.g. Gloucester. It is a measure of the reluctance of the English to use flying buttresses that they were prepared to use iron tie-rods inside as an alternative means of ensuring stability. In the abbey itself those were only complementary to the buttresses; but in the chapter house the whole structure was apparently held together by them at first. In the end, however, it had to be admitted that the expedient was a failure, and within a century the hated buttresses made a belated appearance.

In other ways as well, the chapter house was the building at Westminster where the English tradition re-asserted itself most vigorously. Being centrally planned, it had no counterpart in France, and we are consequently in a much better position than in the abbey itself to see which of the new ideas made the deepest impression on English taste. Without question it was the traceried windows. Although the chapter-house windows must have been contemporary with those of the abbey

36. Salisbury Cathedral, chapter house

choir, they are more than twice as large and occupy practically all the surface on each side of the building. It is natural to compare West-minster chapter house with that at Lincoln. These great windows are the obvious innovation, but there is another difference, hardly less important. In deference to the shape of the windows, the radius of the vault ribs at Westminster has been reduced, and this means that the cone of ribs in the centre has been pushed up into the roof, where it is far less conspicuous than at Lincoln. Both vault and windows at

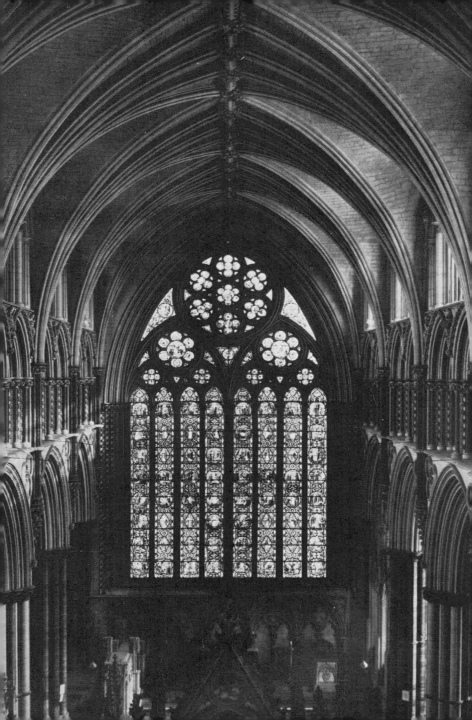

Westminster are nineteenth-century reconstructions, but Salisbury, where the chapter house [36] was a direct copy of the one at Westminster, confirms the impression in every detail. By comparison with the twenty ribs that made the cone at Lincoln, there are only sixteen at Westminster and Salisbury. But whereas there are ten sides at Lincoln there are only eight at Westminster and Salisbury. This means in effect that the sides have been enlarged and the cone reduced; or, in other words, ribs have been sacrificed to windows.

Put like this, the comparison between the Lincoln and the Westminster chapter houses might suggest that there was present from the start an antithesis between two different aesthetic programmes, one represented by the rib patterns at Lincoln, and the other by the window patterns of Westminster. With the advantage of hindsight, we may perhaps feel inclined to be dogmatic about this; but a great deal of experience and experiment was required before the people directly concerned – i.e. the designers – reached this conclusion for themselves. It is true that in the two chapter houses which followed Westminster and Salisbury, those of Southwell and York (both c. 1280), the inference was drawn that central columns and cones of ribs were inconsistent with traceried windows; and the former were duly dispensed with. But it was in the nature of the case that this problem should be more acute in centrally planned buildings than in ordinary churches. And even in chapter houses at least one attempt was made to demonstrate the compatibility of the two ideas. This was at Wells.

The most general reaction to the development of traceried windows was to try and have the best of both worlds; and for at least a generation after Westminster masons went happily about the business of achieving richer and richer effects by making both kinds of pattern more and more complicated. We can see the first signs of this at Westminster itself, in the main vaults of the nave where the full Lincoln pattern was adopted. The three most important designs of the late 1250s – namely, the Angel Choir at Lincoln, the nave of Lichfield, and the choir of old St Paul's – all followed suit. In the Angel Choir [37], which takes its name from the rows of angels over the triforium – a clear indication of Westminster influence – the result was particularly felicitous. Except for a slight modification of the vaults to accommodate an enlarged clerestory, the nave design at Lincoln was readily adapted to receive the new windows. Yet even at Lincoln the designers were aware of the inherent conflict between tracery on the one hand and the implications of thick-wall construction on the other. They repeated the clerestory tracery on the inner side of the wall-passage, and thereby preserved the three-dimensional homogeneity of the wall itself, without losing the essential flatness of the tracery pattern. It was a solution that was followed elsewhere, especially in the north.

The most important of the Lincoln windows, however, was at the east end. Already at Binham in the 1240s the Westminster chapter-house pattern had been used for a façade window. Now at Lincoln we find two of these patterns placed side by side, with another circular pattern – or 'oculus' – above and between them, to form the first really elaborate tracery composition that occupied the full height and width of a cathedral façade. A little later at old St Paul's there was an equally impressive and no less influential east window combining the West-minster rose with a series of lancets. Once the type had been created, a wonderful succession of similar designs followed. Almost at once the

38. Selby Abbey, east end

39. Beverley Minster, screen

great window was accepted as the dominant feature of church façades. In west fronts it replaced the old idea of a screen of niches, and so made possible a new version of the Norman two-towered façade. The west front of Exeter (begun *c*. 1327), which contrives to have both a screen and a great window, might almost be regarded symbolically as the point where one idea gives way to the other. But it was in the north, where the deeply rooted tradition of cliff-like east ends provided ready scope for ambitious schemes, that the most impressive of these great windows were made. Intact, restored, or in ruins, we find them in Yorkshire at Ripon, Guisborough, Howden, Selby [38], York, and in Cumberland at Carlisle. For a hundred years the designing of tracery patterns was one of the chief forms of creative activity in England. The geometrical principles on which they were based became steadily more and more involved, and by the second quarter of the fourteenth century the rigid formality of the earliest examples had given way to a luxuriant and almost lyrical freedom. At York, Selby, and Beverley [39], for instance, we find heart-shapes, and raindrops, and tongues of flame which anticipate by more than half a century the French Flamboyant tracery which was based on these motives.

The lead given by the great windows was closely followed by the smaller windows of the aisles and clerestories. In becoming denser and more elaborate, window tracery followed the same law of development which we have already seen operating in the cases of pier profiles, arch mouldings, and vaulting ribs. The building which marks the critical stage in the assimilation of tracery to these older forms of decoration was Exeter.

Exeter Cathedral was started before 1280 and, although it took more than eighty years to complete, its design was fixed in the early stages and hardly altered except for details. It is clear that the designers set out with the Lincoln idea of an all-over surface pattern in mind; but they also set themselves the task of intensifying it to a very much higher degree. This is most apparent in the handling of the vault ribs. The

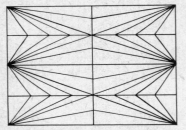

40. Exeter Cathedral, nave vault system (not to scale)

maximum of seven in each diverging set of ribs at Lincoln has become eleven at Exeter [40]. The vaults are now so thick with ribs that there is hardly any exposed surface between them. Moreover, every part of the vault is covered, not just the centre. By comparison with Lincoln, this was going to extremes; and if the main arcades had been as light and open as those of Lincoln the building would have seemed top heavy. To compensate for this exuberant vault pattern it was therefore necessary to stress the main arcades as well; and so it is that we find at Exeter [41] piers and arch mouldings as bulky and obtrusive as any at Wells or Worcester. The vaults and arcades are in fact so prominent that to all intents and purposes Exeter looks like a two-storeyed building. It is not surprising to learn that the original design made no provision for a middle section. The unobtrusive triforium that we now see was introduced in the course of construction. Despite its presence, Exeter still looks like a long vista through a forest.

In earlier Gothic churches the middle section had often been the place for a display of coloured marble shafts. But by the end of the thirteenth century the vogue for this particular kind of ornament was passing, and the triforium became henceforth increasingly redundant. As it did so interest shifted to the arcades below and the clerestory above. The thickening and coarsening of the rounded forms in the piers and mouldings at Exeter are evident enough. But any gain in the clerestory fails to register, because the clerestory is lost to view among the vault ribs. The windows are set back behind a wall-passage, and the tracery has not been repeated on the inside as in the Angel Choir. As a result their contribution to the general effect of the interior is disappointing. The aisle windows are equally discreet. Yet when they are examined in detail it is clear that the windows are every bit as elaborate as the masonry, and there is no doubt that they were intended as a complement to the stonework in achieving an ideal of total decoration.

But they failed to do so. Exeter remains a brilliant piece of masonry in which there happen to be windows. There is no organic unity between them; there is not even an element of deliberate contrast between stone and glass. Impressive as it undoubtedly is, Exeter was not the *tour de force* that it was meant to be, and perhaps it was the disappointment that forced English masons to realize that tracery was not just another decorative device to be used at will in conjunction

41. Exeter Cathedral, nave

with an existing repertory. When it comes to the point, shafts, mouldings, and vault ribs are all very similar to one another. Either they are vertical, or they follow smooth curves. And they are all plastic forms. In short, they cohere into a system. Tracery patterns, on the other hand, have a different rhythm. The strips of stone are lighter; their changes of direction more rapid; their intersections more violent. The conditions under which they are seen are totally different. Above all they are flat patterns, and will not readily combine with plastic forms. The most they will do is to provide under favourable conditions an element of contrast. But in a building like Exeter, where the plastic forms were emphasized to an unprecedented degree, they had no chance.

Whether or not there was a general inquest along these lines, Exeter was followed by a remarkable series of buildings, all of which can be regarded as being to a greater or lesser extent reactions. The half century from 1285 to 1335 witnessed the most brilliant display of sheer inventiveness in the whole history of English medieval architecture. Sometimes the works of this period are grouped together under the label 'Decorated Style'. But quite apart from the fact that this is a singularly inept term by which to distinguish one set of English medieval buildings from the rest, it is doubtful whether the notion of stylistic unity which it implies will stand up to analysis. The name Decorated was first used to distinguish windows with elaborate patterns of tracery from the simple lancets which preceded them and the Perpendicular panelled windows by which they were followed. It is easy enough to extend the meaning of the word to include the new kind of vaulting which was invented *c.* 1290, to which the name 'lierne' is given; but whether we can go farther and speak of Decorated buildings, as well as Decorated tracery and vaults, is another matter. By comparison with the impressive similarities between early Gothic buildings on the one hand, and Perpendicular buildings on the other, it is the variety – one might almost say the experimental character of the so-called Decorated designs – that is the salient fact about them. It is true that they often show an interest in complicated spatial shapes and spatial relations, and recently this has been used as a stylistic criterion. But one hesitates to assume that spatial considerations were fundamental. More often than not they seem to have been means to other ends. Perhaps one gets a better insight into the great buildings of this period by regarding them as so many essays in the quest for a new style. One of these avenues of research led directly to Perpendicular,

42. York Minster, nave

and the kind of solution which Perpendicular offered sheds a good deal of light upon the general problem with which the discarded alternatives were concerned as well.

By a curious inversion of the normal order of progress, the two designs which were to be of greatest significance for the future – the nave of York Minster and St Stephen's Chapel in the Palace of Westminster – were the first to follow Exeter. St Stephen's is best left until we come to discuss the origins of Perpendicular. The nave of York [42], however, deserves to be accredited with more importance than is usually attached to it. The chapter house at York had already provided an introduction to the problems of tracery. The decision to abolish the central column cannot have been taken lightly, for it involved a structural difficulty of some magnitude – namely, how to vault the building. Without the column the span became something like sixty feet. This was far beyond the normal limits of English experience, and in the end the York masons handed the task over to their colleagues, the carpenters, who produced a wooden imitation of a stone vault. This was not the first occasion when the carpenters had come to the aid of the stonemasons. It had happened at Lichfield as far back as 1240, and at Henry III's Chapel in Windsor Castle soon after. But the success of the sham vaults at York marks the emergence of timber architecture into the front rank of importance, where it was to remain for the rest of the Middle Ages. If anything were needed to prove the point that in England visual effect was the primary consideration in the construction of vaults this is it. We are often told that vaulting in stone was invented precisely in order to avoid the risk of fire to which wooden roofs were liable. Now the wheel has moved full circle. Eventually the whole of the nave and the transepts of York were given sham vaults as well. Although the nave vault was not put up until the middle of the fourteenth century, it was probably designed along with the rest about 1290. It is very different from the Exeter vault. Instead of a dense rib system there is a comparatively sparse pattern of an entirely new kind. Between the main ribs, of which there are only three to begin with, a subsidiary system of connecting ribs has been introduced. These small ribs, which start and end on other larger ribs, are known as liernes. At York the idea may have developed naturally from the unified pattern on the roof of the chapter house. But there are several other instances from the last decade of the thirteenth century, the choir of Pershore Abbey (1288) having perhaps the earliest dated example. The importance of this kind of vaulting is that it results in a kind of pattern that is distinctly analogous to the kind of pattern produced by window tracery. The main ribs correspond to the mullions of the windows and the liernes to the detailed designs at the top. It is not too fanciful to see in this innovation the germ of the idea of applying a tracery pattern to a roof.

In other respects also York is a complete antithesis of Exeter. The windows are far more prominent. The arcades are high and wide, like those of Lincoln. The upper walls are thin and flat. There is no wall-passage, and the clerestory windows are brought into the plane of the inner surfaces of the nave walls. Even more remarkable is the handling of the middle section of the elevation. York was built as a two-storeyed design. The window tracery of the clerestory comes right down to the string course above the main arcade. The upper parts are glazed; the lower parts, which correspond to the aisle roofs, are not. That is the only concession to the old notion of a structural triforium. When compared with the cathedral designs that preceded it York nave was decidedly revolutionary. This is perhaps concealed by its great height and width, which puts it in a class apart among English cathedrals, and also by the fact that there were few later buildings of the kind to follow its lead. Nevertheless it is the starting-point for late Gothic

43. Wells Cathedral, chapter house

cathedral design in England, as comparisons with the naves of Canterbury and Winchester will show.

The second series of works at Wells, which began in 1285 and continued for half a century, presents us with a much more complex reaction to Exeter. The first of them, the chapter house [43], was almost certainly built by men from Exeter. It has without doubt the finest cone of ribs to be seen in England. There are no less than thirty-two of them; and with the corresponding ribs that spring from the corners of the building the effect is overwhelming. It is just the sort of chapter-house vault that we should have expected from Exeter masons. The windows are definitely subordinate partners in this composition, and the overall effect represents a return to the Lincoln, as opposed to the Westminster, type of chapter house.

The success of this cone of ribs so endeared the motive to the designers of Wells that they retained the idea when they began to remodel the east end of the cathedral. This work falls into three well-defined stages: an extension of the choir; a new lady chapel; and a retrochoir between them. The starting-point for this complicated design was the type of east end which had started at Chichester c. 1187, and which had worked its way across southern England during the thirteenth century to reach Wells via Winchester, Salisbury, and Exeter. But at Wells the customary grid-like arrangements were drastically altered. The Lady Chapel became an irregular elliptical polygon, while the piers of the retrochoir [44] were disposed in the form of a hexagon with very little regard for the main axis-lines of the building. This extraordinary plan only makes sense in terms of the visual effects which it made possible. It is often claimed that the subtlety of Wells arises from the relation between the Lady Chapel and the retrochoir. This is true up to a point, but the clever handling of these spaces was a means to an end, not an end in itself. The relation between them has been described as 'interpenetration'; but this is surely a mistake. The Lady Chapel pushes into the retrochoir, but there is no reciprocation, and neither loses its identity. For real interpenetration it is necessary to look back at Salisbury. At Wells the Lady Chapel is to all intents and purposes a self-contained building. This is evident from its shape, and still more from its vault, which is a unified star pattern based on liernes. We can think of it as an eccentric modification of the York chapter-house idea. The retrochoir flows around this building, but the contrast between them is very marked. They do not rise to the same height; their vaulting is quite different; and even the piers which they have in common

44. Wells Cathedral, retrochoir

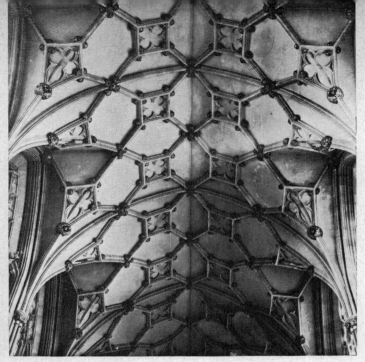

45. Wells Cathedral, choir vault

present different faces in different directions. It is not easy to describe
the Wells retrochoir as a clearly defined spatial entity. Although the
supports form themselves into an elongated hexagon on the ground,
the vaults above them bear no relation to this figure. It is almost certainly a mistake to attempt to think of it in terms of spatial geometry.
Our uncertainty as to its precise limits seems to have been deliberately
provoked. Instead of a spatial configuration, it is objects in space that
we are meant to see. Whichever way we look there are branching cones
of ribs, and beyond them other cones of ribs, with only the aisle windows and those of the Lady Chapel seemingly far away to suggest
where it comes to an end. Although there are some lierne ribs, the
retrochoir does not have a true lierne vault. Fundamentally, it is an
extension of the chapter-house idea, but instead of a single cone we
now have a whole series of them; and their triangular dispositions
allow them to be seen effectively from almost any point of view. There
are so many ribs in play that it proved quite impossible for them all to

be matched symmetrically; and so we find two conveniently placed lion-headed key stones, each of which contrives to swallow a couple of ribs when they have performed their allotted function. In any other context this would have been outrageous, but here it hardly seems to matter at all, where everything else is arbitrary, irrational, and exquisitely mysterious.

As a solution for a particular problem the Wells retrochoir was a triumph of imagination; but its very perfection made it the sort of thing that could not easily be done again. If it had been generalized into a type of church architecture the result would have been a hall-church. But the demands of regularity would have reduced it all to the level of the commonplace. The men who built the extension to the choir of Wells proceeded as though the retrochoir did not exist. Rib-cones are given up altogether, and the vault has become the pattern of squares and hexagons embedded in the solid material of the structure [45]. The texture of this pattern matches that of the window tracery very well. The unity of clerestory and triforium, however, is disrupted

46. Bristol Cathedral, section and plan of east end

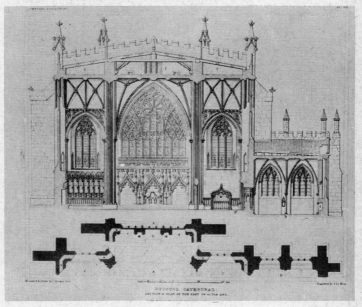

by the wall-passage which was continued from the earlier work, and this is only partially offset by the extension of the triforium downward, so that the niches of which it is composed rest directly on the haunches of the arcade arches. With its strong vertical lines, the choir of Wells seems to share the mood of Perpendicular without actually using any specifically Perpendicular forms. Later, when work shifted to the towers, this Perpendicular quality became more explicit.

It is curious that while this second building campaign at Wells was in progress a kind of hall-church was commenced only a few miles away at Bristol [46]. This was for the choir of St Augustine's Abbey (now the cathedral). Work was already in progress by 1306. It might have been expected that the Bristol designers would have followed the same lines of thought as the men who made the Wells retrochoir. In fact, however, they avoided making any direct allusion to Wells, and to any of the other great building projects of the time in England. The result is undoubtedly the most unusual and original of our great medieval churches.

Much attention has been given to the fact that Bristol has the form of a hall-church – that is, a church with aisles and nave of the same height. But as soon as we compare it with conventional hall-churches in Germany or western France it becomes abundantly clear that the Bristol masons were either being wilfully obtuse, or else they had something else in mind apart from the simple desire to build a hall-church. The aisles and nave at Bristol do not merge to form a unified interior, which is what one expects; and the aisles have a deceptive ambiguity which from some points of view almost destroys the hall-church effect. The only feature of a Continental hall-church about which there can be no dispute at Bristol is the absence of a clerestory. From this it follows that all the windows, except the great east window, are concentrated in the aisles; and instead of being dispersed in two rows, they are now unified, and occupy more or less the full height of the wall. As a counterpart to this bringing together of the windows, the arches of the main arcades and those of the vaults can now form themselves into a single system. What has happened in effect is that ribs and arch mouldings on the one hand, and window tracery on the other, have been rigorously segregated. In other words, the indiscriminate mixing of decorative elements which was so obvious at Exeter has been repudiated. This seems to have been the fundamental idea which inspired the Bristol masons. The thoroughness with which they applied it in detail emerges if we study the windows a little more closely. The only window

47. Bristol Cathedral, south aisle of the choir

which was not banished from the choir proper was the great east window. But here the question of segregation did not arise. The Bristol designers seem to have agreed with their colleagues elsewhere that there was nothing wrong with windows in terminal façades. Indeed, this was the only place for them. To prove the point, they went to the trouble of placing each of the aisle windows at the end of a miniature replica of the structural system of the choir [47]. The design of the individual aisle bays at Bristol is extremely subtle. Each has its own arcade of one arch on either side – i.e. east and west – and its own vaulting system, aligned by a ridge rib running north–south at right angles to the choir. The terminal façades of these bays are occupied by simplified versions of the great east window of the choir. From this point of view the windows are set back from the choir in what appear to be lateral recesses from the central space – detached from, but not wholly unrelated to, the arcade openings. But these aisle bays are thoroughly equivocal. The designers never lost sight of the orthodox conception of a side aisle as a subordinate vista parallel to the main axis of a church. The cleverness with which they contrived to have the best of both worlds, and at the same time ensure the stability of the whole building gives Bristol a claim to be considered the most sophisticated piece of architecture in the whole of Europe at the time. At the points where the thrust of the main vaults is received by the arcade stone girders span the aisles, and allow the outer walls to resist the strain. Below these girders are skeleton arches which support the girders in the middle, but otherwise carry no masonry. To anyone looking along the aisles, the receding vista of these arches gives a strong impression that the aisles are lower than the nave after all; and if the matter had been allowed to rest there the effect would have been similar to that produced by the Burgundian vaults over the side aisles of early Cistercian abbeys like Fountains. But one final note of fantasy was introduced. Part of the masonry between the vaults of each compartment of the aisles was cut away to leave what appears from a distance to be the base of a little cone of ribs resting on the centre of each girder, and hinting at unexpected recesses of space above and beyond. This strange but captivating caprice is perhaps the most wayward thing about this wayward building. The germ of the idea may have been suggested by the free handling of cones of ribs in the Wells retrochoir, but apart from one special adaptation of the motive at Gloucester, there is nothing remotely like it anywhere else. It was one of those brilliant feats of imagination which could transform even a commonplace building into a work of art. But as in the case of the Wells retrochoir, the talents displayed at Bristol were of a kind which could not lead easily to the formulation of a new style.

The same is true of the octagon at Ely. This took the place of the old Norman central tower which fell down in 1322. Several bays of the choir were damaged, and so also were those of the nave and transepts adjoining the crossing. Instead of restoring these it was decided to build diagonal walls across the corners, and turn the crossing into an octagon. The sides of this octagon are not all the same length, but the design can be regarded as a vastly enlarged version of the Wells chapter house, with the central cone of ribs taken out and a lantern placed over the hole that was left. The result is splendidly spacious, and the lantern offers an almost melodramatic solution to the problem of how to combine lighting with vaulting. The vivid shaft of light that passes vertically through the gloom of the vaults creates an effect unlike anything else in architecture, unless it be the dome of the Pantheon. Building the lantern of stone proved a task beyond the capacity of the Ely masons, and once again it was handed over to the carpenters. This time the King's master-carpenter, William Hurley, was summoned from London to devise a solution in wood. The Ely lantern more than confirms earlier impressions of the virtuosity of timber construction, and in this case there is the added interest that its style introduces us to the current taste of London and the court.

By this time, c. 1330, the King's craftsmen were beginning to acquire a nation-wide reputation. At Lichfield a few years before, William Ramsey, the master-mason of all the King's works south of the Trent, had been called upon to perform a similar task. The most outstanding instance of this tendency to fall back upon the King's experts was of course the choir of Gloucester.

These royal craftsmen owed their authority very largely to the fame of one building – St Stephen's Chapel, in the Palace of Westminster. This was started in 1292, and it marks the re-emergence of the Crown as the leading source of architectural patronage. Work on the abbey at Westminster came to a halt before the death of Henry III in 1270; and during the early part of his reign Edward I was chiefly concerned with castle-building in Wales. In their way these splendid castles are themselves evidence for the continued penetration of Continental influences into England. The master-mason in charge of their construction was a certain James of Saint-Georges, who seems to have come from Savoy. Welsh fortified towns such as Conway or Caernarvon are certainly planned like the Savoyard town of Yverdon; while the isolated castles reflect theories of defensive warfare which had been formulated from the experience of the Crusading kingdoms, and had spread across Europe in the course of the thirteenth century. St Stephen's was Edward's first work of pure, as opposed to applied, architecture. It was started shortly after the King's return from a long sojourn in France, and, like the abbey, it has to be thought of as a compound of English and French elements of which one particular French idea turned out to be all-important.

In form the chapel was modelled on the Sainte-Chapelle in Paris. But it was fifty years later than the Sainte-Chapelle, and in the meantime masons of the French court school had developed a new fashion in architectural decoration. In France the problems posed by window tracery never occurred in the acute form that we find in England. This was because from the outset Gothic architecture there had consistently avoided the thick wall. Walls were treated as far as possible as plane surfaces; and consequently when tracery was invented in France it spread with a sort of natural inevitability from the actual window openings to the adjacent masonry. It soon became apparent that remarkably homogeneous effects could be achieved by this means, and during the second half of the thirteenth century the whole aspect of Gothic churches both inside and out was transformed as the possibilities of tracery were exploited. By 1300 the ubiquitous shafts of early Gothic had largely disappeared, and tracery had taken their place as the principal decorative element in church design. From the visual point of view this change was perhaps the chief difference between early and late Gothic, not only in France, but in most parts of Europe as well.

So far as we know, it was at St Stephen's that tracery was first used in this way in England. It seems to have appeared in the form of panels around the heads of the great windows, and short curtains of tracery were carried down over the lower windows. On the strength of these features St Stephen's has been claimed as the first Perpendicular building in England. It is a great pity that it was destroyed in 1834 because the records of its appearance, though copious, are not sufficiently complete to allow us to test this opinion. An equal misfortune was the loss in the Great Fire of 1666 of the chapter house of old St Paul's, which was built c. 1330, and which had close stylistic affinities with St Stephen's. Here, we know what the exterior looked like from a seventeenth-century engraving, but there is no record of the interior.

This is a serious gap in our knowledge, especially in connexion with the precise form of its vault. As a result of these losses we depend entirely on Gloucester for our first adequate impression of what could be done with this new type of decoration.

Building operations at Gloucester seem to have been more or less continuous from *c*. 1318 to the end of the century. They involved the repair of the south aisle of the nave, and the refashioning of all the church east of the nave as well as the cloister. None of this work can be called rebuilding in the Norman or early Gothic sense – it was concerned only with the transformation of the appearance of existing masonry. But a decisive change of style took place *c*. 1330, at the point where the south aisle of the nave was finished and the south transept was taken in hand. The earlier work was essentially conservative and modest in character; but everything after 1330 was revolutionary, and executed on a grandiose and sumptuous scale. The event which precipitated this change was the burial at Gloucester of King Edward II, who had been murdered in 1327 at Berkeley Castle near by. In 1330, after the execution of Mortimer, Edward III belatedly set about restoring his father's reputation. It used to be said that the Perpendicular style was created at Gloucester out of the proceeds of the cult of Edward II. But this cult was almost certainly fictitious, and we now see the Gloucester style of 1330 onward as that of London and the court brought to the West Country under the auspices of the new King's filial piety.

The heart of this new work was the choir [48]. The Norman apse was cut off, and the clerestory removed. But the aisles and galleries remained, and formed a massive frame inside which a delicate scaffolding of tracery was erected, running unbroken from the new and heightened clerestory to levels sufficiently near the ground to make the choir seem entirely shut off from the surrounding aisles and galleries. Unlike the luxuriant patterns of decorated tracery, those at Gloucester are simple and spare. The motive on which the design was based is a rectangular panel with an arched and cusped head. The only virtue of these panels is that they can be repeated endlessly, and applied to any kind of surface, or indeed to no surface at all. Some are occupied by glass; others are backed by solid masonry; and still others pass over the openings of the old Norman walls. The biggest aperture of all is at the east end. This is completely filled with glazed panels to form the first of the great English Perpendicular windows. In fact, the window is slightly wider than the choir – the walls of which have been splayed

out to contain it. It is also slightly bevelled. The usual impression of a
window as a hole in a wall has been completely eliminated here.
Instead the choir seems to terminate directly against a glass screen;
and the whole structure takes on the character of a fragile glasshouse
with parts of the windows blocked in or otherwise obscured.

It is clear that Gloucester choir is no ordinary choir. It is in fact an
enlarged chapel – a sort of Sainte-Chapelle, intended to receive the
remains of the murdered king who in due course, it was hoped, would
become a royal saint. These hopes were not fulfilled; but elsewhere in
fourteenth-century Europe other buildings of the kind are to be found.
Earlier and less elaborate than Gloucester is the choir of the priory-
church at Saint-Thibault, in France [49], where the ducal house of
Burgundy honoured the relics of a local saint. The glorious choir of
Aachen, begun in 1355, was in effect another of these royal sanctuaries,
built to house the shrine of Charlemagne. The case of Saint-Thibault
is particularly interesting because there we find in rudimentary form
the curtain of tracery running from top to bottom of the building:
partly glazed, partly void, and partly backed by solid masonry. If this
represents what French provincial masons were thinking *c*. 1300 the

49. Saint-Thibault, choir

French ancestry of English Perpendicular becomes clear in principle. Nearly all the late Gothic styles of northern Europe, and some of the southern part as well, have their origins in the art of tracery design which the masons of the French court pioneered during the second half of the thirteenth century. From this point of view, Perpendicular marks the completion of the process which started at Westminster Abbey, whereby English Gothic was brought into line with the main stream of Continental Gothic. This is not to say that it ceased to manifest insular characteristics. On the contrary, Perpendicular has been well described as 'the national style of England'. Once more it is a case of Englishmen taking just what they wanted, and no more, from their Continental neighbours; and using what they took in their own way to solve their own problems.

The name Perpendicular was invented with Gloucester in mind; but its obvious appropriateness should not be allowed to obscure the fact that there is a great deal more to the style than the use of a lot of vertical lines. When we compare Gloucester choir with the other experimental buildings of the previous fifty years the quality which is likely to impress us most forcibly is its clarity and straightforwardness. There are no spatial complexities or irregularities; no asymmetry; no illusionistic cunning; no subtle play with half light or indirect light. Everything is what it seems to be, and everything tends to look the same in all directions. Above all, there is a poverty of detail. This was inevitable, granted the voluntary restriction of means which the architects imposed upon themselves. Clearly much was lost. What was gained? If an answer has to be given in one word, it would be: homogeneity. Buildings of the so-called Decorated period had at least this in common – namely, that confronted with the problem of how to combine plastic and linear decorative forms, i.e. shafts, vaults, and tracery, they did so by varying their mutual relations in highly imaginative and sophisticated ways. They refused to sacrifice anything. Perpendicular, on the other hand, confronted with the same problem, solved it by abolishing all the plastic forms. Only tracery was left. Eventually even pier and arch mouldings were turned inside out, as it were, to become a series of lines between adjacent concavities. Gloucester itself did not go quite so far as this, but even so an all-over pattern of an entirely new kind was achieved there. In its own way Gloucester reaffirms that persistent English preoccupation with pattern which had already produced masterpieces at Durham and Lincoln. But now for the first time we can speak of a truly linear pattern, and from this the homogeneity springs. For in this evenly distributed system of lines there are no accents – nothing in particular to distract our attention away from the whole. That is why it seldom takes long to look at a Perpendicular church; but the total impression can sometimes be, as it is at Gloucester, overwhelming.

So far not a word has been said about the choir vaults at Gloucester. That is because they strike the only discordant note in the whole composition. The vaults have what is undoubtedly the most involved lierne pattern ever devised in England. There are no less than three parallel ridge ribs, and several basic rib systems – e.g. quadripartite, sexpartite, etc. – can be detected superimposed on one another, even before the liernes are taken into account. Yet few people would acclaim the result as something visually satisfying. It is evident that the intense congestion was an attempt to match and complete the all-over patterns on the walls and windows below. But whereas lierne vaults accord well with Decorated window tracery, their irregular compartments merely look untidy when they surmount tier upon tier of rectangular panels. There is another factor which interferes with the coherence between vaults and walls. The vault pattern is still conceived in terms of ribs. This is an awkward residue, and there is no doubt that it was felt as such, even though it took a surprising length of time before a satisfactory solution was worked out.

It is not hard to see the crux of the problem. If walls and windows were covered with tracery panels a completely homogeneous interior required that the vaults should be treated in the same manner. But how to apply tracery to a vault? About the time Gloucester choir was being built, not far away, at Tewkesbury, a similar reconstruction was in progress, and there we can see vaults in which elements of tracery were introduced between the ribs to form rose patterns [50] – similar to the rose which appears in one of the clerestory windows. The effect at Tewkesbury is extremely poetic – and it marks a step in the required direction. But Tewkesbury was not built in the Perpendicular style. For that something much more formal had to be found.

The ultimate solution makes it appearance in the cloisters at Gloucester [51]. The name we give to it is 'fan vaulting', but this is perhaps a misnomer. The word 'fan' suggests something semicircular with spokes of equal length. It is true that there are late fan vaults with members that resemble spokes, but to think along these lines is to miss the essential point of the original idea, which is that these vaults are entirely composed of tracery cells. Sometimes ribs are found with

50. Tewkesbury Abbey, choir vaulting

them, but they are always extraneous to the actual fan. Not only are fan vaults made up of cells, but the cells are organized in the form of a self-developing system. Each cell at the base of the fan bifurcates into two, and each of these into two more, and so on. As they grow larger they assume more and more the shape of typical Perpendicular panels; and at all stages there is an element of ordered inevitability which is a perfect foil to the endless repetition of the wall and window tracery. No Perpendicular interior in England can vie with the long vistas of Gloucester cloister, at least from the point of view of uniformity. Here, if anywhere, the aesthetic ideal of the style finds its fulfilment.

Were fan vaults invented at Gloucester? There is something about the complete assurance with which they are handled that suggests that at least some experiments had been made before; but if so, nothing has survived. In the 1360s, at Hereford, we know that the chapter house (now destroyed) was vaulted with a circle of partial fans around a complete fan, in the centre where the thirteenth-century cone of ribs had been. It needs only a little thought to realize how perfectly the principle of the fan was adapted for this purpose, and we are apt to wonder whether it did not originate in such a context. In essence the

51. Gloucester Cathedral, cloisters

cells of a fan vault are generated in the same way as the 'leaves' of thirteenth-century French rose windows – only in three, not two, dimensions. This alone is sufficient to connect the idea with the London *milieu* in which Perpendicular developed at the beginning of the fourteenth century; and in particular we would give much to know how St Paul's chapter house was vaulted. The building was probably too small to have a central column; but in other ways it might have supplied links between the Gloucester and Hereford fans on the one hand and the French rose windows of Westminster on the other. The double cloisters of old St Paul's also remain an unknown quantity. Whether or not fan vaulting began as early as this, the fact that it was not used in the choir at Gloucester has no bearing on the date of its invention. At the outset fans were essentially small-scale decorative forms with no structural utility at all. Accordingly, no one dared to use them for major spans until late in the fifteenth century. The successful effort to overcome this limitation was, characteristically enough, the last great achievement of English medieval architecture.

5 The End of the Middle Ages

The architecture of the long period between 1350 and the Reformation is usually described as Perpendicular; but that should not be taken as meaning that all the buildings looked like Gloucester, or that it was a period of stagnation. The history of Perpendicular architecture is a very complex subject, and no really satisfactory study of it exists. So either a great deal ought to be said about it here, or very little. From the point of view which has been adopted so far in this book the latter is perhaps the more prudent policy. Even so, it is impossible to do justice to the scope of Perpendicular by discussing it in terms of a single stylistic trend, as one can in large measure with the earlier periods. It is true that the masterpieces of the style are still to be found among the cathedrals, abbeys, or the royal chapels which emulated them in both scale and magnificence. But whereas in the twelfth, thirteenth, and early fourteenth centuries there was a constant succession of such works, in the subsequent two hundred years these were comparatively rare and spasmodic. On the other hand, the Perpendicular period was the great age for the building of parish churches in England; and although one is tempted to dismiss parish-church architecture as a debased or simplified version of the grand manner practised elsewhere, there are enough buildings of sufficient merit to justify the invention of a special category of Parish Church Perpendicular. Moreover, it was during this period also that secular architecture, both in its public and private aspect, began to acquire a character of its own, and to display at the highest levels an aesthetic pretension which, if it did not rival those of its ecclesiastical counterparts, at least contained the promise of an importance that was fulfilled after the Reformation. Except in matters of detail this Secular Perpendicular, as it may be called, has little in common with either of the ecclesiastical varieties, and deserves to be accorded a separate status within the family of styles that constitute our late medieval architecture.

In a book of this kind there is little room to discuss all these wider ramifications of Perpendicular; but it must be remembered that as the large-scale works became fewer and fewer, the threads of continuity between them are to be found increasingly among the more modest works of these other categories; and imperceptibly architecture lost a little of its former preoccupation with the niceties of design, and assumed instead something of the highly organized appearance of the modern building industry. For most of the period the men who otherwise would have been the patrons of English architecture were squandering their not unlimited resources on a long series of wars: first, the Hundred Years War, in France, and then, at home among themselves, the Wars of the Roses. While this did not put an end to building altogether, it was inevitably the expensive schemes that suffered most. The worst period of all fell roughly between 1425 and 1475. Not until stable government was restored by Edward IV and Henry VII did circumstances once more favour the most ambitious kind of Perpendicular; and at this level there is a distinct hiatus between two groups of buildings: one belonging to the second half of the fourteenth century and the beginning of the fifteenth; the other belonging to the end of the fifteenth century and the beginning of the sixteenth. It is significant that the patronage of all these buildings was in the hands of the two institutions that were the traditional supports of medieval architecture – namely, the higher clergy and the Crown; whereas the men who paid for the parish churches and the secular buildings were very largely to be found in the ranks of the aristocracy and the prosperous middle classes. The development of this new source of patronage was to be of the highest importance after the Reformation, when for a considerable period both Church and monarchy virtually dropped out of the picture.

It will be convenient to trace the fortunes of 'top level' Perpendicular first, before taking a brief glance at its other manifestations. Among the designers of large churches the immediate reaction to Gloucester was circumspect rather than enthusiastic. The special purpose for which the choir was built set it apart from the ordinary run of ecclesiastical architecture. It remained a chapel 'writ large'. The decorative possibilities of tracery panelling were widely acknowledged, but nowhere else does it seem to have been handled with the same devastating effect. Instead there followed a period of compromise in which the new motive was discreetly and innocuously used in the context of established forms. The result was a kind of hybrid between Perpendicular

52. Canterbury Cathedral, nave

and certain features of Decorated; and during this period the nave of York Minster was probably as influential as Gloucester in determining the designs of great churches. This can be seen in the eastern limb of York itself, begun in 1361, where the elevation and the vaults follow the general lines laid down in the nave, but where much of the detail shows Perpendicular influence. The eastern façade, where work started, is covered with Perpendicular panels, and its principal feature is an enormous Perpendicular window even larger than that at Gloucester. All the window tracery is affected by the new fashion, especially that in the dwarf transepts, which runs from top to bottom of the wall. The detached mullions which form a sort of screen outside the clerestory windows of the Lady Chapel are an inversion of the idea which was used in the Lincoln Angel Choir, but can be provided with French ancestry like other Perpendicular motives.

Another example of compromise is the nave of St Mary Redcliffe, at Bristol (third quarter of the fourteenth century). There the mullions of the clerestory windows are brought right down to the mouldings of the main arcade, and to this extent the effect is closer to the Gloucester conception of Perpendicular.

53. Canterbury Cathedral, nave exterior

The climax of this phase was reached at the end of the fourteenth century when the cathedrals of Canterbury and Winchester received their present naves. In both cases decayed Norman structures had to be replaced or renewed. At Canterbury there was a total rebuilding, and the mason in charge, who was almost certainly Henry Yevele, had more or less a free hand. More is known about this man than any other medieval English mason, and his inventive capacity has perhaps been overrated. Canterbury nave [52] is certainly a beautiful building by any standard, but it owes far more to its proportions than to the novelty of its ingredients. The design owes a general debt to York Minster, and certain specific features to Westminster Abbey, where Yevele had recently completed the nave in accordance with the thirteenth-century style of the choir and transepts. Yevele's distinctive contribution at Canterbury was to heighten the main arcade at the expense of the clerestory. The result was a very subtle compromise between the traditional notion of a great church with soaring piers contributing strong vertical accents, and the spacious homogeneity of a hall-church in which the aisle windows provide most of the light. The tracery of the aisle windows is the most obvious Perpendicular feature of Canterbury [53], with the exception of Bell Harry tower.

At Winchester Yevele's contemporary, William Wynford, had a rather more difficult task. There it was decided not to dismantle the Norman nave entirely, but to retain as much of the old masonry as could be incorporated into an up-to-date design. Although Wynford solved his problem with great virtuosity, the result inevitably suffers by comparison with the serene and noble nave of Canterbury. In particular it was impossible to reduce the piers to the slender dimensions of Yevele's work; and the original thickness of the Norman walls is not entirely concealed by the skilful transition from one plane to the other at clerestory level.

All these buildings, from York choir to Winchester nave, have lierne vaults. As we have seen, there is nothing specifically Perpendicular about the origin of this type of vaulting, and no building in which it appears strictly deserves to be called wholly Perpendicular. Gloucester choir is sufficient proof of its anomalous character. Why then did it go on being used? As no one thought fit to record his views on the subject at the time, we can only speculate; but in the absence of any evidence to the contrary we may guess that the purely ornamental character of the logical alternative – i.e. fan vaulting – had something to do with it. It was one thing to put a fan vault over a cloister walk, or even over a chapter house, and quite another to construct one over the main vessel of a church perhaps forty feet wide and eighty feet high. To do so required skill of a very high order; but even more it required nerve. For we must remember that medieval masons had no means at their disposal for making rational estimates of the strains and thrusts generated in their buildings. They worked within the limits of well-tried rules of thumb which summed up the traditional experience of their craft. Once they transgressed those limits they were lost in the unknown. Lierne vaults had developed organically out of earlier and simpler forms of vaulting. But fan vaulting involved a very considerable break with tradition, and it was only very slowly that men screwed up their courage to put a fan vault over the main span of a church. A tentative move in this direction was perhaps made in the fourteenth-century nave vaults of Hereford Cathedral (replaced at the end of the eighteenth century) where the ribs emerged from cells at the points where they reached the walls. The same sort of thing was done in the transept vaults at Tewkesbury. But at Norwich Cathedral we still find a lierne vault being constructed over the nave in 1464 and even St George's Chapel at Windsor, which was designed for Edward IV, only had fans over its side aisles. By this time, however, the decisive step had been taken successfully at Sherborne Abbey.

The dating of Sherborne is not closely determined. A rebuilding was started early in the fifteenth century; it was delayed and set back by a fire in 1437; and the recasing of the nave [54], with its vault, and the vaulting of the north transept, were the work of the last quarter of the fifteenth century. The fan vault over the choir is certainly earlier than that of the nave, and may very well belong to the first half of the fifteenth century. If so, however, it is curiously isolated, unless some important contemporary works have been lost. Apart from the conoid effect which we find in the vaults of the choir at Winchester, and which represents a transition from lierne to fan, we have to wait until the very end of the fifteenth century and the beginning of the sixteenth for the spate of large-scale fan vaults in which Perpendicular architecture discovered its second and last period of vitality.

The restoration of internal peace and strong government by Edward IV, and with it the resumption of royal patronage on a large scale, initiated what has aptly been called the Indian Summer of English medieval architecture. Three buildings in particular, each of them due to the munificence of the Crown, form a splendid climax to the whole medieval tradition. They are St George's Chapel, Windsor; King's

College Chapel, Cambridge; and Henry VII's Chapel, Westminster Abbey.

St George's Chapel was started, and its design fixed, before the impact of the Sherborne achievement was felt. Consequently the high vaults [55] were given a lierne pattern. This, together with the fact that it has side aisles, makes it far more reminiscent of the late fourteenth-century cathedral designs than Gloucester choir, in spite of the fact that it was meant to be a chapel. It is in fact one of the last great church designs to be carried out in England before the Reformation. The traditional elements, however, do not conceal an internal effect that is more radically Perpendicular than anything achieved since Gloucester choir. This is due partly to the ubiquitous panelling, and partly to the proportions of the building which reproduce in elevation the squared-aspect of the individual panels. This uniformity of appearance is enhanced by the universal use of the flattened four-centred arch throughout the building.

54. Sherborne Abbey, nave

St George's Chapel was completed by Henry VII. Another undertaking left unfinished by one of his royal predecessors provided the occasion for another act of unwonted generosity. This was the chapel of King's College, at Cambridge [56]. The chapel had been conceived by its founder, Henry VI, not so much as an integral part of the college, but as an immense affirmation of his personal piety. It was therefore modelled, not on previous college chapels, like that of New College at Oxford, but on a cathedral choir. The nearest prototype is, in fact, Gloucester, and of all the Perpendicular buildings in England which were influenced by that precocious design, it is the only one which deliberately takes up the problem of the homogeneous Perpendicular interior at the point where it was left at Gloucester, and finds for it a wholly satisfying solution. Essentially the chapel was conceived as Gloucester choir with all the extraneous masonry removed – that is, with all the panels free to be filled with glass. What it would have looked like if it had been completed by Henry VI we may surmise from the Lady Chapel at Gloucester, which was started a few years later, and which was itself a free-standing version of the choir on a smaller scale. But it was perhaps fortunate that the chapel at King's College languished with the fortunes of its royal founder; for when Henry VII provided the money for its completion fan vaults were already a practical proposition. They were started in 1508 by a group of men who had recently had experience of this kind of vaulting at Peterborough. They provided King's College with the finest array of fans ever achieved on a large scale, and the result is the most majestic of all Perpendicular interiors, the only one in fact where vaults, windows, and panelling have been allowed to find a perfect accord, and to define a monumental vista. It is especially fitting that a building which depends so much on its windows should enjoy the rare privilege of preserving its original stained glass.

The classic dignity of King's College Chapel was something that could only be done once, and the third of these late Perpendicular masterpieces, Henry VII's Chapel, is utterly different from it in every respect. Henry VII as a patron of architecture is a paradoxical figure. Not particularly interested in building for its own sake, he nevertheless has three works to his credit that not even Henry III can equal. The completion of the Yorkist Chapel at Windsor and the Lancastrian Chapel at Cambridge may perhaps be regarded as gestures inspired by his policy of reconciliation. But in his own chapel at Westminster he was building for himself, and it is here alone that we find something

of his personal taste. No expense was spared. The old Lady Chapel of
the abbey was taken down, and a new plan laid out which is one of the
most intricate geometrical constructions in the whole of medieval
architecture. For sheer density of ornament there is nothing like this
building anywhere in England. Under it all we can perhaps detect a
basic debt to the design of St George's, Windsor; but whereas there
everything is light, clear, and harmonious, at Westminster there is only
an impression of confused and congested forms which become steadily
worse as we pass from the serried ranks of statues in the middle section
to the vaults above [57]. Nowhere else in England does sculpture play
such an important part in the interior of a great church; and nowhere
are there vaults of such complexity. These almost defy description.
Two fundamental ideas are involved. One is the fan vault, and the
other is the pendant. The history of the pendant motif in late medieval
English architecture is long and fascinating. It originated in timber
work, where there was a certain structural justification for it, although
it was often used as a purely decorative device. It seems to have been
adopted by stonemasons at Oxford in the middle of the fifteenth

56. *Left* King's College Chapel, Cambridge
57. *Below* Westminster Abbey, Henry VII's Chapel

century. It appears in the vault of the Divinity School there [58], and later in what is now the cathedral, where someone had the idea of threading the pendants on transverse ribs. At Westminster the process was taken a stage further by making the pendants the centres of fan-cones [59]. The result is a series of fans which appear to be suspended in space from transverse ribs. The Westminster fans are smaller than the elegant designs at King's College, and the density of the cells is very much greater. Moreover, other fans are introduced between the pendants and the walls, and down the centre of the roof other pendants are suspended, so that the overall effect resembles not so much a church as an exotic cave with rows of fantastic stalactites. As an exultant gesture of defiance at every orthodox conception of vaulting it is no doubt a *tour de force*. But the extravagance verges on the vulgar, and we are left with the impression that the steady intensification of ornament has at last reached saturation point.

Henry VII's Chapel was undoubtedly a special effort, and in its way, like King's College Chapel, it leaves the impression that there was very little left for anyone else to do afterwards. This is confirmed in another way by the last of the great medieval churches to be built in England:

58. Divinity School, Oxford

59. Westminster Abbey, Henry VII's Chapel, vault system

Bath Abbey, which was under construction from 1499 until the Reformation. The great Norman church had fallen into a state of disrepair, and was far too big for the reduced circumstances of the abbey; and, rather than attempt a complete restoration, the Bishop of Bath and Wells decided to build a new, smaller church on the site of the Norman nave. The Bishop was familiar with the court, and his masons, the two Vertues, also came from royal service. The abbey therefore deserves to be grouped with the other royal works of this time; but the resources behind it were less substantial, and it is apt to seem a dull, lifeless building when compared with King's College or Westminster. The Vertues promised the Bishop the most splendid vault in the country; it is unlikely that what they had in mind was the monotonous fan vault which we see today, for the choir seems to have been designed to receive a very shallow vault, perhaps based on a four-centred section, like that of St George's Chapel, Windsor. The fans were a not very happy afterthought, being so attenuated that the cells become monotonous. The man who designed them either did not try or did not wish to introduce the kind of counterpoint patterns which make the vaults of King's College so much more satisfying.

It is always dangerous to speculate as to what might have happened if other things had turned out differently. But it seems fairly certain

60. Beverley Minster

that when the Reformation put an end to the great tradition of church-building it was just about exhausted, and it is difficult to see from what source it could have been renewed, because all the Continental varieties of Gothic were more or less in the same condition. The plain fact is that not many changes could be rung on the theme of fan vaulting and panelling. The aesthetic ideal of Perpendicular was far more rigid and monotonous than that of early Gothic, and if circumstances had been more favourable to large-scale church-building the limitations of the style would have been exposed long before the sixteenth century.

But if Perpendicular provided little scope for variations on the theme of the great church design it found compensation in exploring new fields of design altogether. One of these was church towers. With vaulting and window tracery becoming more and more stereotyped, aspiring masons found an outlet for their talents in transforming the external appearance of the older cathedrals and abbeys. Already in the first half of the fourteenth century Lincoln and Salisbury had set the fashion – the latter crowned by its incomparable spire. During the next hundred and fifty years Wells, Worcester, York, Beverley [60], Gloucester, and Canterbury, to mention only the most familiar, followed suit. The fashion was by no means confined to the great churches. Boston church, in Lincolnshire, Cirencester church in Gloucestershire, the parish churches of Somerset, Merton, and Magdalen Colleges, at Oxford, all testify to the zeal with which this particular form of architecture was followed at other levels.

All these towers are essentially simple in form, depending on their proportions to make an effective silhouette rather than upon the intricacy of their details. In this they are totally different from the fantastic open-work constructions of their Continental counterparts, and as typically English as other aspects of Perpendicular.

The same is true of the Perpendicular parish churches. Many of them – for instance, at Hull and Coventry – are very large indeed. But in construction they tended to be as simple as possible. Hardly any of them are vaulted. St Mary Redcliffe, at Bristol, is quite exceptional. Instead of vaults, fine timber roofs were customary. These made it possible to dispense with elaborate forms of buttressing, and masonry was often little more than the provision of elegant arcades and frames for windows. The churches were extremely light and spacious, and often endowed with rich decoration, as in the sumptuous early sixteenth-century churches at Lavenham, in Suffolk, or Cirencester, in Gloucestershire [61]. But the glory of these churches, and the feature which makes it possible to set them apart as a class of their own, is their timber roofs. Nothing comparable is to be found in the city churches of the Continent, like those of Liège or Nürnberg, which are nearly always vaulted in stone. The use of timber in cathedral architecture has been mentioned from time to time; but there, in spite of its many triumphs, timber was never more than second best to masonry. In parish churches there was no break in the continuity of the use of wood for roofing. In every church, whether vaulted or not, the actual roofing material was carried on a wooden frame; and where there was no intervening web of stone these timbers were given a fine decorative finish.

As carpentry became more ambitious, new methods of timber construction came into use to cover wider spans. The most spectacular of these was the hammer-beam principle, which was used on the most lavish scale, not in churches, but in the great halls of palaces and

colleges. The first and most impressive of all the surviving examples of hammer-beam roofs is that in the hall of the Palace of Westminster [62]. It was devised by the King's carpenter, Hugh Hurland, in 1394, and spans no less than sixty-eight feet. The roof is a superb mixture of constructional and decorative elements, the great baulks of timber offset by free-standing webs of wooden tracery panels.

Hammer-beam roofs continued to be made until well into the sixteenth century, and they tended to become steadily more elaborate. In the hall of the Middle Temple, in London, built in Elizabethan times, two rows of hammer beams were used; and in Edward IV's Great Hall at Eltham Palace, *c.* 1479, pendants were suspended at the ends of the hammer beams. The same device was used again at Hampton Court. Pendants were also used on their own. On a modest scale they embellish the flat ceiling of Crosby Hall, in London; and, much more impressively, the roof of the nave of St David's Cathedral, in Pembrokeshire. What happened when the motive was adopted by stonemasons has already been mentioned in connexion with Henry VII's Chapel at Westminster.

61. *Left* Cirencester Church, nave
62. *Below* Palace of Westminster, hall

The royal halls bring us to the threshold of secular architecture. So far very little has been said on this subject, partly because what has survived is disappointing by comparison with the large number of medieval churches, but also because it has to be discussed in a totally different way. The design of secular buildings varies far more than that of great churches; it has to be thought of far more in terms of function and general effect than in terms of decorative detail or constructional methods. To understand them it is necessary to know something of the kind of life that was lived in them.

The most important thing to realize is the extent to which medieval life was lived in public – at least, by the kind of people who could afford to build themselves fine homes. The basic unit was not an individual or his family, but a group or community. The most obvious examples of this were provided by the monasteries, where the conventual buildings were beautifully organized around their cloisters for the sake of the special kind of corporate life to which the monks were dedicated. But even outside the cloister the great men of state were seldom able to enjoy what we would recognize as private life. They lived the greater part of their lives before a constant audience of their dependants and retainers; and this history of secular architecture in the Middle Ages faithfully reflects this social pattern.

The worldly counterpart to the monastic cloister was the great hall. It was the nucleus of every important medieval residence from Saxon times to the fifteenth century. Around it were grouped the kitchen, storerooms, private chambers, and the chapel. The relation of these components to one another naturally varied. The first sizeable remains that we encounter are embedded in Norman castles. These castles, which were spread in great numbers all over the country, were first and foremost focal points of feudal power, and their dispositions were primarily military. At first they consisted of little more than a mound surmounted by a tower, and a fortified enclosure – hence the name that is usually given to this type of castle: motte and bailey. But castles were also places of permanent residence, and domestic apartments had to be provided for the great men and their garrisons who lived in them. Sometimes these living-quarters were built into the great stone keeps which, in the course of the twelfth century, replaced the earlier wooden towers. In the White Tower, in London, or in the keep of Rochester Castle, Kent, the hall and chapel, etc., can still be seen. But the keep was essentially an ultimate defensive position, and it was not a convenient place in which to live when there was no emergency. Accordingly, a more general practice was to build the great hall out in the enclosure, at some distance from the keep. Thus the hall of Richmond Castle, Yorkshire, stands in a far corner of its bailey. Later, when the modes of warfare changed and the keep lost its importance, it was sometimes transformed into what was in effect a residential block; and in the Pele towers of northern England we have a survival of the idea, the slight fortifications being designed to ward off marauding Scots.

As the king's government became more effective, and feudal war was gradually eliminated, so the need for the physical protection of strong walls became less pressing and emphasis passed from the military to the domestic aspects of castles. Already by the end of the twelfth century castles were being built, like that at Oakham, Rutland, in which the great hall was by far the most important feature of the place. The lead in this process was given by the bishops in the first place, and then by the king. Bishop Pudsey's hall at Bishop Auckland, in County Durham, and Henry III's hall for Winchester Castle, survive to illustrate this trend. Few of the royal castles or palaces preserve much of their medieval form; but in the case of bishops' palaces we are better placed, for at Wells there still stands the rambling and picturesque group of buildings, erected at various times during the thirteenth century, which must have been fairly typical of the class as a whole in spite of certain peculiarities. The domestic hall, the chapel, and the solar, to which a second great hall has been added, are grouped with no apparent system; indeed, they are in some cases barely contiguous. The conception of the great house as a compact and unified building still lay in the future.

From the purely military point of view the climax of English castle-building was reached in the series which Edward I had made in Wales at the end of the thirteenth century. But these stand apart from the evolution of domestic architecture, except in so far as they anticipate certain features of the 'livery and maintenance' castles of the later Middle Ages. After 1300 the feudal levy was no longer a serious military factor. Its place was taken by professional mercenaries, or 'liverymen', who, while being very much better soldiers, were liable to change sides at short notice. To counter the exigencies of this possibility, elaborate precautions were sometimes taken to make it more or less impossible for a garrison to gain access to the private quarters of the lord of the castle. These can be seen perhaps most clearly at Bodiam Castle (1386), in Sussex, where everything was done twice, once for the lord, and once for the men. Bodiam was one of the last

63. Acton Burnell Hall

castles in England to be built for a strictly military purpose, and not every so-called castle of the later Middle Ages went to quite such lengths. At Stokesay (*c.* 1291), in Shropshire, all the fortification was concentrated in a strong tower built on to one end of the hall. We find the same idea on a very much grander scale at Tattershall (after 1431), in Lincolnshire, where the tower itself became the main part of the residence, and its defensive capacity was reduced to a minimum.

The salient feature of house and castle design in the Perpendicular period was undoubtedly the diminished importance of the idea of providing a place of refuge and protection in time of war. Not that warfare disappeared as a social phenomenon in England. On the contrary, the fifteenth century saw more violence than any time since the middle of the twelfth century. But clearly it was not the sort of violence to be resisted with massive fortifications. The typical building of the time was the fortified manor house, such as we can see in the ruins at

South Wingfield (mid fifteenth century), in Derbyshire, where again one large tower, this time built into an orderly plan based on two courtyards, provided the only really strong position in the place. But already, long before South Wingfield, this relative indifference to fortification had produced some interesting experiments. At Acton Burnell, in Shropshire [63], for instance, built at about the same time as Stokesay, Bishop Burnell of Wells, who added considerably to the palace there, built for himself what was in effect a country house. The traditional residential elements were compressed into a neat rectangular plan, much as we find them in the twelfth-century keeps, but with no concessions to the conventions of castle-building other than the use of towers at the corners. These did little more than give the exterior a symmetrical appearance. In the fourteenth century this rather precocious anticipation of the country house of the future proved less of an inspiration than the ideals of chivalry, which required a background of towers and battlements for its pageants, but which were often content with a picturesque sham rather than the real thing. It would be premature to speak of bogus castles while the Middle Ages lasted; but in the distant view of Hurstmonceux Castle (1441), Sussex [64]; in the

64. Hurstmonceux Castle

entrance to Wardour Castle (1393), in Wiltshire; or in John of Gaunt's hall (c. 1390), Kenilworth, there is a definite element of the spectacular, which owes nothing to purely military considerations.

Another factor which helped to distinguish domestic from military architecture in the later Middle Ages was the use of brick. This was introduced into the east of England during the fourteenth century, or even earlier, from Germany and the Low Countries; and by Tudor times it had spread over most of the country, and was used for the largest houses, such as Thornbury Castle (c. 1511), Gloucestershire, and Hampton Court. Brick architecture had its own decorative possibilities, which produced such fantasies as the chimneys of Thornbury [65].

Finally, there was the growing use of large glass windows. Wherever stone walls were the most important consideration, domestic apartments must have been extremely dark and gloomy; and conversely the well-lit house was a sure sign that comfort and convenience had be-

65. Thornbury Castle, chimney

66. Ockwells Manor

come criteria to be reckoned with, even if they had not entirely replaced security and defence. The Perpendicular house never dissolved into glass to the same extent as some Perpendicular parish churches; but the oriel windows which came into general use to light the high tables of domestic halls, the bay windows of the state apartments at Thornbury, and the large areas of wall given up to glass at Ockwells Manor (*c.* 1450), Berkshire [66], or the abbot's lodging at Much Wenlock Abbey, Shropshire, all indicate the point which this new fashion had reached by the eve of the Reformation.

So far as general planning was concerned, the decisive change seems to have taken place when the protective curtain wall of the earlier castles was abandoned. This made it necessary for the domestic apartments themselves to be grouped in a much more orderly way; and from the nucleus of the hall, solar, and chapel we find them spreading around courts, which often presented a continuous wall to the outside

149

world, broken only by a great gatehouse. A tremendous impetus to this kind of design was given by the development of the college system at the universities of Oxford and Cambridge. The universities themselves existed long before anyone thought of endowing permanent institutions where scholars and masters could live together in carefully regulated communities, which is what the colleges were; and it was not really until William of Wykeham founded his New College at Oxford, in 1379, that something like a definitive form was achieved. Wykeham was closely connected with the courts of Edward III and Richard II, and his career as a patron of architecture was one of the most outstanding of the whole Middle Ages. Along with New College he founded a school at Winchester (Winchester College), and as bishop there he was responsible for most of the transformation carried out by William Wynford on the cathedral. His acquaintance with the court style began at Windsor Castle in the 1350s, and he it was who was responsible for introducing the official Perpendicular style into the universities, where it flourished for the rest of the Middle Ages. The essential ingredients for any college were a chapel, a hall, a library, and accommodation for the master, fellows, and scholars. The problem was thus similar to that of housing a family and its retainers, although the nature of the activities which were carried on there, and the greater degree of communal life, gave the chapel and hall of a college more importance than in an ordinary house. The grouping of the scholars' rooms around a court, or quadrangle, with the chapel and hall along one side of it, was a very convenient solution, and the New College design exercised great influence over subsequent foundations at Oxford.

One might have expected that at Cambridge the place of New College would have been taken by King's College, which, in conjunction with Eton, was deliberately planned by Henry VI to match Wykeham's foundations at Oxford and Winchester. But at King's College the chapel consumed almost all the energies that could be mustered, and so far as college design was concerned it had less influence than its contemporary, Queens' College, where the great gatehouse and the use of brick anticipate the Tudor colleges of the sixteenth century.

Of the civic buildings which must have been a prominent feature of prosperous towns in the later Middle Ages, not a great many have survived. The Guildhall, at York, which was destroyed in the Second World War, was a good example. Here and there a medieval inn presents something of its original appearance, as at Norton St Philip and Glastonbury, in Somerset; while the Vicars' Choral Close, at Wells, and the fifteenth-century houses of prosperous wool towns like Lavenham, preserve for us glimpses of a humbler order of domestic architecture. We can hardly be satisfied with what remains. Yet there is enough for us to realize the vitality of Perpendicular architecture. Its fundamental achievement was not the solution of a single stylistic problem, but its ability to cope successfully with a rapidly expanding range of problems presented by a changing and developing society. In this sense it deserves to be called a national style; and it deserves this title more than its predecessors. Admirers of Perpendicular might also think that what came afterwards had no better claim.

Part II

PETER MURRAY

6 Tudor and Jacobean Architecture

Medieval houses must have been very uncomfortable places to live in. By our standards they had hardly any furniture, the chimneys were little more than holes in the roof, and everyone lived huddled together in the great hall, choked by smoke, and frozen by the draughts from the front door. During the sixteenth century things changed considerably, for, with the establishment of a strong government under the Tudors, it became possible to build houses with an eye to comfort rather than defence; and, towards the end of the century, the new Tudor aristocracy, enriched by Church lands, had both the money and the desire to build 'prestige' houses in which to settle their ambitious families. Another factor was the rise of the architect. According to the Oxford Dictionary, the words 'architect' and 'architecture' are first recorded in English in John Shute's *The First and Chief Groundes of Architecture* (1563), which is also the first (and rarest) of English architectural treatises.

In the sixteenth century both France and England became nation-states in the modern sense, and both owed much of this, directly or indirectly, to the spread of ideas from Italy, the home of the New Learning. Henry VIII was pleased with the picture of himself as a Renaissance prince and enlightened patron of all the arts, although he actually did very little apart from employing Holbein as his court painter; and his daughter Elizabeth was both too poor and too mean to do more than encourage her nobles to ruin themselves in building. In fact, in spite of the legends which make every Tudor house built by Italian workmen (and every portrait of Elizabeth painted by Zuccaro), there was very little direct Italian influence on English architecture before Inigo Jones. The French, with much closer contacts, were slow to absorb Italian ideas, but by the time of Philibert de l'Orme (*c.* 1505–70) they had developed a style that took full account of Italian ideas and Italian scholarship without being overwhelmed by them. In England there was little or no court patronage, and, after the break with Rome, no Church patronage either, so that there was no inducement for any really good Italian artists to come here, with the sole exception of Torrigiano, who made Henry VII's tomb, in Westminster Abbey. Cellini's autobiography tells us how the barbarous northerners appeared to a civilized Florentine artist: 'Every day he [Torrigiano] had stories to tell concerning his brave deeds when he was living among those brutes of Englishmen.' Pietro Torrigiano's tomb was made between 1512 and 1518, and it stands in Henry VII's Chapel, built from 1503 to 1519; the tomb is the first pure Renaissance work to be seen in England, under a roof which is the last flowering of Gothic. After the Reformation it was next to impossible to renew contact with the new classicism of Italy, and England depended largely on the hybrid versions current in France and Flanders. Indeed, it is likely that this impure Franco-Flemish style was actually preferred on account of its very elaboration – 'busie and fantasticall', as it would have seemed to the Elizabethans. Probably the finest example of this was Nonsuch Palace, in Surrey, one of the few large-scale undertakings of Henry VIII, begun in 1538 and destroyed in the seventeenth century. Drawings and engravings, as well as a few surviving fragments, all seem to show that the exterior had the almost nightmarish elaboration of the Franco-Flemish style, although some of the decoration was French and some Italianate.

The general type of a medieval house built round its great hall can still be seen at Penshurst Place, in Kent, and in a few other houses. Parts of Penshurst date back to 1340, so that this type of plan was already nearly two centuries old at the beginning of the sixteenth century. A diagram based on Penshurst shows the two most important aspects of this plan:

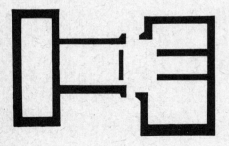

67. H-plan based on Penshurst Place

The reason why this plan is called the H-type is immediately obvious, and this arrangement of the hall in the centre, with the private room or rooms of the owner on one side and the service block on the other, was so sensible and practical that it lasted unchanged for centuries. The only important modification of it is the slightly smaller E- or half-H-plan, in which two of the projections are omitted, and the centre of the E is the front door, thus: ⊓. The H-plan is based on the idea that the whole household ate together in the great hall, which was the centre of the life of the house. At one end of the hall (here the left) there was a dais for the master, and a way into the private rooms; at the opposite end of the hall was a screen which separated the hall from the screens-passage, which in turn led directly to the kitchen, buttery, and other service rooms, while at either end of the screens-passage was a main doorway. Clearly this type of plan is admirable, so long as the builder does not mind having the front door off-centre and is prepared to make the wings of different shapes and sizes according to their function – 'expressing the plan', as it is called. The struggle between the convenience of the traditional form and the desire for a symmetrical plan and façade determines much of the architectural history of the Elizabethan and Jacobean periods, and, as one might expect, the new ideas come in gradually, and as decorative details rather than structural ideas. This can be seen in one of the greatest buildings of the age, Hampton Court, and also in houses like Layer Marney Hall, in Essex, and Sutton Place, near Guildford.

Layer Marney has a great gatehouse, built for show rather than for defence, and is decorated with terracotta window mouldings and crestings on the sky-line which are purely Italian in feeling. Terracotta can hardly have been well known in this country when Layer Marney was built, about 1520, since it had probably been introduced by Torrigiano himself only a few years earlier. The same kind of importation of decorative details occurs at Sutton Place, which was begun about 1523. The plan was originally rather French, with a central court and the traditional English gatehouse in the middle of the entrance side, but there are two new features in the plan itself in addition to the Italianate terracotta decoration. In the first place, the front door is set in the middle of the hall block, and not at the end of the screens-passage, thus obtaining symmetry at the cost of convenience (and probably draughts); and, secondly, there is a long gallery. This was undoubtedly copied from Hampton Court, for Sir Richard Weston, the builder of Sutton Place, had been to France and was at

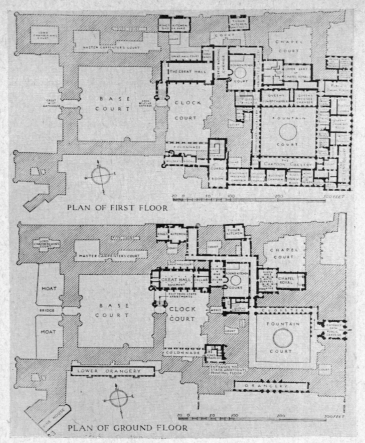

PLAN OF FIRST FLOOR

PLAN OF GROUND FLOOR

68. Hampton Court Palace, plan

the Field of the Cloth of Gold, so that he was acquainted with the ways of the court. The Long Gallery at Hampton Court was built by Cardinal Wolsey, and it is a curious fact that no one has yet been able to explain its purpose. It is said that it was for the cardinal to take exercise in on wet days, but that hardly explains the speed with which it was copied in other great houses of the sixteenth and seventeenth centuries.

158

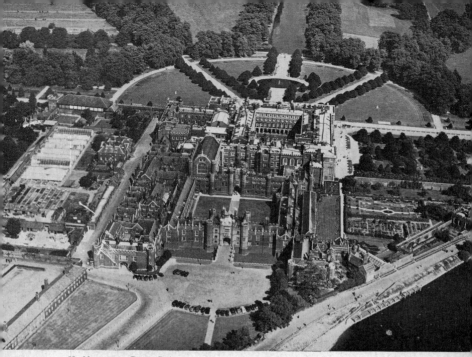

69. Hampton Court Palace

The Palace of Hampton Court was begun in 1514 by Cardinal Wolsey on an enormous scale – his household numbered nearly five hundred – and he continued work on it until, in a desperate effort to stave off disaster, he gave it to Henry VIII in 1529. After Wolsey's fall Henry began to enlarge the house into a royal palace, and work continued until 1540. Later still, under William and Mary, Wren added further ranges of buildings.

The original house was planned as a series of courts [68 and 69], exactly like a monastic or collegiate building, and the same design was used for the cardinal's other great foundation, Christ Church, Oxford, begun in 1525. As one passes from the Clock Court to the Base Court one goes through Queen Anne Boleyn's Gateway, which still bears the arms of Cardinal Wolsey in terracotta as well as part of a series of terracotta roundels of the Roman Emperors. These are of very high quality, and were probably the first such decorations in England; they

70. Hampton Court Palace, roof of the Great Hall

are the work of Giovanni da Maiano, and were paid for in 1521, but
the building accounts show that the actual structure of the palace was
the work of Englishmen. Under Henry VIII the Great Hall built by
Wolsey was greatly enlarged and enriched, and the wonderful
hammer-beam roof [70] was built between 1531 and 1536. The structure, which is of a type invented in the fourteenth century at Westminster Hall, was probably the work of the King's master-carpenter,
John Nedeham, but the superb carving is by Richard Rydge. These
elaborate pendent lanterns once more show the influence of Italian
art, but again it is a question of Italian details on an English body.
The ceiling of Wolsey's Closet, however, shows an attempt at an
Italian coffered ceiling, but it is quite clear that the result is an English
version, and not a copy of anything recognizably Italian. The rest of
the closet consists of traditional linenfold panelling with Perpendicular tracery in the windows.

Henry VIII died in 1547, and the next two years were dominated by the Lord Protector Somerset. Until his fall, in December 1549, Somerset was responsible for a marked French influence in place of the waning Italianism, and his Somerset House, begun about 1547 and demolished in the eighteenth century, was one of the most influential buildings of its day. Old Somerset House seems to have derived from the work of contemporary French architects such as Philibert de l'Orme or Jean Bullant, whose Château d'Écouen of *c.* 1545 was perhaps the actual model for the Protector's architect.

Longleat House, in Wiltshire, is one of the progeny of old Somerset House, and one of the finest examples of English architecture in the age of Elizabeth I, but before we come to it a short digression on the Thorpes, the Smythsons, and John Shute is necessary. When Somerset fell he was succeeded by the Duke of Northumberland, who sent John Shute to Italy in 1550 'to confer with the doings of the skilful masters in architecture, and also to view such ancient monuments thereof as are yet extant'. Shute was, so far as we know, the only English architect of the sixteenth century to have a first-hand knowledge of classical and modern architecture in Italy, but it was not until 1563 that he published the results of his travels in *The First and Chief Groundes of Architecture*, a short treatise based on the most influential of all Italian treatises of the earlier sixteenth century – Serlio's *Regole generali di architettura . . .*, translated into English in 1611. In 1562, the year before Shute's book appeared, Vignola's treatise on the architectural Orders was published, and this is perhaps the closest parallel with Shute. Whatever he may have learned and seen, however, Shute died in the year his book came out, and so we do not know what influence he may have had. On the whole, Flemish and German pattern-books, such as those of Ditterlin and Vredeman de Vries, the latter published in 1563, probably had more influence in England than Shute's rather uncertain classicism, and it was probably in imitation of such pattern-books that the two great collections known as the Thorpe Drawings (London, Soane Museum) and the Smythson Drawings (London, Royal Institute of British Architects) came into existence. Both collections may have been the work of more than one member of each family, and they can no longer be considered as evidence that the men who made the drawings actually built the houses. The most important members of each family were John Thorpe (*c.* 1563–1655) and Robert Smythson (*c.* 1536–1614).

Longleat was one of the first of the great Elizabethan houses – the 'prodigy houses', as Sir John Summerson calls them – and it is certainly one of the great achievements of English architecture. Its builder was Sir John Thynne, who had been in charge of the works at Somerset House, and who had also visited France. He had considerable experience of building, and, as we have seen, Shute may have had something to do with the original planning. The mason at Longleat was Robert Smythson, and through him Longleat exercised an enormous influence on other houses, but it is impossible to say how much the design of Longleat owes to him. The position is further complicated by the fact that there was a fire in 1567 and we do not know how much of the earlier house was incorporated into the new model made in 1568. The latest view is that the present house dates from 1572, and that the top storey – formerly thought to have been added after Thynne's death in 1580 – was part of his original intention. Both in plan and in elevation the most striking thing about Longleat is its symmetry and restraint, for the plan [71] shows that the east, west,

71. Longleat House, plan

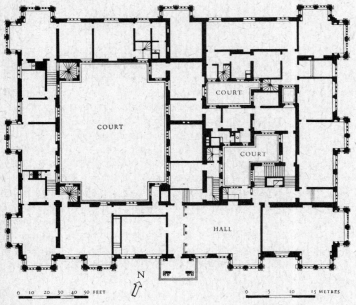

72. Longleat House

and north sides are designed with three projecting bays each, one in the centre, and one at each end, so arranged that the angles of the building appear strengthened, without using the more common device of angle-towers such as we find in French work deriving from Serlio's plan for the Château d'Ancy-le-Franc (1546). On the south, or entrance, front there are five projections – two bay-window units on either side of the front door, which still leads into the screens-passage and the centre of the house. This plan is based on internal courts rather than an adaptation of the H-type, but the much larger number of private rooms now considered necessary was bound to lead to several changes in design.

The first impression of the façade [72] is of the amount of glass, the second of its horizontal extent. The proportion of window to wall increased enormously during the reign of Elizabeth I, perhaps partly on account of greater security, but the fashion changed again under James I, and smaller windows came back. These large windows recur in other houses related to Longleat, for example Hardwick Hall, in

163

Derbyshire (another Smythson house), and so too does the horizontality – indeed, this is a permanent feature of English architecture,
and can be found in Inigo Jones at his most Italianate. In fact, the basic
element of the Longleat façade is really a vertical one, consisting of
two tall rectangular windows separated and flanked by three pilasters.
Each of the bay windows is made up of three of these units one above
the other, and this is the most conclusive proof of Longleat's descent
from Somerset House, where such units occurred in pairs at the sides.
The essential horizontality is maintained by the entablatures of the
pilasters and the string-course linking the bases which together
produce the bands across the front of the house; in addition to this the
roof is flat, with only very restrained decoration in the crestings over
each of the bay windows. All through the decoration is surprisingly
simple and classical in feeling, which is more than can be said for
Burghley House, Northamptonshire. This was begun as early as 1556,
but the main front and the court are later. The plan is that of Longleat,
with the addition of a gatehouse and angle-towers. The court is dated
1585, and is much more French – we know that Lord Burghley sent to
Paris for de l'Orme's books, and there is a resemblance to de l'Orme's
Château d'Anet – but the detail is Flemish rather than French in
character.

Not far from Burghley are the ruins of Kirby Hall, begun in 1570. It
used to be thought that the house was designed by John Thorpe,

73. Kirby Hall

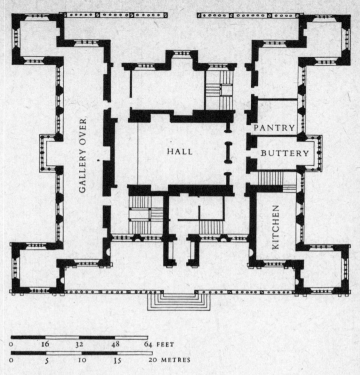

GALLERY OVER

HALL

PANTRY

BUTTERY

KITCHEN

| 0 | 16 | 32 | 48 | 64 FEET |
| 0 | 5 | 10 | 15 | 20 METRES |

74. Wollaton Hall, plan

because his drawings in the Soane Museum include a plan of Kirby inscribed: 'Kerby whereof I layd ye first stone Ao 1570', but Sir John Summerson has shown that he was only about seven at that date, so that he may have laid the first stone if his father was master-mason there, but hardly otherwise. The plan of Kirby is very French in that it consists of a court with an entrance front and loggia, two long wings of lodgings for guests, and then the house proper, with the porch in the centre leading into the great hall on the right. On the left of the porch are two floors, but, to maintain the symmetry of the façade [73], the windows run right down like those of the great hall, which actually rises the full height of the house. On the walls of this front, and also down the side wings, there are Ionic pilasters of a Giant Order (i.e.

165

one that runs through two or more storeys). This is the first use of such pilasters in England, and indeed the Giant Order was first used in Italy only a few years earlier. The porch, with its fantastic gable, is dated 1572, except for the balcony window, which was inserted in 1638.

After 1580 two large and important houses were built, both of them being linked with Longleat. They were Wollaton Hall, near Nottingham (now owned by the Corporation), and Hardwick Hall, which is now national property.

Wollaton is almost certainly the work of Robert Smythson, since he is buried in Wollaton Church, and his tombstone calls him *Gent., Architector and Survayor unto the most worthy house of Wollaton*. The owner was a coal magnate, Sir Francis Willoughby, and Professor Pevsner has suggested that this may have something to do with the extreme elaboration of the decoration, which, with its profusion of Netherlandish strapwork motives, might almost be Victorian. Wollaton is undoubtedly derived from Longleat, but the plan [74] is quite different, and very curious. The general shape seems very close to the Serlio type, which may have been the starting-point for Longleat itself, but Wollaton, like Burghley, has the angle-towers; what is odd,

75. Wollaton Hall

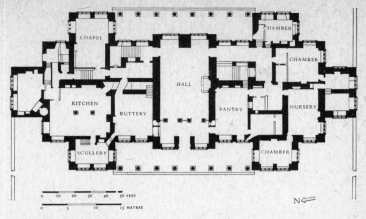

76. Hardwick Hall, plan

however, is the fact that the central court in Serlio's plan is here filled
in by the great hall. This has the advantage that the front door no
longer opens directly on to the screens-passage and thus the hall, so
that there must be a welcome reduction in the draught; on the other
hand, the hall is surrounded on all sides by other rooms, and could
not be lit except by carrying the walls up above the main block,
and using a sort of clerestory. This in turn made the hall block into
the principal external feature, rising up like a great tower, and this
probably suggested the curiously medieval features of the angle-
turrets, and the tracery in the windows of the 'great chamber' above
the hall [75]. Wollaton was built between 1580 and 1588. Two years
later Elizabeth, Countess of Shrewsbury, known as Bess of Hardwick,
a much-married lady and an impassioned builder, began her great
house at Hardwick. It was built at great speed, and was finished in
1596. The architect is unknown, but there are links with both Longleat and Wollaton, so that Robert Smythson is a highly likely candi-
date, especially as he is known to have done some unspecified work
for the house and the plan [76] shows yet another variation on the
great-hall theme. The old H-plan is adapted for the general shape,
but at Hardwick the hall is made to run back at right angles to the
front door instead of forming the cross-bar of the H. By this means
the screens-passage is made into a vestibule at the same time as it

167

fulfils its original purpose of communication with the kitchens. Externally [77] Hardwick is very like Longleat in its proportion of window to wall – the local description is 'Hardwick Hall, more glass than wall' – and it also has something of Longleat's restraint in the detailing, although the treatment of the towers recalls a plainer Wollaton. The interiors of Hardwick are important, since they contain some of the finest surviving Elizabethan decorative work in the gallery, and especially in the Great Presence Chamber, where the coloured plaster frieze is a unique survivor of a barbaric but cheerful form of decoration [78].

Charlton House, Greenwich, built from 1607, was one of the few imitations of the Hardwick arrangement of the hall on the door axis. Charlton also has an elaborate doorway, which is the only recorded instance of an almost literal borrowing from one of the plates in Wendel Ditterlin's architectural extravaganza. The date of Charlton takes us into the reign of James I (1603–25), and to a certain extent it is possible to distinguish Jacobean from Elizabethan architecture, for during James's reign many family houses were built, large in size, but not so exuberant as the Elizabethan ones, more sober in their decora-

77. Hardwick Hall

78. Hardwick Hall, Great Presence Chamber

tion, and usually built of brick, or brick with stone dressings, instead of the stone favoured by the Elizabethans. The windows tend to be much smaller, and they are usually long rectangles instead of the upright shape in fashion earlier. Most of these houses were built by the second or third generation of the new aristocracy, now comparatively settled, and they include such great houses as Knole, in Kent, Bramshill House, in Hampshire, Audley End, in Essex, and, perhaps most typical, Hatfield House, Hertfordshire.

Hatfield was built by Robert Cecil, Earl of Salisbury, the second son of Lord Burghley, Elizabeth's minister. Like his father, Cecil was the leading politician of the day and a great builder; Hatfield was far too large for his needs, but it could house the entire court on a royal progress if necessary. The house was built between 1607 and 1612, of brick and stone, and is much less extravagant than Burghley as well as more comfortably planned. The plan shows that the great hall was

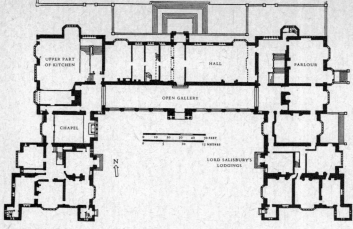

UPPER PART
OF KITCHEN

HALL

PARLOUR

OPEN GALLERY

CHAPEL

N

LORD SALISBURY'S
LODGINGS

79. Hatfield House, plan

80. Hatfield House

retained [79], complete with a screens-passage, because this was the house of a great personage, but at the same time the half-H-plan is developed to give a series of rooms in each of the wings, with the ends of the wings expanded to three rooms thick. It was thus impossible to retain a symmetrical disposition, but this can hardly be seen when one is looking at the house [80]. The south front is much more classical in appearance, with a stone loggia and a central clock-tower, and it is now thought that this is one of the earliest works of Inigo Jones, since there is a payment to him in the Hatfield accounts of £10 in February 1610 'for drawinge of some Architecture'. The other people concerned in the design were Simon Basil, the Royal Surveyor; Robert Lemyinge, who certainly supervised most of the work; and Cecil himself. Much of the interior has been altered, but the splendid wooden staircase with its open well still exists, and was one of the first and finest of its kind.

Many other Jacobean houses of the same general type as Hatfield still exist. To take only one smaller example, there is Aston Hall (1618–35), now part of Birmingham City Museums. Swakeleys (c. 1629–38), Middlesex, now a sports club, is also an example of the compact type of Jacobean house, many of which still exist. All these are traditional buildings, almost completely untouched by the new classical style of Inigo Jones, even though the Banqueting House stood in Whitehall for all to see.

7   Inigo Jones, Webb, Pratt, and May

Inigo Jones is the first British architect who is a clearly definable artistic personality. This is because he appears as a completely new phenomenon, the highly educated Renaissance ideal artist who was able to work for the most exalted patrons without sacrificing his independence. The enormous gap between Jones and, say, Robert Smythson is not so much one of artistic achievement as of intellectual attitude: Smythson was a tradesman who expected to be told what to do (although not how to do it), whereas Jones was an artist who expected his patron to take an intelligent and informed interest in what was being done for him.

This emancipation came ultimately from Italy, where such a change in the status of the artist had taken place a century earlier, and it was Jones's good fortune that he was able to study there, and that, on his return, he was to find royal patrons, in James I, and, above all, in Charles I, who both understood and sympathized with this attitude. Charles I, for all his insistence on the Divine Right of Kings, understood that great artists have an even closer relationship with the Creator. We know that Inigo Jones was not the first British architect to study in Italy – John Shute preceded him by half a century – but he was certainly the first who understood what he saw, and gave himself wholeheartedly to the new ideals based on a fervent study of classical antiquity. Jones learned to speak Italian, and it is important to realize that the whole basis of his art was the knowledge of the great Italian theorists rather than his memories of actual buildings; above all his own style and his own theories were formed by a single book, *I Quattro Libri dell'architettura*, by Andrea Palladio, published in Venice in 1570. Jones founded his style on Palladio, and a century later the whole course of English architecture was modified by Campbell, Kent, and Lord Burlington, when they chose to base themselves on

Jones and Palladio. The *Quattro Libri* was not, of course, the first Italian textbook to make a profound impression on English architects; as we have seen, Serlio was one of the main factors in the Elizabethan and Jacobean styles, but it is true to say that Serlio's *Regole generali di architettura* . . . was always used as a pattern book, as a source for individual motives of decoration. Palladio's treatise was far more scholarly, and far more firmly based on the direct study of surviving classical monuments; Jones took over this more intellectual approach, and, in particular, he followed Palladio's system of harmonic proportions. According to this system the long and short sides of a room should bear a simple mathematical relationship to each other, and also to the height; further, each room should be proportioned to its neighbours, and thus to the block of the building as a whole. A simple example is a single-cube room – say fifteen feet long, wide, and high – next to a double cube – in this case thirty feet long and fifteen wide and high.

The other great factor in the creation of Jones's style is his ability as a draughtsman and as a painter. Most of his predecessors had been able to draw, with some difficulty, a 'plat' or an 'upright' – a plan and an elevation – but that was the limit of their ability as draughtsmen. Jones was a trained artist; not, perhaps, a great one, but able to express his ideas on paper with ease, and a good part of his fame actually arose from his skill as a designer of the elaborate costumes and scenery used in the royal masques. Scores of his drawings for these exist, and it is always necessary to judge his architecture in the light of his fame and achievements as a masque-designer. He was probably the only man in England possessed of the technical skill needed for these elaborate productions, and this alone gave him a prestige at court and among literary men that made him seem altogether different from the masons and carpenters who were the usual designers of houses.

Inigo Jones was born in London in 1573, and died in 1652. We know very little about his early years, but he was almost certainly in Venice in 1601, for his copy of Palladio's *Quattro Libri* (now in the Library of Worcester College, Oxford) is so inscribed. Two years later he is recorded as a 'picture-maker' in the Earl of Rutland's service, but it is likely that he had been to Denmark in the interval. There he worked for Christian IV, but it is not known what he did. In 1605 he is documented for the first time as a masque-designer in England, so it is likely that he had worked in Denmark as a designer of this kind, and had almost certainly studied in Italy, the only place where such elaborate forms of stage design could be learned. No painting certainly by Jones is known to exist, and the work done in 1610–12 at Hatfield (if it is his) is so immature that it must be one of his earliest essays in architecture; yet in 1611 he had a job in the royal household, so that it is most likely that his skill in devising elaborate pageants and his knowledge of the high-flown allegories and personifications usual in this type of entertainment, were responsible for his advancement. He is known to have continued to work as a masque-designer until 1640, and for many years he collaborated with Ben Jonson until they had a violent quarrel over their relative importance. Both were prickly, and the quarrel produced some abuse which echoes down the centuries.

Meanwhile he had been back to Italy, about 1605, and he was in France in 1609. In 1611 he was made Surveyor to Prince Henry, his first certain architectural appointment, and in 1613 he was promised the reversion of Simon Basil's Royal Surveyorship. In that year he was once more in Italy, staying in a villa near Padua with Lord Arundel, the finest connoisseur and the greatest patron then in England. From Padua he went on to Rome, and it was at this time that he made some notes in his Palladio, and filled a sketch-book, in which, on 20 January 1615, he made his only general statement on the art of architecture. It is ill-written, misspelled, and tortuous in expression as all his notes are, but it contains a genuine aesthetic as well as a reasoned criticism of Italian Mannerist art of the previous half century, which were both totally beyond the capacity of any other Englishman of the time. This, as much as his few buildings, is the measure of his importance. He says:

And to saie trew all thes composed ornaments the wch Proceed out of ye aboundance of dessigners and wear brought in by Michill Angell and his followers in my oppognion do not well in sollid architecture [i.e. as opposed to ephemeral work such as stage sets.] . . . For as outwardly every wyse man carrieth a gravitie in Publicke Places, whear ther is nothing els looked for, yet inwardly hath his immaginacy set on fire, and sumtimes licenciously flying out, as nature hir sealf doeth often tymes stravagantly, to dellight, amase us sumtimes moufe us to laughter, sumtimes to contemplation and horror, so in architecture ye outward ornaments oft [ought] to be sollid, proporsionable according to the rulles, masculine and unaffected.

Later in the same year he succeeded Basil as Royal Surveyor, a post he held until work was stopped by the Civil War, in 1642. All his major work was done for the Crown. The Banqueting House in Whitehall was built to replace an older one destroyed by fire on 12 December 1619, and the new one was completed in 1622. This and Jones's con-

81. The Banqueting House, Whitehall (in 1781)

temporary work on the Queen's House at Greenwich must have seemed totally alien to every member of the building trades as well as to most of the public (there is a contemporary reference to the Queen's House as 'some curious devise' of Jones's), and indeed they are uncompromising essays in the purest Palladianism. Two preliminary drawings for the Banqueting House exist, and either might well be mistaken for a design for a palace by Palladio, yet the building itself has an unmistakable character of its own. Jones began by deciding to make a double cube – it is $110 \times 55 \times 55$ feet – with a single large room inside, but he then made the exterior like a Palladian palace in two storeys [81], where a contemporary Italian architect would have made the exterior express the interior by using a Giant Order. The two drawings show how he began with a normal Palladian type, with a large pediment in the centre; but such a pediment is intended to mark the entrance front and here the entrance is at the side. He therefore

82. The Banqueting House, Whitehall, interior

abandoned the pediment, and kept his sky-line level, yet he still felt that a central emphasis was desirable, so he used four columns with projecting entablatures over them to stress the three centre bays, and pilasters to articulate the two side bays, doubling them at the ends to close the building. Such subtleties can hardly have been understood by any other craftsman of the day, any more than the perfection of the detailing in the pediments over the windows: straight on the *piano nobile*, and alternating segmental and triangular on the ground-floor range, or the swags at capital level (an unusual motive borrowed direct from Palladio), or the finely channelled rustication of the surface.

Inside [82], the Banqueting House is a beautifully proportioned single room, with a gallery round it at the level of the first entablature outside. The panelled ceiling is as purely Italian as the rest of the building, but what makes this one of the noblest interiors in Europe is the great painted ceiling by Rubens, put up in 1635. As a decorative whole this interior can be compared with the Carracci Gallery in the Palazzo Farnese, in Rome; but one is unique in its time and the other a masterpiece which is the culmination of generations of similar efforts.

83. The Queen's House, Greenwich, plan

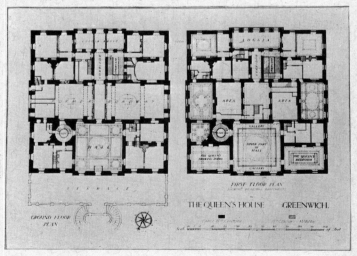

177

The design of the Banqueting House owes its origin to Palladio's conception of a town palace, but Palladio himself was, and is, chiefly famous as a designer of villas for the Venetian noble families, and his designs of this kind formed the English country house of the later seventeenth and eighteenth centuries. This was worked out in detail by Lord Burlington and the Palladians, but the first surviving example of a Palladian villa on English soil is the Queen's House at Greenwich. The Queen's House was actually begun before the Banqueting House, in 1616, but after two years work was stopped until 1630, when it was begun again for the new queen, Henrietta Maria. Her name and the date 1635 appear on the upper part of the north front, so the house must have been finished at about that time. The plan [83] is distinctly odd, for some whim of Queen Anne of Denmark made her choose in 1616 to have her new house built across a public road, the main Deptford–Woolwich highway. Later in the seventeenth century Jones's pupil, John Webb, was called in to add bridges, and thus transformed the house into the simple block we now see [84]. Later still the colonnades were added, and the road itself moved to where Romney Road now is. The plan of the original house was thus an H, but a

84. The Queen's House, Greenwich

different H-plan from those we have seen, since the cross-bar is a bridge at first-floor level only, and the great hall is now the main feature of the entrance front, in the north upright of the H. It is quite unlike any English great hall because it is now a single cube running up through the ground and first floors; like the Banqueting House, this hall is divided at half-height by a balcony which here serves to link all the rooms on the first floor. The first floor is here the *piano nobile* of an Italian villa, and the ground floor, contrary to English usage, was treated as a rusticated basement to set off the columns of the loggia on the south front. The loggia is, of course, a purely Italian idea, and cannot have been used much in Greenwich. Originally the difference between the two floors was emphasized by the fact that the windows on the ground floor were considerably smaller, but they were lengthened at the bottom in the eighteenth century. The shape and size of the windows and the general outline of the building are the only two points which clearly distinguish it from an Italian villa; the windows are, of course, far larger in scale than they would be in an Italian villa where the intention is to keep the sun out, and the shape of the whole house is a long low rectangle of the traditional English shape rather than the cubical block favoured by Palladio.

Most of the interior decoration has now disappeared, but it was probably originally very rich, and we can best get an idea of it from Jones's work at Wilton. Among the other work done by Jones before the outbreak of the Civil War, the most important in the eyes of contemporaries was the huge portico that he added to the front of the medieval St Paul's. This perished in the Great Fire, but we still possess specimens of his ecclesiastical architecture in the Queen's Chapel, Marlborough Gate, and – rebuilt in the eighteenth century – St Paul's, Covent Garden. At Covent Garden, too, he did some town planning that echoed recent work in Paris, and left its mark on English architecture.

About 1628 the young John Webb (1611–72) became Jones's assistant, and later married his niece. Much of Webb's work consisted of preparing drawings for the treatise on architecture that Jones probably projected but never completed; Webb was also the draughtsman for the palace at Whitehall which was planned by Charles I (though there must, at that date, have been an unreal air about the whole thing). The original project of 1638 may have been feasible, but the drawings presented to Charles in captivity, about 1647, can hardly have been more than wishful thinking. These he re-presented to

Charles II, but nothing came of that. The Whitehall Palace designs form a complicated and long chapter in the history of English monumental architecture, but as they were almost all grand projects rather than actual buildings, they need not detain us.

During the Civil War, in 1645, Jones was taken prisoner by the Parliamentarians at Basing House, Hampshire, but was later pardoned, and he and Webb worked at Wilton. The south front of the house was built by Isaac de Caux, but there was a fire in 1647, and Webb and Jones made some repairs which probably included the towers at the ends – a motive to become important in the Jones Revival of the early eighteenth century; more important, Jones designed the two splendid State Rooms, the Single- and Double-cube Rooms. The Double-cube Room [85] was designed to hold the great family portraits by Van Dyck in a setting of the greatest richness, with superb carved swags and pedimented doorcases and a great coved ceiling. This is an important variation on the double-cube theme of the Banqueting House, for he felt here that the true double cube was too lofty, and a compromise was reached which enabled him to set his cornice at what he felt to be the right height, with the cove leading up to the flat of the ceiling at the height required by the double-cube proportion. The richness of this decoration is perhaps more French than Italian, but it is the best evidence we have for the kind of decoration that must once have existed in the Queen's House and elsewhere.

After the death of his master in 1652 John Webb built Lamport Hall, Northamptonshire, and hoped for better days. When the Restoration came he should have had the surveyorship, but it went to the poet Denham as a reward for services to Charles II in exile. The Whitehall Palace plans never materialized, but there was a project for a palace at Greenwich, and some drawings were made by Webb. Once more the project fell through, but one part of it was built, and was later incorporated in the huge scheme for Greenwich Hospital, now the Royal Naval College. This one block – King Charles's Block [86] – was built by Webb from 1665. It is the most important work by him, in a style which owes much to Jones and more to the projects for the palace in Whitehall, but which is nevertheless entirely personal, for it shows a trend towards the Italian Baroque and a sympathy for its aims which we never find in Jones himself. In the Banqueting House there are two small orders to express a double-storey front, and all the units are correspondingly small; at Greenwich Webb built a great mass of rusticated stonework, and then divided it into two storeys by a band

86. Greenwich Hospital, King Charles's Block

of ashlar stone below the sills of the first-floor windows, and another above them. He then tied the whole front together by sets of four giant pilasters, one at each end and the other set in the middle, and these emphases are still further marked by the fact that the end bays have an attic storey over them, and the central entrance bay has attached columns instead of pilasters and a pediment above. This awareness of the unity of large masses derives ultimately from seventeenth-century Italians like Bernini, whose work Webb can never have seen in the original; but his re-interpretation of such ideas makes him the essential link between Inigo Jones and Wren.

Before we come to the work of Wren himself only three houses need detain us – Chevening,* in Kent; Coleshill House, Berkshire; and Eltham Lodge, near London. Chevening has been ascribed to Jones

* Chevening has been made over to the nation, but is not open to the public.

himself, and seems to date from 1630 or later. If these traditions are correct (and it must be observed that an attribution of a country house to Jones is almost always wrong), then Chevening was perhaps the first country house to break with the long, spreading type of plan, with towers at the angles, and other irregularities of outline. It is much more like a town house, since it is a simple block, rather high in proportion, and planned to be two rooms deep. The present house was re-faced in the eighteenth century, and it is therefore impossible to be certain of the original disposition, but it seems to have been earlier than Coleshill. This was one of the most splendid of seventeenth-century houses, but it was totally destroyed by fire in 1952. It was the work of an amateur, Sir Roger Pratt, who spent the Civil War years in France, the Low Countries, and Italy, where he visited Rome with John Evelyn. On his return he began Coleshill for a relative, about 1650, and although Jones was consulted the house was certainly Pratt's work. The plan [87] shows two major innovations. The old great hall has been transformed into a staircase hall, very Italian in feeling, with the very

87. Coleshill House, plan

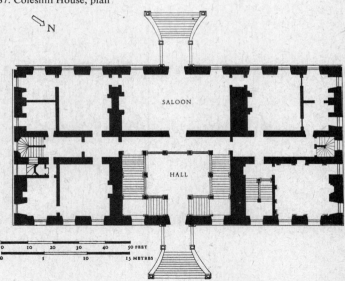

fine double sweep of the stairs climbing round the walls to a landing at first-floor level [88]. Behind the hall was the Great Parlour, but the two were separated by a corridor which ran the full width of the house, dividing it into two intercommunicating ranges. Pratt himself called this type of design 'a double pile', and it may have been invented by him, but, as it is found at Chevening, it is perhaps more likely that Inigo was the first to think of it. Yet when all is said there was a great deal of superb detailing and decoration at Coleshill that was not in Jones's style, and must have been Pratt's. He built little else, and spent most of his life as a country gentleman, but he had a considerable influence, and he helped to popularize a type which was misleadingly to be called the 'Wren type'.

The remaining house was built by Hugh May, in 1663–4, at Eltham in Woolwich (it is now a Golf Club). Hugh May (1622–84) was certainly in Holland during the Commonwealth, was made Paymaster of the Works at the Restoration, and it was for Charles II that he did what was probably his most important work, now lost, at Windsor Castle. His stay in Holland had given him first-hand knowledge of contemporary Dutch Palladianism, and Eltham Lodge [89] reflects

88. Coleshill House, hall

89. Eltham Lodge

very closely the style of such buildings as the Mauritshuis, in The Hague, in its use of brick with stone pilasters, and the Giant Order with a pediment to emphasize the centre. Naturally enough, when the exiled court of Charles II returned from Holland a good many Dutch fashions came with them, and the principal importance of May's Eltham lay in its influence on the smaller English house, and, still more important, on the formation of the style of the greatest architect of the age, Christopher Wren. The Italian and the Dutch styles both contributed to his development although he never visited either country; but the complex evolution of that wonderful mind owes much to Pratt and May as well as to greater men like Jones and Webb.

8 Wren and his Successors

Christopher Wren was one of the three or four greatest Englishmen. This eminence is due as much to the amazing sweep of his intellect as to any single aspect of his work, for the creator of the dome of St Paul's is fit to rank as an artist with Shakespeare; while Wren's own greatest contemporary, Sir Isaac Newton, reckoned him among the three best geometers of his day, and for the first thirty of his ninety years he was exclusively a mathematician and astronomer – a 'natural philosopher', to use the term current in his own time.

Wren was born in 1632, and died in 1723. He came to manhood during the Civil War, and, like many others of his generation, he turned away from politics towards the sciences. Newton was born in 1642, and both he and Wren naturally became members of the Royal Society, founded in 1662, and still one of the great scientific societies of the world; both men became its president, Wren in 1680–2, and Newton from 1703 to his death in 1727. In the second half of the seventeenth century men of this type were sickened by the Civil War, a struggle in which there was evidently a good deal of right on both sides, but in which the moderate and decent men were soon killed or thrust aside by the fanatics. The whole world of scientific experiment – of 'ingenuity' – offered a more rewarding occupation for a man of Wren's talents, for Evelyn had called him 'that miracle of a youth' in 1654, when he was still only twenty-one. Wren was the son of a clergyman, and was brought up in a high church atmosphere. His uncle, Matthew Wren, Bishop of Ely, was bitterly opposed to the Puritans, and was imprisoned by them for eighteen years; he was released at the Restoration, and his sufferings in the Royalist cause may have helped to predispose Charles II in Wren's favour. It seems certain that the personal favour of the King was very helpful to Wren at the beginning of his architectural career, and in fact he soon became virtually court

186

architect, entirely superseding the official royal surveyor, Sir John Denham. Nevertheless, before taking up his architectural career he had already been successively Gresham Professor of Astronomy in London, and Savilian Professor at Oxford, retaining this post until his architectural practice in London took up so much of his time that he had to resign. His mathematical attainments probably caused him to be consulted on old St Paul's for the first time in 1661, but very little is known of this. With his first building, however, we are on surer ground. This was the Sheldonian Theatre, at Oxford, begun in 1664, and given to the university by Archbishop Sheldon as a suitable hall for the conferring of degrees and similar ceremonies. Since the purpose of the building was for solemn public acts, Wren chose a classical amphitheatre as the basic form [90], and, like generations of Englishmen before him, he turned to Serlio for guidance. He adapted the H-shaped plan of the Theatre of Marcellus, in Rome, shown in one of Serlio's plates, and then he added something of his own which is very typical. The Theatre of Marcellus had no roof, but the sun was kept off by an awning of canvas. This was obviously impractical in the English climate, and Wren had therefore to find some way of putting a ceiling over a seventy-foot span, and to do this he turned to a course of

90. Sheldonian Theatre, Oxford, plan

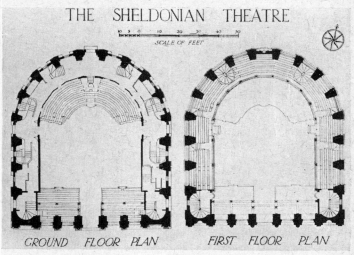

THE SHELDONIAN THEATRE

SCALE OF FEET

GROUND FLOOR PLAN   FIRST FLOOR PLAN

lectures given in 1652 by Dr John Wallis, his colleague as Savilian Professor of Geometry. Wallis had discussed the problems of a Geometrical Flat Floor; Wren simply took his system of supports and turned them upside down, hanging a flat ceiling from a system of roof-trusses, and thus securing, to the marvel of his contemporaries, a clear span of seventy feet totally unobstructed by any supports. To complete the classical allusion, the ceiling was painted to represent the sky with the cords and awning of its prototype. In this, his earliest work, we have already the combination of practical ingenuity and aesthetic feeling expressed in terms derived from classical civilization, which is the hallmark of Wren as an architect.

His next works were for the University of Cambridge, at Pembroke and Emmanuel Colleges, but the turning-point in his career came with great suddenness in the years 1665 and 1666, the years of the Great Plague and the Fire of London, and also the years when Isaac Newton discovered the binomial theorem, and the differential and integral calculi. Wren went to France in the summer of 1665, and spent eight or nine months in Paris and the neighbourhood, returning in February or March of 1666. So far as we know, this was the only time he ever left England, and it was thus the only occasion he ever had to see a fully developed classical style other than that of Inigo Jones – for the rest of his considerable knowledge of contemporary and earlier European work he had to depend on engravings. We know from a letter written from Paris that he bought many of these in France, and he certainly used many more on his return. The letter he wrote is undated, but was probably sent towards the end of his stay, and it contains some impressions which were to influence the course of English architecture:

I have busied myself in surveying the most esteem'd Fabricks of Paris, and the Country round; the Louvre for a while was my daily Object, where no less than a thousand Hands are constantly employ'd in the Works; some laying mighty Foundations, some in raising the Stories, Columns, Entablements, etc., with vast Stones, by great and useful Engines; others in Carving, Inlaying of Marbles, Plaistering, Painting, Gilding, etc. Which altogether make a School of Architecture, the best probably at this day in Europe. . . . Mons Abbé Charles introduc'd me to the Acquaintance of Bernini, who shew'd me his designs of the Louvre, and of the King's Statue. . . . The Palace or if you please, the Cabinet of Versailles call'd me twice to view it: the Mixtures of Brick, Stone, blue Tile and Gold make it look like a rich Livery, not an Inch within but is crowded with little Curiousities of Ornaments: the Women, as they make here the Language and Fashions, and meddle with Politicks and Philosophy, so they sway also in Architecture; Works of

Filgrand, and little Knacks are in great Vogue; but Building certainly ought to have the Attribute of eternal, and therefore the only Thing uncapable of new Fashions. . . . I shall bring you almost all France in Paper, which I found by some or other ready design'd to my Hand, in which I have spent both Labour and some Money. Bernini's Design of the Louvre I would have given my Skin for, but the old reserv'd Italian gave me but a few Minutes View; it was five little Designs in Paper, for which he hath received as many thousand Pistoles; I had only time to copy it in my Fancy and Memory; I shall be able by Discourse, and a Crayon, to give you a tolerable Account of it. I have purchased a great deal of Taille-douce [engravings], that I might give our Countrymen Examples of Ornaments and Grotesks, in which the Italians themselves confess the French to excell.

Probably the most important event of this journey was Wren's short meeting with Bernini, the greatest architect of the day, who was in Paris to design the new Palace of the Louvre and to make a bust and an equestrian statue of Louis XIV. He was accorded almost royal honours (but most of his projects were quietly sabotaged by the French artists); and it is not impossible that this brief interview convinced Wren that architecture was an occupation fit for genius, and by no means lacking in material rewards. The status of the architect in England was still far below that attained in Italy and France, and it needed a great intellect, such as Wren's, to make possible the whole atmosphere of the eighteenth century when architecture took its place among the professions.

Immediately after his return Wren began to prepare a design for the rebuilding of old St Paul's, since the church was then in a very decrepit condition. It is not surprising that the new design was based on the great domed church of the Sorbonne, which Wren had seen on his trip to Paris. His design was accepted on 27 August 1666: on 2 September the Great Fire of London began. The events of those days are best described by John Evelyn in his *Diary*:

27 *August.* I went to S. Paul's church, where, with Dr Wren, Mr Pratt, Mr May, Mr Thomas Chicheley, Mr Slingsby, the Bishop of London, the Dean of S. Paul's and several expert workmen, we went about to survey the general decays of that ancient and venerable church . . . the shape of what stood was very mean, and we had a mind to build it with a noble cupola, a form of churchbuilding not as yet known in England, but of wonderful grace.
2 *September.* This fatal night, about ten, began the deplorable fire, near Fish Street, in London.
3 *September.* The fire . . . was now taking hold of S. Paul's church, to which the scaffolds contributed exceedingly. . . .

4 September. . . . the stones of Paul's flew like grenadoes, the melting lead running down the streets in a stream, and the very pavements glowing with fiery redness, so as no horse, nor man, was able to tread on them. . . .

7 September. At my return, I was infinitely concerned to find that goodly church, S. Paul's – now a sad ruin, and that beautiful portico (for structure comparable to any in Europe, as not long before repaired by the late King)* now rent in pieces, flakes of large stones split asunder and nothing remaining entire but the inscription in the architrave, showing by whom it was built, which had not one letter of it defaced! It was astonishing to see what immense stones the heat had in a manner calcined, so that all the ornaments, columns, friezes, capitals, and projectures of massy Portland stone, flew off, even to the very roof, where a sheet of lead covering a great space (no less than six acres by measure) was totally melted.

It has been calculated that more than thirteen thousand houses were destroyed in the fire, as well as more than one hundred churches and the cathedral itself. Evelyn estimated the homeless at two hundred thousand, and it was this that made the Great Fire so much worse than the second fire of 1940. Fortunately, the Government, headed by Charles II himself, took effective steps to feed the refugees and to start work on the rebuilding: once again, Evelyn's *Diary* tells us how the work of rebuilding was taken in hand:

10 September. I went again to the ruins; for it was now no longer a city.

13 September. I presented his Majesty with a survey of the ruins and a plot [plan] for a new City, with a discourse on it. . . .

* The great portico was the work of Inigo Jones, in the 1630s.

91. Wren's plan for the new City of London

Quick as Evelyn was, Wren was even quicker, for his plan for the new City [91] had been presented to the King a few days earlier. Charles at once appointed a commission for the rebuilding of the City, nominating Hugh May, of the Office of Works, Sir Roger Pratt, and Dr Wren; the City appointed three more of its own nominees. The commission had three main problems to face. They had to provide for the rebuilding, as quickly as possible, of thousands of houses and shops, of sufficient parish churches for the needs of the large population of the City, and for the rebuilding of St Paul's; next, they had to try to improve the planning of the City, since before the fire it had consisted of a noisome huddle of medieval alleys and mean houses, permanently jammed with traffic, and intermittently swept by contagion or fire. Finally, they had to reconcile the claims of thousands of freehold owners with the need for much wider streets and large open spaces, and it was this which made Wren's plan impracticable. The essence of his plan derives from the best contemporary models in France and Italy, and consists of long straight streets, intersecting mostly at right angles, but with a few main vistas centred on large public buildings, such as St Paul's or the Royal Exchange. This rectilinear plan is complemented by a scheme of piazzas – the very word is derived from Italian practice – which form the centres of rings of streets. The plan shows how easy it would have been to cross London from north to south or east to west, with an extra diagonal link from the focal points of the Cathedral and the Royal Exchange; further, the main streets were to be ninety feet wide: far wider than their medieval predecessors. The snag lay in the fact that Wren's plan took little account of the ownership of land, and would have needed extensive powers of compulsory purchase, while in many cases the remains of the burned-out buildings and their cellars would also have had to be cleared at great expense. In the event the owners of the original buildings were allowed to return to their old sites, subject to the restrictions imposed by the Act of 1667, which made it impossible to return to the most insanitary aspects of the medieval City. All the houses and shops were rebuilt at the owners' expense, but the public buildings were paid for by the City and the Companies, and the churches were built out of the proceeds of a tax on coal. Wren's plan may not have had much effect on the aspect of the City, but it was probably one of the reasons for his appointment as Royal Surveyor in 1669, Webb being passed over once again. Under Wren's general supervision work was begun on the new churches in 1670, but it is important to remember that, of the fifty-five

92. St Bride,
Fleet Street

93. St Mary-le-Bow,
Cheapside

94. St Vedast,
Foster Lane

Wren churches, only a handful were designed in detail by Wren himself, since the majority were very largely carried out by the craftsmen of each parish. In most cases Wren provided the plan and, at a later stage, the steeple. The plans are particularly important, since they were all adaptations of the older parish-church sites to suit the new, Anglican, liturgy, a point which he developed at some length in his memorandum on church-building of 1711, insisting on the need for a 'convenient auditory' in which 'everyone should hear the Service and both hear and see the preacher'.

Among the most important survivors of the City churches are St Bride, Fleet Street (1671–8; steeple 1701–3) [92]; St Mary-le-Bow, Cheapside (1670–3; steeple completed 1680) [93]; St Stephen Walbrook (1672–9), and St Vedast, Foster Lane (1670–3; steeple 1694–7) [94]. All these churches were badly damaged in the Second World War, but St Bride,* St Stephen, and St Mary-le-Bow have been restored; St Vedast has been repaired, and its tower – its most important feature – survives. Two other churches are usually counted among the City churches, although, in fact, outside the City boundary: St Clement Danes, Strand (1680–2), and St James, Piccadilly (1682–4).

Basically the City churches are rectangular in plan, but the cramped and awkward sites meant that the shapes were often very odd, and it needed all Wren's ingenuity to adapt them to some more or less symmetrical arrangement. The new Protestant type of parish church did not need a choir, and it was not usually necessary to have any kind of transept, so the type evolved by Wren is that of a hall, with or without aisles, but having galleries to contain extra seats and make it possible to hear the sermon. This type had been evolved in Holland for the Calvinists, but it was also a type used by the Jesuits; like them, but unlike the Calvinists, Wren had to provide an altar – normally against the east wall – and his interiors were also intended to be much more richly decorated than the Calvinists would have allowed. Three plans of the surviving churches will show his ingenuity. In the first, St Bride [95], he was able to use a pure rectangle since the site was clear; the church is therefore a traditional parish type of nave-and-aisles, with the east end a mere salient (since there were fewer clergy to fill the choir), and the emphasis on the entrance tower and spire. Wren attached great importance to the steeples, since they were the landmarks and 'handsome Spires or Lanterns, rising in good proportion

* The St Bride restoration is not in accordance with Wren's design.

193

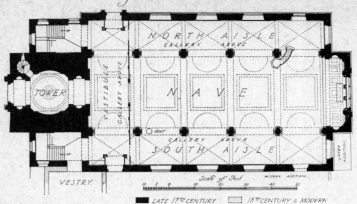

95. St Bride, Fleet Street, plan

above the neighbouring houses . . . may be of sufficient Ornament to the Town'. The second plan, that of St Mary-le-Bow [96], is a variation on the same theme, but we happen to know that it was based on the Basilica of Constantine, in Rome (which Wren would have known from the engraving in Serlio), as well as the general idea of the classical basilica, as described by Vitruvius,* which underlies most of his City churches. The plan looks like an ordinary nave-and-aisles type, with the entrance set at the side under the tower, but the interior shows the great central barrel vault supported on the side piers, which are themselves supported by flat longitudinal arches and smaller transverse ones – precisely the constructional system of the great Roman baths, and the kind of exercise needed by the future architect of St Paul's.

St Stephen Walbrook is perhaps the finest of all the City churches, and is generally regarded as a trial run for St Paul's; certainly it is a different type of plan [97], based on the idea of a dominant dome, then still an innovation in English churches. Several of the City churches were based on the centralized type of plan – a square containing a cross (St Martin Ludgate, Ludgate Hill; St Anne and St Agnes, Gresham Street; St Mary-at-Hill, Lower Thames Street), or an octagon or

---

* The most important architectural writer of ancient times. He lived in the first century B.C.

96. St Mary-le-Bow,
Cheapside, plan

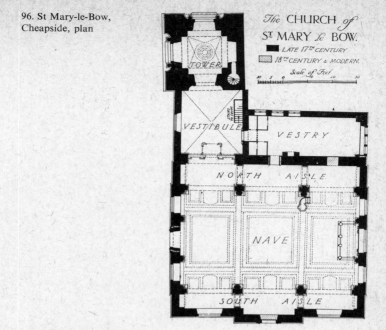

The CHURCH of
St MARY le BOW.
■ LATE 17TH CENTURY
☐ 18TH CENTURY & MODERN.
Scale of Feet

TOWER

VESTIBULE

VESTRY

NORTH AISLE

NAVE

SOUTH AISLE

97. St Stephen Walbrook, plan

CHURCH of St STEPHEN WALBROOK.

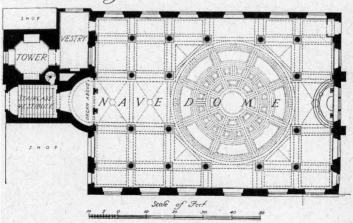

SHOP

VESTRY

TOWER

STAIRCASE
VESTIBULE

ORGAN ABOVE

SHOP

N A V E   D O M E

Scale of Feet

195

similar figure treated as an oval (St Antholin,* Watling Street; St Benet Fink,* Threadneedle Street), or a square covered by a dome (St Mary Abchurch; St Mildred,* Bread Street; St Swithin,* Cannon Street), but St Stephen is a particularly subtle combination of a nave and four aisles with a large central domical space. This gives great variety to the internal spaces [98], and makes the voids between the architectural solids as important as the solids themselves. The dome is carried on a series of arches which spring from eight Corinthian columns set on high bases (originally the pews came up to the tops of the bases); but the columns also carry straight entablatures running in different planes from the arches, linking the central (or domed) church with the long nave-and-aisles one, and giving a constantly shifting series of spatial effects as one moves round the interior. This use of varying ceiling levels in the angles owes much to Dutch Calvinist churches, which Wren can have known only at second hand, but St Stephen differs fundamentally from them in having an altar at the east end, in its much richer furnishing and plasterwork, and in its complexity of spatial treatment – in fact, it is the architectural equivalent of the Anglican compromise between the austerities of Calvinism and the splendours of Baroque Rome. This was precisely what was needed

* Destroyed.

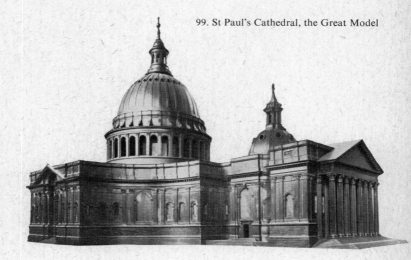

99. St Paul's Cathedral, the Great Model

98. St Stephen Walbrook

at St Paul's, the first cathedral to be built for the Anglican liturgy and for a Dean and Chapter anxious to maintain the high church tradition and to avoid the Puritanism which was so recent a memory.

The rebuilding of St Paul's began in 1675, and was finished in 1710. It is extremely rare for a building of such size and importance to be completed in the lifetime of its architect, and it was particularly fortunate that Wren lived to a great old age, for he seems to have modified the design at almost every stage. After the fire the choir of old St Paul's was unusable, but services were held in the nave until, in 1668, some masonry fell, and it became clear that the building was dangerous. Wren was then asked to prepare a design for a new choir as a preliminary to a complete rebuilding when more money should be available. In the event the Coal Tax was almost all spent on the parish churches up to 1675, when the new cathedral was begun on the increased funds available. Between 1668 and 1675 at least three full-scale projects were put forward, none of them bearing very much resemblance to the executed building, but all of them playing a part in its long genesis. By 1670 the first model had been prepared and approved. It still exists in a fragmentary state, but we can say with certainty of it that it was not really adequate as a cathedral, and that

100. St Paul's Cathedral, the Great Model, interior

101.
St Paul's Cathedral,
plan of the Great
Model design

it had a dome, thus proving Wren's desire to build a domed church comparable to those he had seen in Paris. Certainly he wanted to provide London with a great landmark, as the spire of old St Paul's had once been, and his basic conception was therefore a compact block, building up to a climax in the dome. This idea reached splendid expression in the Great Model of 1673 [99], eighteen feet long, and preserved in the cathedral itself. This is supposed to have been Sir Christopher's own favourite (he was knighted in this year, 1673), and it is easy to see why, for it is great architecture which comes from the antique tradition by way of the great Italians – and in particular it is very reminiscent of the plan which Michelangelo had made for St Peter's and had been prevented from carrying out. The most striking features about the Great Model are the clean sweep of the interior under the dome [100] and the use of deep re-entrant curves for the external walls, contrasting with the dome above, as well as with the portico of giant columns which was clearly intended to recall Inigo Jones's. The Great Model is not quite a fully centralized plan [101] since it has a small dome over the vestibule at the west end, i.e. it has

199

200

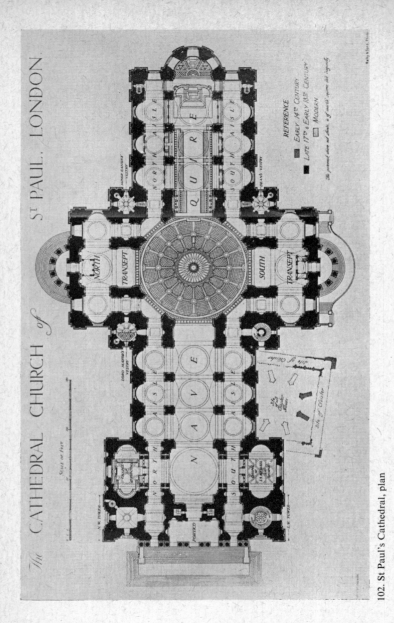

102. St Paul's Cathedral, plan

an east–west orientation. Nevertheless it did not look much like a church to most laymen, and the clergy 'thought the model not enough of a cathedral-fashion'. This probably meant that it did not look like a medieval cathedral, and therefore did not support their efforts to maintain the theory that the Anglican Church was the natural successor to Rome. The model also had the practical drawback that it could not be built in stages, as the money came in. It was therefore rejected, and Wren drew up another plan, known as the Warrant Design, in 1675. It received the royal approval, although the elevation is almost grotesque, and the work began at last. The plan of the Warrant Design is very close to that of the executed building [102] in that it is a Latin cross – 'a cathedral form, as they called it, but so rectified as to reconcile the Gothick to a better manner of architecture', while the exterior is a combination of old St Paul's and Inigo Jones, with an extraordinary dome-cum-spire on the top. Probably Wren did not take the Warrant Design very seriously, for there is a clause in the warrant allowing him 'the liberty . . . to make some variations, rather ornamental than essential, as from time to time he should see proper', and he took advantage of this almost at once. It is true that he never altered the essential Latin-cross plan, but he certainly changed the exterior almost immediately, and he modified the plan to make it approach as nearly as possible to the central type, with the dome in the middle as the focus, rather than the east end. The dominance of the dome must always have been his concern, for early in the 1680s he designed the present upper storey, and shortened the nave [103]. The upper storey is particularly important, for, as an air view shows, the upper part is simply a wall decorated with blind windows, and concealing the buttresses of the roof; nevertheless, the screen wall serves the double purpose of stiffening the supports of the dome (it has the same static function as pinnacles in a medieval flying-buttress system), while it also makes a far better build-up to the dome itself from all points of view at ground-level, most particularly from the east [104], where something of the effect of the Great Model can be realized. All the decorative detail of this work is much influenced by Roman Baroque architecture, and the best example of this is the use of motives taken from Pietro da Cortona's Santa Maria della Pace, in Rome, for the semicircular porches of the transepts. This too was decided early in the eighties, so that the years 1675–85 saw a critical period in the evolution of the cathedral; these were also the years in which he made some Baroque experiments in the City steeples. The west front [105],

except for the towers, was perhaps also designed in the 1680s, but here Wren was severely handicapped by being unable to get stones large enough for a Giant Order. This is the reason for the double order of coupled columns in the portico, always regarded as one of the weakest parts of the design but largely offset by the triumphant Baroque of the great west towers, contrasting with, and yet subserving, the glorious curve of the dome rising above them. They were executed between 1705 and 1708, after the dome itself was largely settled, and they owe a great deal to Borromini's towers at Sant' Agnese in Agone, in Rome.*

* The influence of Borromini is also very marked in the tower of St Vedast, Foster Lane [94], of 1694–7.

103. *Left* St Paul's Cathedral, nave
104. *Below* St Paul's Cathedral, view from the east

In 1697 the dome itself was taken in hand, but there had been projects before that date and the final design evolved only in stages. In the same year Wren's salary was halved by order of Parliament because he had not adhered to the Warrant, which had provided for the completion of the choir before anything else was undertaken. There can be little doubt that Wren realized perfectly well that, if he did as he was told, the nave, dome, and west end would never get built, or at least not in his lifetime, and so he began the western parts before completing the choir. In December 1697 the choir was opened, but it was not until 1711, when an Act of Parliament declared the building complete, that Wren received the arrears of his salary.

From the very beginning Wren had intended to provide a dome, to soar over the roofs of the houses and make a landmark comparable to the spire of old St Paul's, and his experiment at St Stephen was to give him practice in setting a dome on eight arches. The great difficulty which faced him is simply that a dome high enough to serve as a landmark – indeed, to be visible at all from the ground outside – is necessarily set on a high drum, which gives the effect from inside the building of standing at the foot of a factory chimney; on the other hand, a dome which looks right from the inside is scarcely more than a shallow saucer. The solution to the problem had been found at St Peter's more than a century earlier, where Michelangelo provided two separate shells, not concentric. Wren's practical genius took the solution a stage farther, for he designed a semicircular dome [106] with a large 'eye' to close the vista upward, lit by a flood of light from the lantern far above, and he supported the lantern on a great cone of brick and masonry, which is invisible from inside and outside the cathedral. The actual outer dome is a mere skin of lead on a timber framework, and could therefore be designed to satisfy purely aesthetic demands, since the whole of the 850 tons of the lantern was supported on the invisible cone and buttressed by the colonnade of the drum. The colonnade is interrupted at every fourth bay by a solid pier with a niche, so that the monotony of an unbroken peristyle is avoided, additional buttressing is achieved, and a slight feeling of direction is obtained and heightened by the very definite orientation of the lantern itself. In between is the perfect curve of the dome, Wren's masterpiece, and the finest of its kind.

Not the least astonishing thing about St Paul's is the fact that it was only one of the commissions Wren had in hand in the last quarter of the seventeenth century and the first few years of the next. Apart from the

105. St Paul's Cathedral (in 1797)

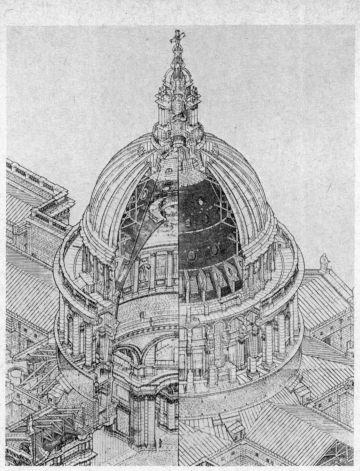

106. St Paul's Cathedral, dome (from a drawing by R. W. Brook-Greaves and W. Godfrey Allen)

City churches, he was responsible for several public buildings ranging from the Library of Trinity College, Cambridge (1676–84) and Tom Tower, at Christ Church, Oxford (1681–2), to Hampton Court Palace (1689–1700, south and east wings), and the two hospitals in imitation of the Hôtel des Invalides, for Army and Navy pensioners at Chelsea

(1682–91) and Greenwich respectively. Greenwich Hospital is his finest work, apart from St Paul's, and is particularly splendid in its setting, rising from the Thames, and leading up the slight slope to the Queen's House. The Queen's House is, in fact, too small and too far away to form a true central feature, but Wren had to retain it, and leave the view from it unobstructed; this he did by setting it at the end of two splendid colonnades crowned by domes, but although it is certain that this splendid vista is entirely Wren's, it is at Greenwich that we first encounter the Wren–Hawksmoor–Vanbrugh problem. Nicholas Hawksmoor (1661–1736) went to Wren in 1679 as a boy of eighteen, and worked as his clerk on all the important buildings from about 1684. After Wren's death he became a major architect in his own right, but his style is only now being distinguished from that of his friend and collaborator, Sir John Vanbrugh (1664–1726), and it is quite certain that all three men, with Wren as leader, were responsible for Greenwich. Greenwich Hospital [107] was begun in 1696 in place of a projected palace, for which Webb had already built the wing now called King Charles's Block, and Wren was in charge of the new building. The design was altered in 1699, the year after Hawksmoor

107. Greenwich Hospital

108. St Mary Woolnoth

was made Clerk of the Works, and the year in which Vanbrugh burst
into architecture. Captain Vanbrugh had been a regular soldier who
was arrested in France as a spy and imprisoned in the Bastille; next he
became a playwright, producing his best comedy, *The Provok'd Wife*,
in 1697; equally suddenly he became an architect, in 1699, when the
Earl of Carlisle commissioned him to design Castle Howard, in Yorkshire. It seems that he had no practical experience, and he therefore
collaborated with Hawksmoor, but the design may well have been his,

for in 1702 the Earl of Carlisle got him the Comptrollership of the Works, which made him Wren's principal colleague. From 1703 he was a director at Greenwich, and in 1716 he succeeded Wren as surveyor there; it is perhaps not unfair, therefore, to call Greenwich Hospital, or the Royal Naval College as it now is, the principal work of the Wren School. Another similar work is the Orangery at Kensington Palace, of 1704, but here there is even less evidence to connect it with Vanbrugh, and present opinion tends to ascribe the new features here to Wren's 'late manner' or to Hawksmoor.* Vanbrugh's main contribution to English architecture lies in the dramatic power of his imagination, which gives a personal stamp to all his works, even though the details may be by Hawksmoor. Vanbrugh had an intuitive sympathy for the ruggedness of medieval buildings – for what he called 'the castle air' – which no other architect of his day had; Hawksmoor had a similar feeling for the grandeur of ancient Rome, but his architecture is more sophisticated, one might almost say introverted, than the expansive theatricality of Vanbrugh at his best – compare, for

* Dr K. Downes in his *Hawksmoor* (Zwemmer, 1959), definitely attributes it to Hawksmoor.

109. Seaton Delaval Hall, north front

The North front of Seaton Delaval in the County of Northumberland the Seat of Francis Delaval Esq.   design'd by S.r John Vanbrugh K.t 172

110. Blenheim Palace

example, St Mary Woolnoth, Lombard Street [108], with the main front of Seaton Delaval Hall in Northumberland [109], since here the two artists are using almost identical forms. Castle Howard, Blenheim Palace, Oxfordshire – where the dramatic setting is Vanbrugh's but many of the finest touches are Hawksmoor's – and the gaunt, romantic ruin of Seaton Delaval are Vanbrugh's major works, and it was at Blenheim [110] that he was able to build on a titanic scale, since he conceived it 'much more as an intended Monument of the Queen's glory than a private Habitation for the Duke of Marlborough' – this was because the Crown paid for some of the palace, but not as much as the Duchess thought was right. The palace was begun in 1705, and the quarrel between Vanbrugh and the Duchess grew to such a point that in 1725 he was refused admittance to his own building.

If Vanbrugh was an inspired and slightly flamboyant amateur, Hawksmoor was a dedicated professional, supremely competent but

111.
St George,
Bloomsbury

at once diffident and aloof; his friend Vanbrugh spoke no more than the truth when he wrote, in 1721: 'Poor Hawksmoor, what a Barbarous Age have his fine, ingenious, parts fallen into. What wou'd Monsr. Colbert in France have given for such a man?'

Perhaps his best-known work is his completion of the western towers of Westminster Abbey, in the Gothic style he used for the outside of All Souls College, Oxford (1715–40); but there the interiors are in the classic manner he loved and truly understood, as may be seen in the Clarendon Building (1712–15), also in Oxford. His finest works, however, are undoubtedly the London churches built for the Commission of 1711: St Alphege, Greenwich; St Anne, Limehouse; St George-in-the-East, Stepney;* St Mary Woolnoth, Lombard Street; Christchurch, Spitalfields; and St George, Bloomsbury. This last [111] was built between 1720 and 1730 and has a noble portico which challenges comparison with that of St Martin-in-the-Fields. It is, indeed, the contemporary of St Martin's, and we have left the Age of Wren, and moved into a new century, a new reign, and an entirely new conception of architecture.

* Severely damaged in the Second World War.

212

9   Gibbs and the Palladians

Towards the end of Wren's very long lifetime there was a sharp reaction against much of what he stood for; and when he died, in 1723, there was a new and alien dynasty on the throne and a new approach to architecture which he may well have found distasteful. The architecture of James Gibbs, who built one of the most famous of all English churches – St Martin-in-the-Fields – formed a link between Wren and the eighteenth century, and it was Gibbs who helped to spread Wren's ideas all over Britain, and indeed all over America as well. While Gibbs was building his church the new school of dogmatic followers of the Italian architect Palladio (1508–80) claimed to be following in the footsteps of Inigo Jones, and, with the powerful support of the Earl of Burlington, they established what was practically an architectural dictatorship. Before we turn to their ideas and works it will be easier, with Wren fresh in our minds, to consider the life and achievement of James Gibbs. He was born in Aberdeen, in 1682, and he died in London, in 1754; unlike his fellow-Scot and bitter rival, Colen Campbell, Gibbs was certainly a Tory (and probably a Jacobite), and a Catholic into the bargain. All this, on top of being a Scot in London at the time of the Hanoverian Succession and the Jacobite Rising of 1715, was not calculated to advance any man's career, and it was perhaps fortunate for Gibbs that Campbell died in 1729.

We now know that Gibbs went to Rome as a young man, in 1703, to study for the priesthood at the Scots College there; after about two years, however, he abandoned his studies and finally began to work under Carlo Fontana (1638–1714), one of the leading exponents of Late Baroque architecture, and a notable teacher. His Italian training was Gibbs's greatest asset when he set up in London early in 1709, for he was almost the only architect then working in England who had not only been to Rome and studied both ancient and modern build-

112. St Mary-le-Strand and Somerset House (in 1796)

ings there, but had also had a regular academic training under a distinguished master. This training, of course, made him sympathetic to the English Baroque practised by Wren, and he was thus well qualified to carry on the Wren tradition. His first great work was the church of St Mary-le-Strand, only a few yards west of Wren's St Clement Danes, and clearly showing the influence both of Rome and of Wren.

St Mary-le-Strand [112] was built under the Act of 1711 which provided for fifty new churches – the Act responsible for the Hawksmoor churches – although only twelve were actually built. Wren was appointed one of the commissioners under the Act, and it was for his fellow-commissioners that he wrote his famous memorandum on church-building. Hawksmoor and Gibbs were architects to the Commission, but Gibbs did not keep his post for long. He was appointed in 1713 and sacked in December 1715, on the return of a Whig government under the Hanoverians. Gibbs's first patrons had

214

been the Earls of Oxford and of Mar – and it was Mar who led the 1715 Rising, and was defeated by John Campbell, Duke of Argyll, at Sheriffmuir. As Argyll was Colen Campbell's patron it soon became clear to Gibbs that he could survive in a Hanoverian and Whig world only by trimming, and from about 1720 onward he came to terms with the Whigs, with the Church of England, and with the architectural principles of Palladianism. He managed to live at first by private practice for Tory patrons, and he also wrote two books – *A Book of Architecture* (1728) and *Rules for Drawing the Several Parts of Architecture* (1732) – both of which were widely read and copied in England and America, and they brought him in, according to his own account, nearly £2000 – a very considerable sum in those days.

St Mary-le-Strand was built between 1714 and 1717, and looks in many ways like a Roman palace or a Baroque church in Rome, such as Fontana's San Marcello. The windows were set high up to keep out the noises of the Strand, and the lower range of blind niches was therefore introduced to balance the composition, and to allow for a double order of columns both outside and inside, although the building is only one storey high. A double range of columns had been used by Sir Christopher Wren in the portico of St Paul's, and both churches were implicitly criticized by Campbell when he published a *Design for a Church, of my Invention* (1717) with the remarks:

In those admirable Pieces of Antiquity, we find none of the trifling, licentious, and insignificant Ornaments, so much affected by some of our Moderns . . . nor have we one Precedent either from the *Greeks* or *Romans*, that they practised two Orders, one over another, in the same Temple in the Outside . . . and whereas the Ancients were contented with one continued Pediment . . . we now have no less than three in one Side, where the Ancients never admitted any. This Practice must be imputed either to an entire Ignorance of Antiquity, or a Vanity to expose their absurd Novelties. . . .

Campbell's design of his own invention is, in fact, little more than a copy of the Roman temple at Nîmes. The richness of texture in Gibbs's design would be welcome to those people who were accustomed to Wren's City churches, and the semicircular portico at the entrance to St Mary-le-Strand may be taken as typical of Gibbs at this date; for it is clearly reminiscent of the famous Roman church of Santa Maria della Pace, but the same idea had been used by Wren, and as it were naturalized, in the half-domes over the side entrances of St Paul's. The beautiful little bell-turret over the main portico of St Mary is also clearly inspired by Wren's City churches, but it has a rather

113. St Martin-in-the-Fields

curious history behind it. The original design did not provide for a steeple, but there was to be a great column, 250 feet high (Nelson's Column is 184 feet), with a statue of Queen Anne on the top, standing in front of the church. When the Queen died the idea was dropped, and Gibbs had to provide a steeple on a structure which had not been designed to carry a great weight, and on top of a pediment: an architectural solecism that he was to repeat at St Martin-in-the-Fields [113].

In 1720 Gibbs took a party of Whig generals on a conducted tour of Wren's City churches, after which they accepted his designs for the rebuilding of the old church of St Martin-in-the-Fields (1722–6). The church as built differs from the early designs, and also from the model preserved there, but the essentials – the internal planning and the combination of a steeple with a portico – remain unchanged.

In plan the church is a long rectangle with a big portico at the west end, the entrance front being divided into three equal bays, the central one giving access to the church under the steeple, and those at the sides being provided with staircases and separate entrances on the north and south sides, each expressed by deeply recessed giant columns set between giant pilasters. These recesses are repeated at the east end, where there are also stairs and entrances to the Royal Pews (St Martin's is the royal parish church). On the outside there are two rows of windows set between the giant pilasters, and framed with a characteristic series of heavy blocks round the openings; unlike St Mary-le-Strand, the two ranges of windows here serve the purpose of lighting two levels inside, the upper ones giving on to the galleries which run round three sides of the church. The use of galleries to increase the seating accommodation was an idea taken from Wren's churches – in this case, St James's, Piccadilly, and St Bride's – with the central columns dividing the nave from the aisles, and carrying the galleries at the same time. The most unusual feature is the narrowing of the church at the east end to form the chancel, the incurved diagonals providing opera-box openings for the Royal Pews. The splendidly ornate plasterwork of the interior [114] is by the Italians Artari and Bagutti, who worked for most of the leading architects of the time; another example of their work for Gibbs can be seen in the little church of St Peter, Vere Street (off Oxford Street), built in 1723–4, and to some extent a trial run for St Martin's.

Externally, the best-known feature of St Martin-in-the-Fields is the combination of steeple and portico, which has always pained

114. St Martin-in-the-Fields

architectural purists, since no classical building ever had a steeple, and the very idea of a vertical element riding over a portico is fundamentally unclassical. Gibbs himself said,

> Steeples are indeed of a Gothick Extraction; but they have their Beauties, when their Parts are well disposed, and when the Plans of the several Degrees and Orders of which they are compos'd gradually diminish, and pass from one Form to another without confusion. . . .

and he seems to have seen no reason why he should not combine these beauties with the different ones inherent in the fashionable huge porticoes six columns wide.* The first hexastyle portico (to give it its proper name) was built by Campbell at Wanstead House, in Essex, before 1720, but, at the time when St Martin's was going up, others were being applied to churches by Hawksmoor at St George's, Blooms-

---

* Wren's Memorandum advocates both steeples and porticoes.

bury, and by John James at St George's, Hanover Square. Gibbs gave considerable thought to the problem of combining such a portico with a steeple, as may be seen in the side bays, where the two recessed columns marking the side entrance also seem to support the steeple over them. In the choice of forms for the actual steeple he was clearly working in Wren's manner, not only in the steeple as it now exists, but also in the alternative designs engraved in his *Book of Architecture*. The beauty of its subtle transitions, from the square base, rising out of the body of the church and proportioned to the pediment in front of it, up to the final concave-sided obelisk spire, has made it one of the best-known and most imitated of buildings. One of the earliest and most faithful copies was by Henry Flitcroft – officially a Palladian, and nicknamed 'Burlington Harry' – in his St Giles-in-the-Fields (1731–4), at the other end of Charing Cross Road. Derby Cathedral (1723–5) by Gibbs himself, is based on the same idea.

Outside London Gibbs's most important work was for the Universities of Oxford and Cambridge, although one of his last works was to provide a free design for the West Church of St Nicholas, in his native Aberdeen. At Oxford he took over from Hawksmoor, and built the Radcliffe Camera [115], or Library, between 1737 and 1749. He was very proud of this splendid building for the Tory University, and he published a book of engravings to commemorate it, in 1747.

The Camera consists of two concentric cylinders, the inner of which rises above the outer, and is covered by a dome reminiscent simultaneously of St Peter's, in Rome, and St Paul's, in London. In fact, the circular design had been projected by Hawksmoor in 1715, and he in turn was drawing on a design by Wren for a circular building near St Paul's and another for a projected Mausoleum in memory of Charles I, which Wren had designed in 1678, before Gibbs was born. In spite of this, and in spite of the air of Ancient Rome which Hawksmoor imparted to the whole scheme, Gibbs can take the credit for the Radcliffe Camera as it stands, beautifully sited on an open piazza behind St Mary's Church, and with University buildings on the other three sides. In a largely Gothic area it combines something of Ancient Rome with still more of the Rome of the Renaissance and the Baroque – which Gibbs had known at first hand – and it adds to this an indebtedness to Wren that never lapses into servile imitation; this, perhaps, is no bad epitaph on Gibbs himself.

The architectural equivalent of the victory of the Hanoverian dynasty and of Whig principles is provided by the almost complete sway of Lord Burlington's circle over the whole field of English architecture. In literature and in the common-sense philosophy of John Locke and his disciples there was a marked impulse towards the virtues of moderation and harmony, and a tendency to play down the more dramatic style of artists like Wren and Vanbrugh – the difference between Milton's *Paradise Lost* and Pope's *Essay on Man* is essentially the same difference as that between St Paul's and Chiswick Villa: both are perfect of their kind. Pope was to become a friend of Lord Burlington, who was only seventeen when the *Essay on Criticism* was published in 1711, but it contains the lines:

> Learn hence for ancient rules a just esteem;
> To copy Nature is to copy them . . .

and this equation of classical antiquity with the very laws of Nature was later part of Burlington's own creed. In 1731 Pope dedicated Epistle IV of his *Moral Essays* to Burlington, now his friend, and in it he addresses Burlington directly:

> You too proceed! make falling arts your care,
> Erect new wonders, and the old repair;
> Jones and Palladio to themselves restore,
> And be whate'er Vitruvius was before . . .

Inigo Jones, Palladio, and Vitruvius – the seventeenth-century Englishman, the sixteenth-century Italian, and the ancient Roman – were to be the tutelary deities of the new movement, and when we see why Pope specified these three names we can understand what Lord Burlington's life-work was, and the nature of the architectural revolution accomplished by him and his two closest associates, Colen Campbell and William Kent.

The great victories won by British troops under Marlborough – Blenheim, Ramillies, Oudenarde, and Malplaquet– were all gained between 1704 and 1709, and culminated in the Peace of Utrecht of 1713; the peace had two interesting consequences, for it meant that the Continent was once more open to travellers, and it confirmed the already high opinion of themselves held by Englishmen in the early eighteenth century. The Grand Tour had already begun to form an important part of the education of a rich young Englishman, and for the rest of the century it was to remain the most important single factor in the process of civilizing him. Usually he went to France, and then on to Venice, where he might stay several months, and so on to Florence and Rome, where a year was not exceptionally long to stay,

115. The Radcliffe Camera, Oxford

and so to Naples, and then home. Travelling was difficult and expensive, so that this one long trip was all he ever undertook; but it broadened his mind, and brought him into contact with the remains of classical antiquity – and he had been brought up on a diet of little else but Latin and Greek literature. The new feeling of national pride in the place won by British arms in European affairs easily combined with his classical upbringing to form the idea that Vitruvius, the only architect of the ancient world about whom anything much was known, should be the guide of the British architect, the more so since Inigo Jones had brought the classic tradition back to England, and had interpreted it according to Palladio. Palladio's book *I Quattro Libri dell'architettura* was first published in 1570, and was based on the treatise by Vitruvius, so that he naturally fell into place beside the other two, and one of the most important English translations of his *Four Books* began to appear in 1715.

In the same year the then unknown Scottish architect Colen Campbell published the first volume of his *Vitruvius Britannicus* – the title is significant – a collection of large engravings of British buildings of the seventeenth and eighteenth centuries. The last volume he supervised himself came out in 1725, so that the eighteenth-century buildings are all earlier than that date, and quite a number of them are designs of Campbell's own which were never executed. The Preface to Volume I is a manifesto of the new Palladian movement, and has a familiar ring. He says that foreign things are often praised more than English, although it is fair to admit that architecture owes much to Italians:

... above all the great *Palladio*, who has exceeded all that were gone before him and surpassed his Contemporaries; whose ingenious Labours will eclipse many, and rival most of the Ancients. ... With him the great Manner and exquisite Taste of Building is lost; for the *Italians* can now no more relish the Antique Simplicity, but are entirely employed in capricious Ornaments, which must at last end in the *Gothick*. ...

It is then with the renowned *Palladio* we enter the Lists, to whom we oppose the famous *Inigo Jones*. Let the *Banqueting-House*, those excellent pieces at *Greenwich*, with many other Things of the great Master, be carefully examined; and I doubt not, but an impartial Judge will find in them all the Regularity of the former, with an Addition of Beauty and Majesty, in which our *Architect* is esteemed to have outdone all that went before. ... And here I cannot but reflect on the Happiness of the *British* Nation, that at present abounds with so many learned and ingenious Gentlemen. ...

The three people who created and carried on the new movement were Colen Campbell (*d.* 1729), Richard Boyle, third Earl of Burlington and fourth Earl of Cork (1694–1753), and William Kent (1685–1748). There can be little doubt that the actual creation was the work of Campbell, for there are several designs of his in *Vitruvius Britannicus* of 1715 which are expressly stated to be in the manner of Inigo Jones or Palladio (*Designs for the Duke of Argyll and Lord Islay*, both of them Campbells); and in 1715 Lord Burlington was making his Grand Tour in Italy, and Kent was living in Rome, working as a painter and as a guide to the English visitors. Campbell's first big work was Wanstead House, near London, begun in 1715 but demolished a century later, which was chiefly important for its great hexastyle portico, claimed to be the first in England. This was copied from the fronts of antique temples, since Palladio had thought – quite wrongly – that ancient houses must also have had such porticoes.

Lord Burlington seems to have taken a great interest in the new movement from the moment he returned from Italy in 1715; and he helped with the publication of the second volume of *Vitruvius Britannicus* (1717), employed Campbell to remodel Burlington House in Piccadilly (parts survive as the Royal Academy), and, finally, became his pupil in architecture. In 1719 Burlington returned to Italy to visit Palladio's buildings in Vicenza, and to buy many of Palladio's drawings (they are now in the Royal Institute of British Architects). When he returned to London he brought Kent back with him, and the two men became lifelong friends and partners, with Burlington acting as the general designer and Kent concentrating on interior decoration, furniture design, and the layout of gardens.

The first two important buildings were both Campbell's, and were both designed before 1723, when they were well advanced in building. They were Houghton Hall, in Norfolk, for the Prime Minister, Sir Robert Walpole, and Mereworth Castle, in Kent. Houghton was designed as a house of great state and magnificence for the most important politician of the day, but it was completed by others, and Campbell's original ideas were considerably modified. He intended the house to be very like Wilton – that is, very like Inigo Jones – and the finest remaining part of his design is undoubtedly the Stone Hall, a cube of forty feet, which recalls the Queen's House, but has a cold and antique magnificence of its own. Much of the decoration at Houghton was actually due to Kent, and to the great sculptor, John Michael Rysbrack.

Campbell's masterpiece is the strangely named Mereworth Castle, which is basically a close copy of the famous Villa Rotonda outside

116. Mereworth Castle

Vicenza, begun by Palladio in the 1550s, and one of the most famous of
all his works. Campbell published his own design, and invited con-
noisseurs to compare it with the Palladian original, so there can be no
question of his copying another man's work and hoping nobody would
notice. In fact, the differences between the two are quite considerable,
the most important being that, to Palladio, exact symmetry was of
supreme value, and he therefore made all four sides of the house exactly
the same, repeating the great entrance portico on all sides and
arranging the rooms identically in each quarter of the square plan.
Campbell kept the square plan, with a central dome, but only two of his
porticoes (the main entrance and the garden one) have steps up to
them, the side pair being purely decorative. The house was originally
intended, like one of Palladio's villas, to be used only for short periods,
and so there were not many rooms. The two principal ones are the
central, circular hall, which is superbly decorated in the Italian manner

by Bagutti with swags and statues, and the Long Gallery which runs the whole length of the house on the garden front. The hall is very like the hall of any of Palladio's villas, but they were designed to keep out the heat of the Italian sun, and Campbell provided no chimneys (since Palladio's villas obviously did not need any); but he arranged for the smoke to escape from the top of the lantern of the dome by means of an ingenious arrangement of flues between the two shells of the dome. The gallery is more traditionally an English type of room for receiving company, and here Campbell kept closer to the model provided by Jones, but the detailing and the general richness of effect are Campbell's own contribution, and make Mereworth [116] unmistakably an eighteenth-century English house, and not just a copy of a sixteenth-century Italian one.

Palladio's Villa Rotonda and Campbell's Mereworth inspired another and finer imitation at the hands of Lord Burlington himself, in his own villa at Chiswick, then just outside London [117]. This was begun before 1726, by when Burlington and Campbell seem to have quarrelled, and was the work of Burlington himself, except for the help he received from Kent in the interior decoration and in the layout

117. Chiswick Villa

of the garden. It is the first example of their happy collaboration.*

Chiswick Villa is a more subtle and sophisticated version of the Villa Rotonda than Mereworth, partly because Burlington had actually seen the villas of Palladio, and also the remains of ancient Rome, and Campbell had not; partly because Burlington used Palladio, not merely as a model to copy, but as a guide to understanding the achievements of Roman architecture. The plan of Chiswick Villa [118] is complicated, more complicated than either Mereworth or Palladio's villa; and for two reasons, for the plan of Chiswick is fundamentally different from that of the Villa Rotonda in that it is not symmetrical and has a variety of room-shapes. The important difference is in the abandonment of Palladio's guiding principle of symmetry, for the Villa Rotonda is biaxially symmetrical – that is, strictly symmetrical about the north–south axis and also the east–west one. The villa at Chiswick, more sensibly if less mathematically, has one main or entrance front, one garden front, and two identical side fronts, and each façade is treated according to its function. Thus, only the entrance front has a portico, but it is a grand hexastyle one, flanked by imposing double stairs. The garden front also has a stair, but the façade is more decoratively treated, with three large windows looking out on to the garden. The plan also shows that the design of the house is strictly symmetrical about the main axis – which runs through the house from the portico to the garden – but there is also a variety of room-shapes, some rectangular, one round, and one – the main room on the garden side – a long rectangle with apses at each end. Finally, the great central hall is octagonal. This variety of spatial treatment does not derive from Palladio's example but from classical antiquity, for the Romans built many of their great baths with such shapes, and Lord Burlington knew this from the drawings of the ruins made by Palladio himself; these were the drawings purchased by Burlington in Italy in 1719, some of which he published in 1730.

For all its grandeur Chiswick is quite small, since it was intended to be no more than a *villa suburbana* in the Roman sense, and in accordance with this classical ideal it has only one main storey, and was never intended to have suites of bedrooms for guests. The interior is both rich and classical, and is mainly the work of Kent, as is also the garden with its temples, statues, and canal in imitation of the Brenta canal which runs by so many of Palladio's villas. This particular piece

* It has recently been superbly restored by the Ministry of Works, which is now responsible for its upkeep.

226

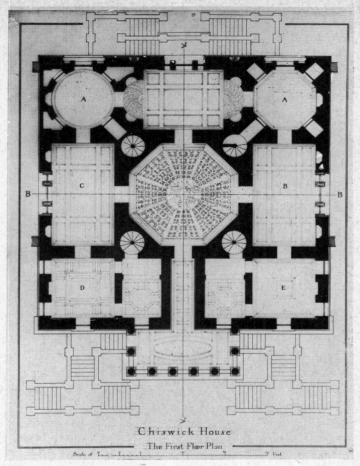

Chiswick House

The First Floor Plan

Scale of [   ]   3 Feet

118. Chiswick Villa, plan

of Italianism must surely have been the work of Kent, the history-painter from Hull whose Roman years had left such an impression that he could write in a letter:

I am still at work here the days being so short and cold to an Italian constitution that I keep my little room, only twice a week that I go to the

119. Holkham Hall

Operas where I am highly entertain'd, and then think myself out of this Gothick countery. Engagements I have for more work makes all these power-spirited [i.e. poor-spirited] English daubers raile, and make partys against me . . . [Hogarth and Thornhill certainly railed against him – see, for example, Hogarth's engraving *Burlington Gate*].

Soon after this, in 1730–2, Lord Burlington was able to build another rigidly classical reconstruction of an antique basilica as the Assembly Rooms at York, but the last of the great works produced by Burlington and Kent in partnership was the huge house for Thomas Coke, later Earl of Leicester – Holkham Hall, in Norfolk [119]. This is not far from Houghton, and was intended to be even grander and more classical. Some of the design may be attributed to Coke himself, who had made a Grand Tour, met Kent in Rome, and returned filled with an ambition to collect editions of Livy, classical sculpture, and to have a suitably antique house to put them in. Building did not begin

120. Holkham Hall

until 1734, and went on for nearly thirty years, after both Kent and Burlington were dead, but the house is their monument. Several designs by Kent for the main façades are known, but none was executed without modification; it seems that Kent would propose some rich and imaginative design, which would then be pared down, and made more austere, by Coke or Burlington or both. An example of their passion for antiquity is the fact that the house is built of brick; Coke, in Rome, had picked up a piece of ancient brick, which is tawny in colour, and different in size and texture from modern English brick, and had brought it home as a souvenir. He found that it could be reproduced at a near-by brickworks, and so the 'classical' brick was used for the house instead of stone (which would admittedly also be dearer). Nowadays the vast expanse of this rather dreary brick, made much barer by the fact that all the windows have had their glazing-bars* removed and plate-glass inserted – thus ruining the careful balance of void and solid, and the feeling for the texture of the wall as a whole, that are among the principal subtleties of good eighteenth-century building – inevitably makes one think of barracks; but the contrast with the interior is all the stronger. It must always be remembered that the eighteenth-century Whig liked a contrast between an austere exterior (which he would have equated with the Roman virtue of *gravitas*) and pomp and magnificence in the interior. When the architects were Burlington and Kent it happened all the more that the two aspects should be so contrasted, and, for sheer state, there is hardly another room in England to rival the hall at Holkham [120]; and it is a highly informative sidelight on the great Whigs that such a room should be built in a country house for the reception of antique statues. Three points about the design serve to give an idea of its richness and complexity: first, the change of level from the main floor to the saloon at the end is used to provide the main element in the design – the rise of the stair and the vista through the colonnade beyond. The change of level provides a high base on which to set a colonnade – that is, an antique basilica type which has an internal colonnade and a richly coffered roof: the elaborate frieze is taken from the Temple of Fortuna Virilis, in Rome. The apsidal end and the coffering above are also antique, but the idea of a vista through a colonnade is taken from one of Palladio's churches, for Burlington wrote of San Giorgio Maggiore, Venice: 'An open intercolumniation discovers the choir, it ends in a semicircle – most beautiful.'

* The glazing bars were originally gilt.

230

The ceiling owes much to Inigo Jones, being based on one of his drawings owned by Burlington; and thus it is possible to see, at Holkham, the combination of Vitruvius, Palladio, and Jones which Pope recommended in the passage quoted earlier.

Kent died in 1748 and Burlington in 1753, and the stricter forms of Palladianism died with them; but their ideas were to remain profoundly influential for at least the rest of the century. Sir William Chambers is sometimes called 'the last of the Palladians', and he certainly remained true to ideals of Roman classicism; his work is discussed in the next chapter. Perhaps even more important was the influence exerted by the Palladians on much less exalted architects, on speculative builders, and on country gentlemen building with the help of local craftsmen. Their work still exists in large quantities in almost every old town, and the traditions they started were often carried on for generations. The most famous of them were architects of national importance such as John Carr (1723–1807) of York, and, perhaps the most famous of all, the two Woods of Bath. John Wood the Elder (1704–54) and his son John (1728–81) were responsible between them for most of the building of Bath; and above all they were responsible

121. The Circus, Bath

for the development of the town in an orderly way as the finest piece of large-scale town planning then attempted in Britain. The layout of such schemes as Queen Square, the Circus [121], and the Royal Crescent assure their fame more than any single building, fine as are Prior Park or the New Assembly Rooms – for these street designs established the standard type of town layout in Britain.

10 Chambers and the Adam Brothers; the Greek, the Gothick, and the Picturesque

After Lord Burlington died in 1753 the rest of the century was dominated by two architects who had just enough in common to dislike each other heartily: they were Sir William Chambers and Robert Adam. Nowadays there are people who would claim that Robert Adam was the greatest of British architects, greater even than Wren, but this would certainly not have been the case in the eighteenth century, except in the Adam family circle, for two of his brothers spent their whole careers in fostering Robert's genius, and in making sure that the rest of the world was aware of it and of the Adam Revolution.

Both Chambers and Robert Adam were ambitious Scots who settled in London at almost the same moment with the intention of becoming the leader of what was gradually developing into the architectural profession; without the other one, either of them could have done this, but, in fact, the two rivals had to share the distinction between them, Chambers getting most of the official honours and Adam most of the publicity. The situation was not unlike the rivalry between their contemporaries, Sir Joshua Reynolds and Thomas Gainsborough, and this professional rivalry alone would have made them antagonists, but their antagonism was much sharpened by their disagreement over what constituted good architecture; for, as we might guess, Sir William Chambers, R.A., was an upholder of tradition as well as one of the principal Founder Members of the Royal Academy and its first Treasurer, and Robert Adam was an innovator who was never elected to the Academy.

William Chambers was born in 1723 in Gothenburg, Sweden, the son of a Scottish merchant who had settled there. While he was still very young he was sent to England to be educated, and then, as a young man, he sailed to China in the service of the Swedish East India Company. Not until he was twenty-six did he take up architecture, and then he spent a year studying in Paris and another five years in Italy. In 1755 he returned to England and set up in practice. The fact that he had been to China was useful to him when he was first making himself known, for he wrote a book about Chinese buildings which caught the public taste, and as a result he was commissioned to lay out Kew Gardens and to build some ornamental and exotic temples there, including the Pagoda, which still stands in the Gardens, now rather forlorn. He also had the good fortune to be appointed architectural tutor to the Prince of Wales (who became George III in 1760) and was thus soon well established. In 1761 he was made one of the two Architects of the Works – but the other one was Robert Adam. His years in France and Italy had given him great prestige in his profession (a prestige also possessed by Robert Adam), and they also meant that he was in touch with the latest developments in Paris and Rome, where most of the leading architects were his personal friends; he was able, therefore, to supply a cosmopolitan touch which enlivened the Palladian tradition he inherited from Kent and Burlington, a tradition which was beginning to wear thin by the time George III came to the throne. Chambers, like Reynolds, was able to give fresh intellectual authority to the classical tradition they inherited, and the Royal Academy was important in the lives of both men. It was founded by George III in 1768, with Chambers playing a leading part in the negotiations which preceded the actual foundation. Reynolds was knighted and made the first President, but Chambers was made Treasurer, a position which gave him great power, greater in some ways than Reynolds enjoyed, since he was responsible to the King. Although he was not knighted the King allowed him, in 1770, to use a Swedish knighthood that had been conferred upon him as if it were an English one.

In spite of all this, if Chambers had died then he would have been forgotten now, for his masterpiece was not begun until 1776 and took ten years to build; indeed, a good deal of it was not built for many years after that. This is Somerset House, in the Strand, intended from the beginning to be a grand public building, housing part of the Civil Service, and also some of the learned societies under royal patronage, including the Royal Academy itself. There had been no great public building of this kind in England since Greenwich Hospital, and one of the first things Chambers did was to revisit Paris to study French government buildings at first hand. Detailed analysis of Somerset House reveals how much he learned from his renewed study of French

122. Somerset House, north side of the courtyard

work, but it also shows how much he had learned from the whole European tradition, for his masterpiece is a wonderfully complex arrangement of ideas and details taken from the entire range of architectural history as it was then understood – that is to say, Roman and Italian Renaissance and French seventeenth- and eighteenth-century work, but certainly not Greek or Gothic, both of which Chambers loathed. Somerset House is learned, it is rich but sober, grand but restrained: it is a great building but not an original one.

Nowadays it is difficult to see the building as Chambers designed it, except from inside the main quadrangle [122]. This is because the east and west sides were built in the nineteenth century on space which Chambers left for expansion (the east wing, by Sir R. Smirke, is now King's College, in the University of London); the south front, facing the river, has had its effect entirely altered by the construction of the Embankment; while the north front, facing the Strand, though untouched, has had its scale and importance totally disrupted by the towering cliff of Bush House opposite. Almost all the interior is inaccessible, and is, in any case, now divided up into the dreariest kind of Government offices.

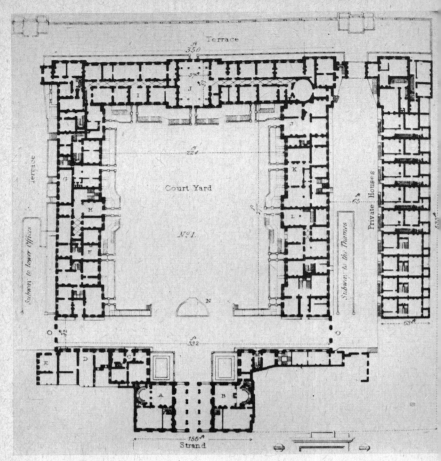

123. Somerset House, plan

The plan [123] is governed by two factors: the need to house the
Government offices and, separately, the learned societies, including
space for the Academy exhibitions and schools; and, secondly, the
difficult site. The ground slopes steeply downward from the Strand to
the river, and at the same time the river frontage is much longer than

the Strand one. For this reason the Strand front* is a separate block containing the learned societies, and is rather more elaborately treated than the rest of the composition or, as Chambers himself puts it:

> The vestibule opens to the most frequented street in London, is a general passage to every part of the whole design, and the apartments are intended for the reception of useful learning and the polite arts, where, it is humbly presumed, specimens of elegance should at least be attempted.

This sedate eighteenth-century prose exactly reflects the character of the architecture, which is a splendid restatement of an Italian palace theme, with references to the parts of old Somerset House then believed to be by Inigo Jones, and to contemporary French designs as well. All the details are beautifully executed, and the rich decorative sculpture was commissioned from Chambers's fellow-R.A.s. The surviving interior details show the same conscientious craftsmanship.

The Government offices proper lay on three sides of the central court, with the south block as the principal one, much longer on the river side than the court side. It has a small dome over a central pediment, but these are hardly big enough in scale to go with the court side, and far too small to go with the long river-front. This is enormously long (planned to be some 800 feet), and Chambers has done his best to break the monotony by subtle alternations of smooth and rusticated stonework, by the very dramatic river arches which originally served as a base for the whole, but are now stranded on the Embankment, and above all by the 'bridges' with open screens of columns which punctuate the ends of the façade. It is in details like the ranging of columns over the arches on the court side or the alternation of rusticated and smooth wall, column and window, on the river side that Chambers shows his mastery of classical design. Somerset House makes no grand gestures, but it is beautifully modulated, and it was its builder's answer to the self-advertisement of the Adams' riverside scheme at the Adelphi, a few hundred yards to the west.

Chambers died in 1796. Robert Adam was born in 1728, and died in 1792. He was the second son of William Adam, perhaps the best Scottish architect of his day, and a man of some substance, for his eldest son, John, became a landowner, and both Robert and James made their Italian journeys in considerably more state than young architects could normally afford. Robert matriculated at Edinburgh University in 1743, but his architectural career did not really begin

* See illustration 112.

until 1754 when he went to France, and then on to Rome, where he stayed until 1757. There he met many of the English lords and gentlemen who were making the Grand Tour and who were later of great help to him in his career. In 1757 he went to Spalato (now called Split) in Dalmatia, and in five weeks he and his assistants measured and drew the ruins of the Palace of the Emperor Diocletian (284–305), publishing the drawings as a book in 1764. His object in doing this was twofold; he wanted to produce a book which would make his name known when he set up in practice, since this was the usual way for an ambitious young architect to get himself talked about, and, at the same time, he wanted to break away from the usual type of such books. He wanted to study the remains of ancient domestic architecture, rather than the baths and temples which had been studied so often before, and he also wanted to publish drawings of palace ruins outside Rome itself, for this was the time when discoveries were being made in places as far away as Asia Minor and Greece. In fact, Robert Adam was himself essentially a domestic architect – a builder of town or country houses – and he was able thus to justify some of his new ideas on the grounds that they had classical authority. He succeeded in making his name known, for he set up in practice in London in 1758, although the book was not actually published until six years later. Almost at once he broke away from the rigidity of Lord Burlington's followers, and introduced a whole series of new, elegant, decorative motives, some based on Pompeian themes (Pompeii and Herculaneum were discovered in the mid eighteenth century), and some based on Italian Renaissance forms (which, in turn, were based on classical ones). This was the greater part of the Adam revolution, and it very soon became the common property of most London architects and builders: indeed, it has lasted almost to this day. The remainder of the revolution consisted of ideas connected with what the brothers called 'movement', which in itself had close links with the theory of the Picturesque. The first volume of the *Works in Architecture of Robert and James Adam*, published in 1773, explains what they set out to do: 'We flatter ourselves, we have been able to seize, with some degree of success, the beautiful spirit of antiquity, and to transpose it, with novelty and variety, through all our numerous works.' They pride themselves on having brought about 'a greater movement and variety in the outside composition and in the decoration of the inside an almost total change'; they have banished 'the massive entablature, the ponderous compartment ceiling, the tabernacle frame', and in their place they have 'adopted a beautiful variety of light mouldings, gracefully formed, delicately enriched and arranged with propriety and skill'. The book was published when they were meeting with difficulties, and it is easy to detect the note of self-advertisement, yet it is none the less true that most of these qualities were theirs; above all, that of movement in the outside composition which is more fully defined in connexion with the south front [124] of Kedleston Hall, Derbyshire (*c.* 1765–70 but never completed):

Movement is . . . the rise and fall, the advance and recess with other diversity of form, in the different parts of a building, so as to add greatly to the Picturesque of the composition. For the rising and falling, advancing and receding, with the convexity and concavity, and other forms of the great parts, have the same effect in architecture, that hill and dale, foreground and distance, swelling and sinking, have in landscape. That is, they serve to produce an agreeable and diversified contour, that groups and contrasts like a picture, which gives great spirit, beauty, and effect to the composition.

The fully developed Adam style may be studied in a number of houses, for they were very busy architects, but two of the best are Osterley Park House, Middlesex, and Syon House, Brentford, in

124. Kedleston Hall

Middlesex, both near London, and both begun quite soon after Robert set up in practice. Osterley was begun in 1761, and was worked on for more than eighteen years, while Syon was begun in 1762, and finished in 1769. Both were old houses which were more or less drastically remodelled to bring them up to the much higher standards of comfort and luxury demanded by the eighteenth century. Syon was an Elizabethan house, a hollow square in plan, and therefore containing a series of rooms, each of them long and narrow, and opening one into the other. Adam proposed to fill the square internal courtyard with a great rotunda for the reception of guests, but this idea was dropped, and his executed work consists of a series of rooms beginning with the entrance hall, and continuing through an ante-room, dining-room, and drawing-room to the Long Gallery, which takes up the whole of the back of the house. The hall is very large and formal, almost entirely white, with a black-and-white marble floor and a high ceiling, since it runs the whole height of the house. Because of uneven floor levels there are short flights of steps at either end, one of which leads to the ante-room [125]. This was intended as a waiting-room for liveried servants, and it forms the strongest possible contrast to the severe hall, for it is quite small, nearly square in plan, and lavish in gilt and coloured decoration to the point of vulgarity (Adam also worked for the same family at old Northumberland House, in London, and a fragment now in the Victoria and Albert Museum shows that the decoration used there, of gilt lead and metal foil under plate glass, was vulgar in the extreme). The ante-room at Syon contains twelve columns of antique marble dredged from the Tiber and ranged round the walls; this is purely for decorative effect, but the arrangement of one side, with the columns standing well away from the wall instead of against it, allowed Adam to make the room appear square although it is actually $30 \times 36\frac{1}{2}$ feet. After the highly coloured ante-room comes the dining-room, followed by the Red Drawing-room, which is little more than an ante-room to the Long Gallery and was intended to keep out the smell of food and the noise of the gentlemen drinking after dinner. The Long Gallery was, of course, part of the Tudor house, and was adapted by Adam as a drawing-room 136 feet long, but only 14 feet wide and 14 feet high. He met this difficulty by splitting the room up into five main bays opposite eleven windows, so that the apparent length is reduced. The decoration is also kept very low in relief, but at the same time intricate, so that one looks at it piece by piece.

125. Syon House, the ante-room

126. Osterley Park, propylon

127. Osterley Park, Etruscan Room

In 1761 Adam began work at Osterley (now a department of the Victoria and Albert Museum), not far from Syon, and, like it, a Tudor house which was now to be modernized. A large part of one side of it was knocked down to make the splendid double portico, or propylon [126], which gives entrance to the central court, and stands opposite the front door. It is derived partly from the Propylaea, at Athens, and partly from the Temple of the Sun, at Palmyra, both of which were known to Adam from books published a few years earlier. This choice of non-Roman models shows a breadth of taste that Chambers disliked; but it is also part of the movement known as neo-Classicism, which was being formulated in Italy and France in the middle years of the century, and of which Adam was one of the leading British exponents. The so-called Etruscan Room at Osterley [127], designed about 1775–9, is a good example of this style, which was also very much in vogue during the 1770s, when several Etruscan rooms were decorated. Almost all have perished. They were called Etruscan

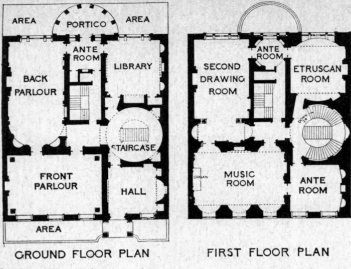

GROUND FLOOR PLAN   FIRST FLOOR PLAN

128. Home House, plan

because they were based on the colour schemes of early Greek vases, which were then thought to be the work of the Etruscan forerunners of Roman civilization; the vases themselves were copied, and the new style spread, by the great potter, Josiah Wedgwood, who called his new works Etruria (a name they still bear). The flat decoration with strong colours, based on reddish-brown, black, and yellow, and the more or less Greek motives employed in the Etruscan Room at Osterley, are not only important as an example of a once fashionable style; they are also evidence of the truly international position occupied by Robert Adam in the neo-Classic movement which dominated the architecture of the whole of Europe in the second half of the eighteenth century.

In 1768 the brothers began a great scheme for the building of medium-sized houses for professional people on top of warehouses and vaults beside the Thames and running up to the Strand. This was called the Adelphi (Greek for 'the brothers'), and was a most ambitious undertaking, but unfortunately it was dogged by bad luck, and nearly ruined the Adam family. Most of it was pulled down in 1936. In the 1770s Robert designed a number of large and splendid town

129. Home House, the staircase

houses, a field in which he was unsurpassed, and which helped to regain some of their losses. The finest surviving house of this group is Home House, 20 Portman Square, London, built for the Dowager Countess of Home, in 1773–7, and now the Courtauld Institute of Art in the University of London [128].

The plan is splendidly adapted to the purpose of the house – that is, the provision of a suitably dignified setting for the formal lives led by the wealthy people who inhabited these great houses. Home House is not very big – it was built for a childless widow in her seventies – although it has a wide frontage. The ground floor is divided up into a hall, which leads into the centre of the house, occupied by the stair well, and from this point the house opens out into parlour, dining-room, and library, with a small service stair tucked away inconspicuously, but centrally placed. The stair well is most important, since it is the only means of lighting the centre of the house, and the dome at the top is used to flood the grand staircase with light [129]. The need to gain light dictated the placing of the stair well, and that in turn meant that the front door was placed off-centre, an abandonment of the symmetrical façade that would have been unthinkable to a Palladian thirty years earlier. The three large windows to the left of the front door can now be used to light a single room, which, since it faces south and looks out on to the square, was the general living-room. The arrangement of the dining-room and the library shows equal care for planning, coupled with subtle variations of shape in the rooms themselves, making for variety or 'movement', as Robert Adam called it.

On the first floor there is a sequence of rooms leading from the Countess's boudoir, through a very highly coloured music room with a most elaborate ceiling into a ballroom, and so through a tiny ante-room into the Etruscan bedroom, now restored to its original colour scheme, like the one at Osterley. These were all state rooms, and so they present us with the Adam style at its most decorative. They show the greatest attention to detail, such as the ormolu door handles, and even the doors themselves, which are inlaid with satinwood, holly, and ebony on a mahogany framework. A set of very highly finished drawings for Home House is in the Soane Museum, London, among the collection of some eight thousand Adam drawings there, and they give a very good idea of the meticulous way in which Robert Adam designed everything down to door-knobs and candlesticks. This tireless attention to detail is a good part of the secret of the unity of style, the feeling that every part fits every other part, so that no change could be made without spoiling the whole effect, which is what made Robert Adam famous, and will continue to keep him so.

Towards the end of his life Adam had a chance to realize his desire to build on a grand scale, to show that he could do more than build admirable houses. His work in Fitzroy Square, London, and, above all, in Edinburgh, shows what he could do, but unfortunately it was completed and altered by others: the General Register House of Scotland (1774–92), at Edinburgh, was his answer to Chambers's Somerset House, although it was actually begun a little earlier. Adam's work at the university was begun in 1789, but was drastically altered in 1815 and again later, and finally his splendid layout of a whole group of houses and a church, Charlotte Square, was also altered, although enough of it remains to serve as an example of large-scale planning.

So eminently successful an artist was bound to be imitated, and the first man who caused him some trouble was James Wyatt (1746–1813), whose Pantheon in Oxford Street, now demolished, was a nine days' wonder in 1772, when it was opened as a place of entertainment. His name was made overnight – Horace Walpole, in one of his bursts of enthusiasm, called it 'the most beautiful building in England' – but

130. Strawberry Hill

131. Fonthill

132. Hagley, Doric temple

Wyatt was little more than an imitator of Robert Adam, and his reputation suffered later because of his haphazard conduct of his business affairs, and later still because of his incursions into the Gothic style. Heaton Hall, now part of Manchester City Art Gallery, is a good example of his 'Adam' style, and even has an Etruscan Room, but he is better remembered as the architect of Fonthill Abbey, Wilt-shire, and the restorer of Salisbury, Durham, and other cathedrals where his activities gained him the nickname of 'Wyatt the Destroyer' from later generations of antiquaries. In fact, the eighteenth century regarded Gothic architecture as rude and barbarous until, about the middle of the century, Horace Walpole and others began to build in the 'Gothick taste', just as Chippendale, for example, was designing Gothick chairs. All through the second half of the century the Gothick was an amusing style for small and unimportant buildings, and was never intended to challenge the absolute supremacy of the Roman

249

classical style. It was simply a new thrill, like the Gothick novels of Walpole, Beckford, 'Monk' Lewis, and others; indeed Horace Walpole's Strawberry Hill, Twickenham [130], begun in 1753, and William Beckford's Fonthill Abbey were the two great monuments of the style, and it has nothing in common with the passionate revivalism and religious enthusiasm of the nineteenth-century Gothic Revival, which would have seemed ridiculous and ill-bred to the eighteenth. Wyatt's work on the cathedrals was, in fact, necessary to stop them falling down, but he seems to have been quite insensitive to their beauty, although his own Fonthill was plainly based on Salisbury. This architectural fantasy [131] was built for the eccentric millionaire, William Beckford, between 1796 and 1807. It soon became a legend in the Wiltshire countryside, and when, in 1825, its 276-foot-high tower fell down nobody can have been very surprised. Nothing now remains of the Abbey.

The two great revivals of the nineteenth century were the Greek and the Gothic, and oddly enough both of them originated as eighteenth-century fashions within a few years of each other. The 1750s saw the first Gothick experiments, and also a few Chinese buildings, but in the sixties the Greek style began to make itself felt. This was rather less of a fashion and more of a serious attempt to widen the accepted range of architectural motives, and that was why Sir William Chambers was so bitterly opposed to it. In fact, it soon became accepted on the Continent as more correctly antique than Roman architecture itself, although a few people continued to claim that it was no more than a bad imitation of Roman work. The Greek style was introduced into England by James 'Athenian' Stuart (1713–88) and Nicholas Revett (1720–1804), whose book *The Antiquities of Athens* was announced as being prepared as early as 1748, although the first volume did not appear until 1762 and the second, more important, one was not published until just after Stuart's death in 1788. The impact of this important publication did not really make itself felt until early in the nineteenth century, partly because neither Stuart nor Revett was sufficiently active or ambitious to change the course of architectural history; indeed Stuart was extremely dilatory over the commissions he was given, and frequently went off drinking with the workmen, as one exasperated employer complained. When the Greek revival of the nineteenth century got under way it was said, quite wrongly, that:

the chasteness and purity which Stuart and Revett had, with some success, endeavoured to introduce into their buildings in England, and in which their zeal had enlisted many artists, had to contend against the opposite and vicious taste of Robert Adam, a fashionable architect, whose eye had been ruined by the corruptions of the worst period of Roman Art.*

Finally, the Picturesque. This was not strictly an architectural movement, but it had a great effect on architecture because of its close connexion with landscape-gardening. In reaction against the formal layout of the French garden a new style was evolved (still called *le jardin anglais* on the Continent), which was claimed to represent a new kind of beauty, the wildness of Nature tamed a little by the order imposed by the artist – the ordered wildness of such great seventeenth-century painters as Claude and Gaspar Poussin. To the eighteenth century a picturesque landscape was one which looked as though it might have come out of a picture, and not, as it usually means nowadays, a landscape fit to put into a picture.

As a result of this desire to make Nature imitate Art dead trees were planted in gardens and sham ruins built to close a vista and other amiable absurdities committed; some were Gothic and some Greek [132], and some even Chinese, but from the point of view of architectural history what matters about the Picturesque is that it taught people to look at a building and its setting, and it encouraged visual sensibility.

* J. Gwilt, *An Encyclopaedia of Architecture*, 1842.

11   Holland, Soane, and Nash: the Regency

The last years of the eighteenth century saw a variety of experiments in different styles, culminating in the style we usually call Regency: admittedly an amalgam, but possessing a distinct character of its own, and quite different in intention from the deliberate revivalism of the Greek and Gothic men of the early and middle years of Victoria's reign. One of the most important architects of the later eighteenth century was Henry Holland (1745–1806), whose style was very largely based on contemporary French work, thus distinguishing him from the Adam brothers and Wyatt, and recalling rather the practice of Sir William Chambers. Unfortunately little of Holland's work survives, so that he tends to be overlooked, but his position as architect to the Whig oligarchy surrounding the Prince of Wales before he became Prince Regent means that Holland must be considered as helping to form the Regency style. He began as a speculative builder, and became the son-in-law of 'Capability' Brown, the most important landscape-gardener of the late eighteenth century. In 1776 he was commissioned to design Brooks's Club, which still stands almost unaltered in St James's Street, and because this was the headquarters of Whiggery, he gained a strong connexion which was to culminate in the commission for Carlton House. At that moment there was a French fashion among the Whigs, and Holland's own tastes coincided with it. He must have studied the latest French architectural books – he did not go to France until the eve of the Revolution – and we know that he employed many French craftsmen, who may have had a considerable share in his buildings. Between 1783 and 1785 he was employed by the Prince of Wales to enlarge and alter Carlton House. Although it was demolished in 1826, we know what it looked like, and the plan shows that Holland disposed his interiors very skilfully. The Corinthian portico survives, with some alteration, as the portico of the National Gallery, but it was originally set back from the street with a screen of Ionic columns in front of it, which must also have added to the French appearance. Another work by Holland which has connexions with the Prince Regent was the original house at Brighton (1786–7), later to be expanded into the Brighton Pavilion, and which, in fact, is still the core of that otherwise very different building.

Properly speaking, the Regency lasted only ten years (1811–20), but it is usual to think of it as beginning in the architectural sense rather earlier, at about the beginning of the new century, and lasting until the end of George IV's reign, in 1830. This is probably because of the two great figures who dominated the architectural scene during those years – Sir John Soane and John Nash. John Soane was born in 1753, the year Lord Burlington died, and he died a few months before Victoria came to the throne, in 1837. His very long life thus covers the whole course of English architecture from the decline of strict Palladianism to the rise of equally strict dogmas, whether Greek or Gothic, but he himself combined motives – sometimes Greek, sometimes Adamitic – with a freedom and eclecticism hardly equalled even by the Adamses themselves. His approach was at least partly due to the fact that he was one of the first architectural students of the Royal Academy, where eclectic methods were taught, and partly also to the publications which made Greek and Gothic architecture better known. He was one of the earliest professional architects and did much for that sense of professionalism which so greatly raised the status of architects during the nineteenth century. His professionalism was no doubt partly because he was born plain John Soan, the son of a bricklayer, near Reading. In 1768 he came to London as the pupil of George Dance the younger, the City architect. Dance built relatively little, but his masterpiece was Newgate Prison, begun in 1770, and the dramatic imagination displayed in it explains his influence on Soane and other advanced young architects. Dance had been in Rome, and was much influenced by the etchings of Piranesi, whose scrupulously accurate plates of the great Roman ruins are also imbued with a brooding sense of decayed grandeur which was very much in harmony with neo-Classic ideals, and which recurs in the most unexpected places in eighteenth-century architecture. These romantic overtones to apparently purely classical works are among the principal elements in the very sophisticated attractions of the architecture of both George Dance and his greater pupil, Soane. In 1772 Soane went to widen his experience by working for Holland, and in the same year he entered the Royal Academy Schools and won the Silver Medal. He followed this up by winning the Gold Medal in 1776, and was awarded a travelling scholarship to Italy in 1778. In Rome he made exact measured drawings of the major antiquities, thus satisfying the requirements of the new, more accurate, architectural scholarship, and at the same time he satisfied some of his own inner needs by drafting grandiose projects, such as that for a British Senate House, which continued to haunt his imagination. Soane got as far as Paestum, where he saw the Greek temples, but he was prevented from going on to Greece itself by an offer of employment from the eccentric Bishop of Derry (later Earl of Bristol). He returned to England in 1780, thus losing a year of his scholarship, only to find the offer was not serious. After this bitter disappointment he had a hard struggle for some years until the turning-point of his career came in 1788 with the Surveyorship of the Bank of England. He held this post for forty-five years, and rebuilt the whole Bank, an undertaking even more complicated than Wren's rebuilding of St Paul's. The Bank gave him an income and status as one of the leading architects of the day, and in return he created a masterpiece that even now has not been totally destroyed, in spite of the efforts made since the 1920s.

As soon as he was appointed he made a thorough survey, discovering extensive rot and damage, and a rebuilding programme was put in hand which lasted from 1792 to 1800, when a second, larger programme was begun. The size of the Bank was nearly doubled when this second stage was completed in 1827, but the problems facing the architect were more complicated than a mere expansion. The mob had tried to set fire to the Bank in the Gordon Riots of 1780, so the first consideration was security; this meant that the new building had to be carried on piecemeal, behind strong walls, and it also meant that fireproof construction had to be employed, and, above all, no windows could give on to the street. On top of this was the very awkward site, roughly triangular, which made an adequate wall-treatment difficult – the longest wall was 451 feet long, windowless, and lacking any kind of natural climax such as a portico.

The structural problem was solved by the most ingenious use of Roman constructional methods based very closely on the great baths, using very light shell domes with top lighting in a dynamic system that owed a great deal to such Gothic cathedrals as Ely, which Soane knew and admired [133]. The decorative motives, on the other hand, are freely adapted from the Greek as well as from more usual Roman

254

133. Bank of England, Dividend Office (as it was)

134. Bank of England, Tivoli Corner

sources. The resulting halls were superbly personal architectural expressions of their function, but they were hardly ever accessible, and most of them have been destroyed. Sir John Summerson has described their soaring quality as 'the Gothic miracle rediscovered at the heart of the Roman tradition', but most of Soane's contemporaries were shocked by his free treatment of classical detail, and would probably have agreed with the anonymous author of an imaginary epitaph on Sir William Chambers, who called the Bank

> A Fabric . . . in a barbarous style,
> Of which, though pretending to originality,
> The peculiarities are borrowed
> From the example of the Dark Ages. . . .

Another critic more pithily described his pilasters decorated with incised ornament in an austerely Greek manner as 'scored like loins of pork'.

On the outside Soane's worst problem was probably the very acute angle made by the junction of Princes Street and Lothbury, which is also one of the most prominent parts of the whole façade. He experimented with various angle-treatments from 1804 until he evolved the highly sophisticated construction known as Tivoli Corner [134], completed in 1807. This, which has suffered badly in recent years, can still be seen. Its name comes from the fact that Soane decided to use the most ornate form of the Corinthian Order, that found in the Temple of Vesta, at Tivoli, in order to give the maximum effect of richness to the acute angle covered by the segment of the temple in a way which shows that he had not been blind to the Rome of the seventeenth century. Inside his 'temple' there are two unfluted columns for contrast and to get the maximum effect of shadow, while the movement of the design as a whole is completed by the curious semi-Greek sarcophagus which serves as a finial, and is based on a concave rectangular form opposing the curved and convex shapes below; in short, the extreme acute angle of the corner seems as though it were deliberate, and not a difficulty to be overcome.

The Soane of this period, from the 1790s to about 1815, was the most original genius in architecture then alive. Unfortunately, much of his work has been lost, but there are still three buildings by him, all in London, which are easily accessible. They are Pitzhanger Manor, Ealing; the Picture Gallery and Mausoleum of Dulwich College; and Soane's own house in Lincoln's Inn Fields.

Pitzhanger Manor (now Ealing Public Library) was built about 1770 by George Dance for himself, and was bought by Soane in 1800 as a country house for his own family [135]. He retained two of the rooms built by his master, but between 1800 and 1803 he made several important alterations, the most important being the main front. This he treated as a revised version of Robert Adam's south front of Kedleston, but he went back to Adam's original model, the Arch of Constantine in Rome, and set free-standing columns in front of the wall, supporting nothing but statues. In spite of his apparent closeness to the classical prototype, Soane's effect is much less Roman than Adam's; in other words, the Soane revolution was more fundamental than the Adam one. The tiny entrance hall at Pitzhanger has a ceiling which also affords the strongest possible contrast with Adam, for it is a subtle essay in the enclosure of space, like the inside of a sarcophagus hollowed out and seen from below, and it has none of the ornament or colour that Adam used to give accent to his ceilings.

The Picture Gallery at Dulwich was built between 1811 and 1814, much altered in the nineteenth century, destroyed by a flying-bomb, and rebuilt in 1953 from the original designs. It was one of the first 'modern' picture galleries with top lighting, and is still one of the most satisfactory. In his later years Soane was much occupied with what he called 'the poetry of architecture', and a good deal of this seems to have been due to the Picturesque movement. Part of his poetry lay in spectacular effects of light, sometimes filtered through coloured glass and sometimes reflected by small pieces of mirror-glass set in odd places. At its worst this has a rather tawdry mock-Romanticism, as in the Monk's Parlour in his own house; at its best it can have a wonderful sense of lightness and space, as in the 'hanging ceilings' lit from the sides so that they appear like tents suspended in space. Again there are examples in his own house, now the Soane Museum [136]. Originally Soane lived at No. 13 Lincoln's Inn Fields, but he spread into parts of Nos. 12 and 14, and from 1812 he designed and altered his house to fit it for a museum for future generations of architectural students. It is crammed with every possible object that could interest a romantic yet austere architect in the early nineteenth century – an Egyptian sarco-

135. Pitzhanger Manor

136. Sir John Soane's Museum, Breakfast Room

phagus and Hogarth paintings, the drawings of John Thorpe as well as those of Robert Adam, and, of course, all his own drawings and models.

Soane was an architect of genius, a scholar using the classical tradition who yet evolved an intensely personal style in the last years of the eighteenth century. John Nash (1752–1835), the favourite architect of George IV, is perhaps best described as an architectural impresario, a creator of townscape, and an organizer of genius who knew little, and cared less, about the finer points of architectural scholarship. Nash, though an exact contemporary of Soane, was a nineteenth-century man, and it is a curious fact that he achieved nothing until he was about fifty-five. He set up as a speculative builder on a legacy of £1,000, and went bankrupt; then he met the landscape-gardener Humphrey Repton and became his architectural partner, learning from him the principles of Picturesque disposition that he was

137. Regent Street as it was

to apply in so revolutionary a way to houses in towns. He made a mysterious marriage in 1798 – it was said to a lady that the Prince of Wales was anxious to see married – and from then on he had money and the patronage of the Prince.

At the beginning of the nineteenth century there were numerous schemes described generically as 'metropolitan improvements' which were part of the 'neatness and elegance' of the age of Jane Austen. Such an opportunity arose with the falling-in of the Crown leases in Marylebone and the decision to redevelop the park. The first schemes for what we now know as Regent's Park were formulated in 1810–11, and with them – it was Nash's stroke of genius – a scheme to drive a great north–south road up from the Houses of Parliament and·the Carlton House area to the new park, where the Prince could have a *guinguette*,* and a Triumphal Way to link it with Carlton House. The new park was to be dotted with neat villas which could be let to Members of Parliament, lawyers, and similar prosperous folk who would need a direct road to Westminster. Thus Regent Street came into existence. Nash was also responsible for further improvements – in St James's Park for example – and projected even more, for the Regent's Park that we still possess is much less than he planned. In 1811 he laid out a group of nine cottages, all different, to form the artificial Blaise Hamlet, near Bristol, and this truly Picturesque adaptation of

* A country cottage.

260

138. Cumberland Terrace, London

Repton's principles of irregularity and apparent extent were tried out in it, and then in Regent's Park. The beauty of Nash's scheme was that it consisted of maintaining the park as an open space but dotting it with forty-odd villas, so disposed that, according to Repton's principle of apparent extent, each was invisible to its neighbours and appeared to possess the whole park; the genius of the scheme lies in the way this garden-city was to join on to London (which ended at Marylebone Road) by means of the formal links of the terraces, and above all the square and half-circus at the top of Portland Place. Behind the new quarter was a canal and a barracks, and a whole service district was planned near Albany Street.

To the south the existing Portland Place was incorporated bodily, and the link with Carlton House was made by means of Regent Street. This swerves alongside the 'narrow Streets and meaner Houses occupied by mechanics and the trading part of the community' to the east of the Hanover Square district, marking its changes of axis by eye-catchers – All Souls, at Langham Place; Oxford Circus; the splendid sweep of the Quadrant at the junction with Piccadilly Circus [137], and then the formal straight stretch down to Waterloo Place and Carlton

139. The Pavilion, Brighton

140. Chichester Terrace, Brighton

House Terrace. It is sad that the scheme was no sooner finished than Carlton House was demolished, and Nash was involved in the building of Buckingham Palace. This caused great scandal over costs, and he was called before a Select Committee. Very little survives of Nash's Palace, but the Marble Arch, which he intended as an entrance, now stands on its own as an eye-catcher at Tyburn. As a palace-builder it is perhaps fairer to him to enjoy his more imaginative flights, such as

Cumberland Terrace, Regent's Park, or Brighton Pavilion. In the first case [138] he has contrived a perfect stage-setting, with a whole terrace of serious houses dressed up with a pediment, and made to pretend, for the benefit of the Royal Villa opposite (which was never built), that they are one big palace. Much the same air of make-believe surrounds the Pavilion, at Brighton [139], which began life as an ordinary villa by Holland. About 1805 Sezincote House, in Gloucestershire, had been built in the 'Hindoo' style, and Repton seems to have proposed something similar for the Royal Pavilion. The Regent approved, and Nash was commissioned to execute the work in a vaguely Oriental style. In 1816 Coleridge's Kubla Khan 'a stately pleasure dome decreed', and some time afterwards the bulbous dome appeared on the sea front at Brighton.

With the death of George IV, in 1830, Nash disappeared. He died in his own East Cowes Castle five years later.

Most of the houses in and around Regent's Park were not designed by Nash, whose talents were absorbed in laying out the whole, and in complicated financial transactions connected with it. Among the architects responsible for the houses was Decimus Burton (1800–81), who later built the Athenaeum Club and the open screen of Ionic columns at Hyde Park Corner. He was, however, only one of the many talented men then working in a style influenced by Soane and Nash, and there were hundreds of builders all over the country who put up houses and whole streets, many of which still survive. John Buonarroti Papworth (1775–1847) was responsible for much of the splendour of Cheltenham in the years 1824–32, and scores of streets and houses in London, Clifton, Tunbridge Wells, and, above all, Brighton [140] and Hove, still remain as testimony to the vitality of the Regency style.

Part III

PAUL THOMPSON

12   Victorian Architecture

However strongly one may feel that Victorian architecture could achieve great things, there is no doubt that a discussion of it must start with an apology. The medieval and Georgian architecture which now survives is no more than a winning fragment, aged and softened by country air, of the civilization of church and aristocracy. It had its sordid side, but that has now vanished. Victorian architecture, the architecture of an industrial age, dismal with a century of urban soot, survives in such quantity that it is still the commonest setting for modern existence. As such, it is rightly resented. Nobody will be sorry when most of the six million Victorian houses still in use have followed the mud and timber huts of the medieval peasantry and the reeking rookeries of the Georgian towns into oblivion. There will be little regret for most Victorian factories, offices, and shops. But this certainly does not mean that there was no great architecture in the period, or that Victorian architecture as a whole, in so many ways foreshadowing our own problems and our own solutions, cannot be interesting and illuminating.

Victorian architecture was the product of a dramatically changing and expanding society. Building had been the slowly evolving expression of traditional needs and traditional crafts; now it was suddenly faced with the unprecedented demands and the unprecedented possibilities of an industrial age. The slowly growing population of England and Wales, which had perhaps trebled in the six hundred years up to 1780, suddenly exploded, trebling in the next seventy years, and trebling again between 1850 and the present day. The volume of building is closely connected to the size of population, so that the expansion of the building industry in the first half of the century was more rapid than ever before or since. This sudden expansion changed the whole character of building.

As in other rapidly growing industries, the small craftsman and the jobbing builder, whose main interest was a good reputation and steady work, gave way to the large contractor, whose main concern was quick profits. While the craftsman had been paid *pro rata*, the contractor worked to a lump-sum contract. The result was that during the nineteenth century standards of execution declined seriously. Shoddy speculative building has, of course, a long history: it can be found before 1700, and it is still commonplace today. The relentless commercial pressures undermining standards of good craftsmanship, so pathetically and brilliantly described by Robert Tressall in *The Ragged Trousered Philanthropists* (1914), have continued to lower the standard of detailed execution since the Victorian period. It would be difficult today to approach the technical finish of the best Victorian work. On the other hand the worst effects of this continued decline have been countered by the wider application of building by-laws since 1875. The Victorians did not have this protection, and it is therefore no coincidence that 'jerry-building' was a new Victorian word.

At the same time the Industrial Revolution had entirely changed the types of building required. The population expansion was chiefly in the towns, and it brought with it new needs for mass housing, for factories and railways, for town halls and offices, for water works and hospitals, for schools and libraries, for museums and cemeteries: the new communal demands of an urban society overwhelming the old work of cottages and country houses.

The scientific advances which made the Industrial Revolution possible also extended the technical possibilities of architecture. The old local boundaries of materials were broken. First the canals brought Welsh slate to London, carried brick into stone country. By the 1840s the quicker, cheaper transport of the railways had widened the choice of materials still further, so that for even a relatively inexpensive building a whole range of slates and tiles for roofing – red and grey and purple – of red and yellow bricks, knapped flints, limestones, sandstones, and granites for walling, of decorative grey and pink and green marbles from Derbyshire, Devon, Ireland, or Italy, could be readily obtained in almost any part of the country. For all but the very cheapest building local materials must now be a conscious choice. In addition new materials were introduced. Iron was in common use from the late eighteenth century, plate glass by the mid nineteenth century, and by the 1860s experiments were being made with steel and concrete. For decoration there were new synthetic materials, such as glass mosaic and mastic infill.

The growing powers of machinery enlarged choice still further. Thus, while in the past ornament had been a handmade luxury, machinery could now cut and even carve stone and provide pre-cast decorations in iron and other materials. There was still in Victorian England the same contrast as in the past between the care and expense taken with a minority of buildings and the cheapness of the majority, but it was no longer true that cheapness meant simplicity. Mean essentials could now be veiled by cheap ornament.

Machinery not only undermined the old craft basis and significance of ornament; it challenged the whole traditional method of building. It is true that in the Victorian period the old methods were adapted or distorted rather than wholly superseded, so that in 1900 the industry was still dominated by craftsmen, bricklayers, stonemasons, carpenters, and plumbers, even if there had been many changes in their ways of working. But already by the 1840s whole buildings were being prefabricated. Factory-made wooden churches were made for the slums, factory-made iron houses and warehouses, even clock towers and ballrooms, were exported to America and the colonies. And in the great iron and glass railway stations and Crystal Palace exhibition buildings of the 1850s industrialized building showed both a technical virtuosity and an aesthetic expression beyond the range of traditional building. The British Museum was completed in 1847 after twenty-five years building, and the Houses of Parliament, started in 1840, were to take as long. The Crystal Palace, which rivalled them in scale, was put up in nine months by a systematic use of prefabrication, standardization of parts, application of machine tools to wood-working, and efficient site management. The same contractors – Fox, Henderson and Company – went straight on to undertake to build the first half of Paddington Station in five months. This time they were over-optimistic, taking just over a year. But who could deny that these two iron and glass buildings were as impressive in their own way as any traditional Victorian building?

The scientific and technical advances which were thus undermining the old limits of taste imposed by materials, craftsmen, and costs were paralleled by equally destructive advances of scholarship in the arts. Historicism was not a new Victorian architectural phenomenon. Georgian Palladianism was a revival based on historical precedent. The Adam style was firmly based on studies of Diocletian's palace, the Greek revival on the rediscovery of classical temples. Nor was the Victorian variety of styles new. Eclecticism was typical of eighteenth-century taste, the park with its Gothic grotto and Doric temple, the thatched rustic cottage, the Chinese chairs and the Moorish pavilion. Hawksmoor, Vanbrugh, Adam, Wyatt were all willing to design in more than one style. The Victorian situation differed only in degree; but this difference was vital. As a whole Georgian knowledge of architectural history was limited and imprecise. During the first half of the nineteenth century interests widened and at the same time became more scholarly. Gothic and Romanesque, Moorish and Byzantine, as well as classical architecture were taken seriously. The historical sequence of architectural styles was defined. Helped by improved transport, architects systematically toured England and the Continent recording the styles of different periods in different regions. The result was that the educated architect who could previously have made an easy personal choice of manner within a relatively limited but loosely defined pattern of general design, was now sharply aware of a bewildering choice of style and period, of sharply defined limits of period and national precedent, and of the need for a conscious exercise of personal originality if his creative talents and the functional effectiveness of his designs were not to be hamstrung by archaeology.

It is often suggested that Victorian taste reflects the rise of a middle-class patronage lacking the education of the Georgian aristocracy. The difficulty of this explanation is that the Victorian aristocracy and royal family, who were still the leaders of taste in early Victorian England, showed no more discrimination than the middle classes. And in fact the Victorian middle classes were probably better informed about architecture than the Georgian gentry. Certainly they travelled far more frequently and extensively, to France and Germany, Spain and even Turkey, as well as to Italy, helped by improved roads, by newly constructed railways, and by magnificent guide books. Equally, they produced and circulated far more architectural books. No English critic of architecture can have reached a wider audience than Ruskin.

Victorian architects shared in this increase of travel and reading. They founded numerous local architectural societies at which papers were read and problems discussed. They supported a weekly architectural press which, beginning with the launching of the *Builder* in 1842, had expanded to five or more titles by 1900. They founded the first modern schools of architecture.

Yet in spite of this indubitable expansion of knowledge and education it is true that Victorian architecture in part reflects an educational failure. Georgian buildings were generally put up in a neat conventional manner in traditional local materials, whether the builder used a trade copy book or his own instinct. It did not matter that he was little educated. Victorian builders, with their wider choice of styles, materials, and ornament, were much more likely to suffer from lack of architectural education. In the later nineteenth century it was common for even the simplest builder's terrace, which a century before would have had no architectural pretensions whatever, to be distorted by misunderstood ornamental conceits. Moreover, it had become much less easy to acquire a sufficient education than in the eighteenth century. The Georgian architect or gentleman required only a visit to Italy and the perusal of a short shelf of books to be a cultured man. Sufficient technical experience could be readily obtained as an architect's pupil or builder's apprentice. But this old informal educational system was overwhelmed by the expansion both of knowledge and demand in the nineteenth century. While historical knowledge was so rapidly expanding and new technical improvements such as fire-proofing, sanitation, and central heating had constantly to be assimilated, only a remarkable architect could have kept up with the times sufficiently to give a pupil an adequate training. At the same time the expansion of the building industry and the growth of middle-class patronage produced an unprecedented demand for architects. The architectural profession increased more than tenfold between 1820 and 1870. In this situation the properly-trained pupils of able architects were easily outnumbered by men with little or no professional training whatever. In spite of their architectural schools and their weekly press the Victorians never caught up with this problem. Only the restriction of entry to the profession to those who were qualified could have imposed an adequate education on all Victorian architects. But the formal organization of the profession was only beginning with the foundation of the (later Royal) Institute of British Architects in 1834, and restriction of entry was not to be achieved until 1938. Because of this there is no doubt that much Victorian architecture exhibits the vices, as well as the virtues, of ignorance.

It was particularly serious that no efforts were made to extend formal architectural education beyond the limits of professional training. Unlike literature and art, architecture has never acquired a place in secondary education, and in universities it is conceived only as a professional training. The architectural patron has remained self-educated. Worse still, when specialist training and growing professional class consciousness resulted in a rigid division between nineteenth-century architects, engineers, and builders, no attempt was made to share a common training in design. This reduced the potential influence of technical advance on architectural design and meant that builders and engineers, who were responsible for more building work than architects, could hardly receive a proper aesthetic training.

On the other hand, a proper training would have been no panacea. Bewildered by the aesthetic abundance and technical advances which confronted them, the Victorians failed to find satisfactory new principles of design. Victorian theorists were torn between various doctrines which they could not reconcile. The authority of historical precedent, the correct use of a national or local style in local materials, conflicted with the belief that history was a storehouse of collective experience to be raided at random. The laws of nature taught the need for 'realism' in architecture, the functional basis of beauty, the virtue of honestly displayed natural materials, the excellence of naturalistic ornament. But the challenge of new materials and new functions could not both be met with functional honesty and be moulded by a historicist vocabulary. Similarly the inherited respect and desire for ornament conflicted with functional frankness, and the belief in naturalism with the archaic simplicity and geometric ornament of old examples. There was a belief in old craft traditions, a hope that craftsmen of mediaeval vitality might be rediscovered, a realization that the Industrial Revolution had destroyed the security and integrity of craftsmanship: a romantic feudalism which was to lead through Pugin, Ruskin, and Morris into socialism. Running sometimes with but usually against this school of thought there was a faith in *laissez-faire* progress, in commerce and machinery, a belief that good designs would be mass-produced if designers could be better educated, a belief that a scientific study of structure, colour, and ornament in nature and history could produce laws of design for a scientific age. Running across all these theories was the conflict between the need for order and authority and the need for originality, for a distinctive Victorian style.

Some of these Victorian theories have been incorporated into the theory of modern architecture, some have been discarded. But in their time they all seemed plausible, and most Victorian architects held a personal mixture of contradictory viewpoints, of historicism and functionalism, believing both in authority and in originality, veering uncertainly through their careers from one inclination to another. Thus one can find Paxton, the brilliantly original function-alist designer of the Crystal Palace, as a complacent architect of half-timbered cottages, Italianate villas, and Elizabethan manors, and Gilbert Scott, the most prosperous of Gothic revivalists, as an admirer of pure engineering, declaring that 'if we had a distinctive architecture of our own day worthy of the greatness of our age, I would be content to follow it', boldly proclaiming that 'one great effort is still before us: we have yet to make our style thoroughly our own, and divesting ourselves of the shackles, though not of the aid of precedent, to strike out boldly and fearlessly for ourselves'. The fascination of Victorian architecture is in this unpredictable variety, in the flashes of insight and originality which sprang from its confusion.

The confusion of Victorian architecture makes it difficult to treat it, as most architectural history, as a sequence of stylistic development. Certainly there were fashions in styles, which can help to indicate the date of a building. At the start of the period, in the 1840s, the most popular styles were Greek revival, Romanesque, Tudor and Eliza-bethan, Italianate, and archaeologically correct English Decorated Gothic. By the 1850s the Greek and Romanesque had all but dis-appeared, and new fashions developed for eclectic and original Gothic, drawing on Italian, French, and German sources, for a free classical style mixing Renaissance motives and Gothic shapes, and for a heavy version of French Renaissance. These styles carried on into the 1870s, but at the end of the 1860s correct English Gothic came back into favour and the domestic 'Queen Anne' fashion began. The 1880s were marked by a craze for Dutch gables, the 1890s by a fashion for flamboyant Gothic and a Baroque revival. Behind these superficial fashions can be detected three major phases: an early Victorian style marked by an earnest historicism and plainish materials; a high Vic-torian phase between the 1850s and 1870s of revolt from archaeology, with a preference for bright colours, contrasted materials, and coarse strong sculptural shapes; and a lighter late Victorian style marked by smoother, softer textures, gentler colours, and fussier, more delicate ornament. But all these fashions can only be rough guides; the pace of change was so rapid that there were always survivors of older styles being built in each phase.

Moreover, for certain types of building there were clear stylistic preferences which showed remarkable persistency. Church schools, for example, tended to be Gothic, while Board schools were usually built in a version of the 'Queen Anne' style. Consequently a list of

273

141. Albert Docks, Liverpool

stylistic phases needs to be supplemented by a list of building types. Thus a wave of workhouse building followed the reform of the Poor Law in 1834. Although starting earlier, model housing and prisons first became important in the 1840s. Similarly, the 1852 Interment Act resulted in numerous new cemeteries. A conspicuous series of mental hospitals was built by the Lunacy Commissioners between 1844 and 1860. Railway stations were most frequent in the same period. Church schools were typical of the mid century, while Board schools began in 1870. Crystal Palace exhibition buildings gave frequent opportunities for iron and glass in the 1850s and 1860s, winter garden pavilions at the resorts in the 1870s and 1880s. Public libraries and municipal housing first became common in the 1890s. The history of these building types, so closely reflecting the progress of Victorian social history, is in many ways more interesting than the superficial succession of favourite styles. Both of these methods

274

would, however, be too lengthy and too complex to be used in a brief introduction to Victorian architecture. It will be more rewarding to select a few of the more significant types and styles for special consideration.

Since we are discussing the architecture of the first industrial age, it will be best to start with industrial building. Here the extremes of the Victorian achievement are at once obvious. The squalor of much early industry is undeniable. On the other hand, because the effect of historicist fashions was more slowly felt in utilitarian buildings, the Victorians here made their most important contribution to the functional tradition which is regarded as one of the sources of modern architecture.* The biggest group of these buildings – dock and railway warehouses and sheds, maltings and breweries, textile mills, flour mills, linseed mills – are designed in a style evolved for industrial building in the late eighteenth century. Although often the internal structure was of iron, the outside was solidly built of local brick or stone, with long regular rows of windows, often with white cast-iron frames. The effect of these buildings comes from their honest simplicity and frequently breathtaking scale. There are, of course, many variations, due to the colour of local stone or brick available and the building's function. In silk mills the need for light resulted in long continuous window strips, strikingly modern in feeling. Warehouses are often given dramatic scale by weatherboarded wooden sack hoists which project over recessed doors running up the whole height of the building. Variety is also introduced by the distant reflections of architectural styles, by pilasters of brick in another colour or gables echoing Palladian pediments, by the cast-iron stumpy Doric columns which allow dock warehouses a ground floor open to the quayside, or the massive arcading typical of warehouses and commercial buildings in London. This tradition of industrial building is not usually thought of as typically Victorian, but many of the best examples come in fact from the Victorian period. Most of the little stone mill towns in the steep valleys running up into the Pennines from Halifax are wholly Victorian. The finest of the Liverpool Docks by Jesse Hartley, the Albert [141] and Stanley Docks, date from the 1840s and 1850s, the great warehouses at Sharpness Docks from the 1870s, the maltings at Mistley in Essex from still later, and the street warehouses in Bristol by W. B. Gingell (12 Temple Street)

* See J. M. Richards, *The Functional Tradition in Early Industrial Buildings*, London, 1958.

and E. W. Godwin (104 Stokes Croft) from *c.* 1860. There are numerous other examples which are undated.

The same difficulty in dating explains the fact that the Victorian contribution to similar pre-industrial functional buildings – farm sheds, barns, watermills, and windmills – has been generally ignored. Where these can be dated, the same simplicity and use of local materials, often weatherboarding, or Norfolk flint and pantiles, can be found. But the need for them was rapidly declining, and equally striking visual solutions for new functions are more typical of the nineteenth century. Circular engine houses for the railways, the steep, slated, flat-capped pyramids of malt kilns [142], the majestic simplicity of railway viaducts, show the inventiveness of the industrial tradition.

Perhaps the most important aspect of the functional tradition was its frank acceptance of new materials. Surprisingly few experiments with concrete are known – in fact the most striking early British

142. Malt kilns, Mistley

143. Royal Albert Bridge, Saltash

144. Palm House, Kew

example of its use is a church, St Barnabas, Oxford (by Arthur Blomfield, 1868). But the use of iron, steel, and glass was pioneered in utilitarian buildings. The most spectacular experiments were in bridge-building: Robert Stephenson's tubular Britannia Bridge of 1845–50 crossing the Menai Strait; Isambard Kingdom Brunel's Royal Albert Bridge [143] of 1857–9, curving across the Tamar estuary at Saltash on tall granite piers, a strange construction combining suspension and sausage-shaped tubular arches; and Sir John Fowler's steel-cantilevered Forth Bridge of 1890. Stephenson's High Level Bridge at Newcastle upon Tyne (1845–9), the remarkable latticed metal railway arches on the Penrith–Darlington railway, and Brunel's Clifton Suspension Bridge, Bristol (1829–64), are less inventive but equally impressive.

278

The iron and glass roofs which were taken up by exhibition buildings and railway stations derived from greenhouse construction, and fortunately the finest of their ancestors, the Palm House, Kew (by Richard Turner, engineer, and Decimus Burton, architect, 1844–8), still survives [144]. The elegance of its thin white repeating panels and easy curves is unforgettable. The Crystal Palace and the exhibitions which followed have disappeared, but the parallel development in railway stations can still be traced. They form a splendid series. The first great surviving station is Newcastle Central, by John Dobson and Thomas Prosser (1846–55), a triple-curved roof resting on two rows of iron pillars which follow the long curve of the tracks. The contrast between the style of this train shed and the fine late classical façade of the station, and the ruthless thrusting of the tracks through the old castle grounds, are striking illustrations both of the uncertainty and the confidence of the Victorians. King's Cross, London, the next in date, by Lewis Cubitt (1851–2), is exceptional among major stations in that the arches of its twin train shed were of laminated wood (replaced by steel without altering the design in 1869), and that this twin train shed was frankly expressed by two great arched windows as the main element in the façade. Paddington, by Brunel and Digby Wyatt (1852–4), has no façades at all, but a careful attempt was made to integrate the platform buildings and train shed with a prickly kind of metalwork decoration. This curiously fascinating detail, together with the spatial grandeur of its three aisles and double transepts, makes this the finest of the early railway stations, one of the best of all Victorian buildings.

Of later British stations, the finest is St Pancras, London, by W. H. Barlow and Sir Gilbert Scott (1868–74). Barlow was a friend of Paxton, and had helped him design the Crystal Palace. His train shed spans 243 feet and rises to 100 feet at its slightly pointed apex. This slight suggestion of an arch, together with the complete elimination of any distinction between wall and ceiling, gives the huge structure a strange lightness. The main façade by Scott, a wild example of high Victorian brick Gothic, encrusted with chimneys, crocketed towers, and crenellated gables, makes one of the most romantic skylines in London, a complete contrast to the severe simplicity of the train shed. Yet it would be a mistake to think that Barlow did not want this contrast. Just as Scott could admire the aesthetics of pure engineering, Paxton had been a fierce advocate of Scott's Gothic design for the Foreign Office, and the use of the same style – though not of course the same

design – at St Pancras [145] seemed wholly appropriate at that date.

On a smaller scale, Victorian cast-iron buildings can be seen all over the country in innumerable railway stations. The smaller stations of the old Great Western are especially good. Covered markets, which with their flagged alleys and diverse stalls are the Victorian version of the pedestrian shopping precinct, are also often interesting for their iron roofs. Some, such as Halifax Borough Market (by Leeming and Leeming, 1892), are spatially quite ambitious. More frivolous examples are provided by seaside piers and bandstands in parks. Rarer, but more important, are cast-iron commercial buildings in which the frames are exposed in the façade. Iron skeletons were common, but they are only occasionally revealed. In shops sometimes the framework is used to make a continuous window, with goods displayed on each floor. Examples can be found in country towns such as Whitchurch, Shropshire, and Swanage, Dorset. Ground-floor metal shop fronts are relatively common, although some are very fine, such as Asprey's, New Bond Street, London. Similarly, with offices, especially where cramped building made lighting difficult, masonry is occasionally reduced to a minimum and cast-iron detailing

145. *Left* St Pancras Station
146. Chatham Naval Dockyard

frankly used. Glasgow has several examples, but probably the most brilliant is Oriel Chambers, Cook Street, Liverpool, by Peter Ellis (1864). Warehouses of this kind are rare, but there are some startling cast-iron weatherboarded boathouses in the Portsmouth and Sheerness Naval Dockyards. At Chatham Naval Dockyard [146], the former museum – built in 1867 – with its rigid vertical repeating elements, strikingly anticipates modern design. And since cast-iron made its mark with an exhibition building, a mention must finally be made of the Bethnal Green Museum, whose iron naves were originally erected as the South Kensington Museum by Young and Son in 1855–6, ridiculed as the 'Brompton Boilers', and transferred to Bethnal Green in 1871. Their unpopularity illustrates how the Victorians, while able to welcome functional design in temporary or utilitarian buildings, fiercely rejected it when 'architectural' quality was thought to be required.

This attitude helps to explain the mixed achievements of the Victorians in housing. The best Victorian housing falls into two groups. The first is traditional. In the countryside, until the agricultural depression of the 1870s, the more conservative builders continued to use local stone or brick, even thatch, far more widely than is usually thought. Often a largish village with a street of shops, like Blakesley in the golden iron-stone Northamptonshire hills, or pale brick Cottenham in the Fens, or even a little red brick town like Pewsey in Wiltshire, seems by the sash windows and door frames to be largely Victorian in detail, yet has all the anonymous integrity of an earlier period. Even the much more self-conscious *cottage orné* or model village, with its crinkled bargeboards and twisted chimneys, very likely comes from an early-nineteenth-century pattern book, and certainly belongs to a pre-Victorian tradition. It is only the country houses and the houses built for the more self-conscious professional middle classes which usually betray their date.

In the towns it is equally remarkable how late the classical tradition of terraces and crescents often survives. In London most of Belgravia, Pimlico, Bayswater, and Notting Hill was built up in the 1840s and 1850s in white stucco. The detail became more Italianate, but drastic attacks on the tradition, such as R. C. Carpenter's Tudor Gothic Lonsdale Square of 1838 and Gough and Roumieu's distorted compressed Milner Square of 1841–3, both in Islington, had little influence before the 1860s. Outside London other notable examples in the classical tradition are Park Town, Oxford (by S. L. Seckham, 1853–5), and Decimus Burton's Calverley Estate at Tunbridge Wells (1827–52), both of which mix classical crescents with Italianate villas; Adelaide Crescent, Brighton (1830–60); the Esplanade, Sunderland (1855–60); and the severe Grecian terraces of Alexander Thomson in Glasgow: Walmer Crescent (Paisley Road, 1858), Moray Place (Strathbungo, 1860) [147], and Great Western Terrace (the Great Western Road, 1870). It is this same classical tradition which gives a pleasant integrity to the pioneering working class housing of Henry Roberts, such as the model dwellings in Streatham Street, Bloomsbury (1849). At the other extreme, tenement building in Glasgow fused the local terrace tradition with the grim drama of industrial warehousing.

In complete contrast is the second group, the housing, mostly built for the middle classes, of the Gothic revivalists. It can be studied in Victorian vicarages all over the country, or in a middle-class suburb like North Oxford, with its generous detached houses set out in curving, blossoming, tree-lined roads. The most ornate houses, with Venetian Gothic windows, big porches, wrought iron roof crests, and circular turrets are a coarser version of the high Victorian church style, which will be mentioned later. Most, however, are more

147. Moray Place, Glasgow

148. Red House, Bexleyheath

restrained, and in the freedom of their internal planning, the big plate-glass windows, the bold simple massing of steep gables and tall chimneys, the imaginative use of ordinary materials – perhaps creamy brick walls with red bands between the floors and above the windows, and blue slate roofs with red ridge tiles – they frequently approach a wholly original Victorian functionalism. When the material used is stone or tile-hanging the result is more conventional, although it can often have the attractiveness of local vernacular building. The houses designed by William White at St Columb, Cornwall (*c.* 1850), Lurgashall, Sussex (1852), and Great Bourton, Oxfordshire (1862), are especially charming examples. Where red brick was used, especially in the hands of William Butterfield and G. E. Street, the result was a more original style, the design relying on honest simplicity, with sash windows, hipped gables, and battered chimney breasts. There are notable parsonages at Hensall and Pollington in Yorkshire by

Butterfield (*c*. 1854) in this style, and it was used by Philip Webb in Red House, Bexleyheath [148], designed for William Morris in 1859.

This red-brick style had a long and healthy influence on English architecture. The excellent London County Council housing built at Millbank (1897–1902) [149] and Boundary Street, Bethnal Green (1890s) owes much to the personal influence of Philip Webb. Attractive working-class terraces and cottages were built much earlier by Butterfield at Baldersby, Yorkshire, Braunstone, near Leicester, and Ashwell, Rutland (*c*. 1855–60). In their integrity and humanity these buildings stand out from the mass of industrial jerry-building as well as from the mean barrack tenements provided by mid-Victorian philanthropy. Philip Webb's brick houses at 19 Lincoln's Inn Fields (1868) and 1 Palace Green, Kensington (1863), also prepared the way for the ousting of stucco by brick in west London. The 'Queen Anne' terrace houses of Tite Street and Cadogan Square, Chelsea, designed by Norman Shaw, E. W. Godwin, George and Peto, and others in the 1880s, were but a fanciful fashionable development of the same style. With its characteristically late Victorian pretty white woodwork, fretted skyline, light classical detail, and subtle textural play of brick,

149. Millbank Estate

terracotta, and tile-hanging, the 'Queen Anne' style is often exceedingly attractive, even if its plainer antecedents, less encumbered by arty ornament, are architecturally sounder. One of the earliest and best examples is Shaw's Swan House, Chelsea Embankment (1875), with a typically varied window pattern: light, late-seventeenth-century-type oriels projecting on the first floor, the second floor again projected with alternate very tall slim oriels and sash windows, a band of broader shuttered sash windows above, and then dormers. A very complete group of similar houses is at Bedford Park, Middlesex, the first planned garden suburb, laid out by Shaw in 1875, with the houses chiefly designed by Godwin, M. B. Adams, and E. J. May. In the home counties, especially Surrey and Sussex, Shaw and his followers proved very popular, reviving the local tradition of brick and tile. While mid-Victorian architects like William White had successfully used this vernacular manner for humbler country schools and rectories, Shaw now used it on a grander scale in country houses. A characteristic example, now a hospital, Banstead Wood, Surrey (1884–90), with its rows of white bays and jutting red gables and its tall ribbed chimneys, has a sensitive domesticity surprising for so large a building.

The parallel development of the red-brick style in school building was equally important. Street and Butterfield had used it for village schools such as Eastbury, Berkshire (c. 1851), and Pollington, Yorkshire (c. 1854), and it was taken up by E. R. Robson for the London Board schools after 1870. Here the simple brick detail, the flexible planning, and the big sash windows proved wholly successful, and influenced Board-school design throughout the country.

Board schools are perhaps the most easily acceptable of the larger, ambitious buildings – churches, country houses, town halls, and other public buildings – which are today the most prominent examples of Victorian architecture. They veer between deliberate meanness and wild ostentation. The meanest, such as hospitals and prisons, are chiefly interesting for their planning. The majority, while feeling the need for ornament and display, were built without the extravagance which could have given them quality, so that they tend to be fussy but barren. The combined effect of pretension and economy is especially obvious in Victorian churches. Even so, there is a number of important buildings of real architectural quality in this group.

Firstly, there are the direct fruits of serious historicism. Many of the leading Victorian architects were considerable scholars, and were capable of designing evocative buildings in period styles. The grandest architecture of the Greek revival, the British Museum, London (by Robert Smirke, south front 1842–7), and the National Gallery of Scotland, Edinburgh (W. H. Playfair, 1850–4), is Victorian. St George's Hall, Liverpool (by H. L. Elmes and C. R. Cockerell, 1839–54) and the Fitzwilliam Museum, Cambridge (by George Basevi and C. R. Cockerell, 1837–47) [150], are perhaps closer to Roman, and certainly handled with Baroque mastery.

Equally dignified, but freer in design are the Ashmolean Museum, Oxford (1839–45) and the branch Banks of England, Castle Street, Liverpool; King Street, Manchester; and Broad Street, Bristol (c. 1845), all by C. R. Cockerell. The last echoes of the Greek revival can be seen in the great Corinthian porticoes of Baptist tabernacles in now dingy south London streets, and even at this level it can give surprising pleasure.

The Italian Renaissance style which succeeded it is seen at its best in Charles Barry's clubs and palaces: the Reform Club, Pall Mall (1837), Bridgewater House, next to St James's Palace, both in London (1845–9), and Cliveden House, Buckinghamshire (1850). Less

150. Fitzwilliam Museum, Cambridge

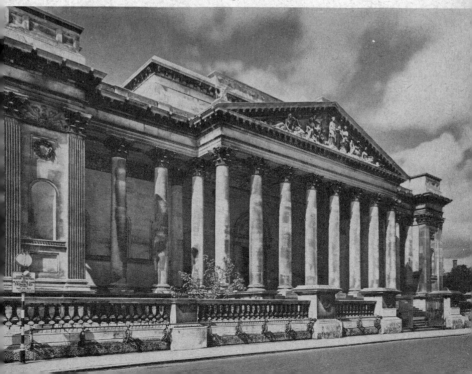

151. Houses of Parliament

accomplished but nearly always decent versions of this style are
numerous in banks and offices and London clubs and, when discreetly
handled and of good stone, can be impressive. Fine country examples
are the Corn Exchange, Cirencester (1862), and the National Provincial Banks in Sunderland and Stockton by John Gibson (1876–7).

Tudor and Elizabethan design was based on much less knowledge
and open to more abuse, but the daring reminiscences of Wollaton
Hall by Barry at Highclere, Hampshire (1842–4), by Paxton and
G. H. Stokes at Mentmore, Buckinghamshire (1852–4), and of
Burleigh House at Harlaxton, Lincolnshire, by Anthony Salvin
(1834–55), are remarkably successful. The Houses of Parliament
(Barry, 1835–60) [151] are somewhat similar both in intention and in
effect, although they are in fact a happy mixture of a romantic sky-
line, classical symmetry in the river front, and delicate late Gothic
detail.

288

This Gothic detail was designed for Barry by A. W. N. Pugin, the apostle of Gothic principles in architecture, and it is his most sympathetic work. The early Victorian church Gothic is on the whole very disappointing, except perhaps in Pugin's Cheadle (1846), where just for once he was allowed sufficient money to realize his dreams. Some of the early Tractarian country churches are pretty, and there are two good town churches at Leeds (St Peter, by R. D. Chantrell, 1839–41, and St Saviour, by J. M. Derick, 1842–5), but there is nothing outstanding before the former Catholic Apostolic Church (now London University church), Gordon Square, London, by Raphael Brandon (1850–4), which is rich Early English on a cathedral scale. On the other hand, the later churches of G. F. Bodley, such as St John, Tue Brook, Liverpool (1868–70) and St Augustine, Pendlebury, Lancashire (1874), and of J. L. Pearson, especially St Augustine, Kilburn, London (1870–80), St John, Upper Norwood (1881–7), St Stephen, Bournemouth (1881–1908), and Sutton Veney, Wiltshire (1862), are always sensitive and often magnificently spacious. Pearson nearly always vaulted his churches. A more original group of late Victorian churches, with enormous traceried east and west wall windows and fresh sensitive detailing, are by Norman Shaw (Holy Trinity, Latimer Road, London, 1887) and J. D. Sedding (St Clement, Bournemouth, 1873, and Holy Trinity, Sloane Street, London [152] 1888–90). Sedding's churches have the added attraction of arts-and-crafts fittings which often betray the seeds of future Art Nouveau.

Early Victorian Gothic was more successful with secular buildings, schools, convents, and parsonages. Butterfield's Cumbrae College, Scotland (1849–51), and R. H. Carpenter's Lancing College, Sussex, begun in 1854 and carried out by his son and William Slater with a soaring chapel, are perhaps the best. There are also Gothic castles, notably Salvin's at Peckforton, Cheshire (1846–50), and Pugin's Alton Castle, Staffordshire (1847). A later castle, built on old foundations by William Burges at Castell Coch, Glamorgan, complete with portcullis and weird furniture (1875–90), is even classified as an ancient monument and in the care of the Ministry of Works.

There are other Victorian revivals which also produced successful historicist buildings. Castles were built in the Norman style, although the most spectacular, Penrhyn Castle, Wales (1827–37), by Thomas Hopper, is just pre-Victorian. Of neo-Norman churches, those by Benjamin Ferrey have quality. A Pisan Romanesque style was strikingly used by T. H. Wyatt and D. Brandon in their basilica at

Wilton, Wiltshire (1843). One of the noblest of all Victorian buildings is J. F. Bentley's great severe, domed, brick, Byzantine Westminster Cathedral (1895–1903). Another attractive late Victorian revival, treating seriously a motive popularized by Norman Shaw, is represented by the Dutch-gabled, brick-and-terracotta Harrington and Collingham Gardens, Kensington, by George and Peto (1881 onwards).

Much more could be mentioned: but it is time to leave the safety of historicism for high Victorian originality. The Victorians wanted their own architectural style and, failing to see how close to a new style they had come in utilitarian building, they looked for it in a free eclecticism, an original reinterpretation of period styles. The mid-Victorians reacted strongly against the drabness, the meagreness, the pedantry of their predecessors. The high Victorian style is thus characterized by a free mixing of period motives, exciting experiments with coloured materials, a liking for tough, masculine, sculptural shapes, the 'reality' of frankly exposed structure, and 'vigour and go' in architectural detail. It was a difficult and dangerous style,

152. Holy Trinity Church, Sloane Street

153. Wheatley Church

which too easily degenerated into mere coarseness. This is particularly true of high Victorian ornament. On the other hand, the Victorian revival of craftsmanship in architectural sculpture and stained glass produced its finest results in this period. The wonderful naturalistic sculpture of the O'Shea brothers at the Oxford Museum (by T. Deane and B. Woodward, 1855–97, with a unique Gothic glass-and-iron courtyard), and by Thomas Earp in churches such as St Paul, Herne Hill, London (G. E. Street, 1858); or the stained glass by Saunders at Studley Royal, Yorkshire (Burges, 1871–8), by Powell's at Waltham Abbey, Essex (restored for Burges, 1859), by Holiday at Westminster Abbey (south nave aisle, third from west, 1868), and by William Morris at Selsley, Gloucestershire, St Martin, Scarborough (both for Bodley, 1861–2), and Lyndhurst, Hampshire (for William White, 1862), are all high Victorian in context and outstanding in

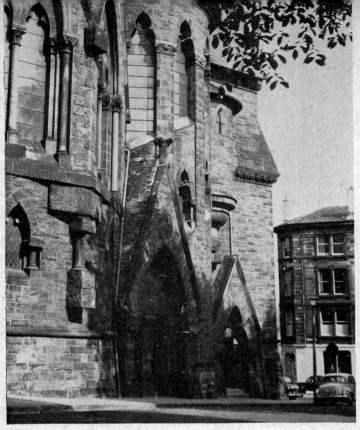

154. Barclay Church, Edinburgh

quality. The craftsmanship of this period is little known, but it repays investigation.

There are a great many varieties of high Victorian style: indeed, each well-known architect created his own manner. James Brooks built a series of churches in east London in the 1860s: bare brick vessels with long roofs, lancet windows, and strong arcades, a few Early English details such as detached shafts, but the whole effect relying on spatial simplicity. This is the style at its most severe. Some church exteriors by Street, especially the sturdy, thick, boldly modelled spires of SS Philip and James, Oxford (1859–63), and

155. St Augustine, Penarth

Wheatley, Oxfordshire (1856) [153], achieve a comparable monumentality. Street's brick interior at Westcott, Buckinghamshire (1867), is as severe as Brooks's, but usually his are richer, often with rough stone walls and the pulpit a moulded white stone cylinder. Pulpits, like fonts, frequently gave church architects a chance to explore abstract sculptural forms. The same sculptural feeling in architecture appears especially powerfully in the work of F. T. Pilkington: Trinity Church, Irvine, Ayrshire (1864), St John's Church, Kelso (1865), and Barclay Church, Edinburgh (1864). The last [154] is of rough grey granite, its walls curving irregularly, massively

293

buttressed gabled doorways leaning squeezed in the angles, thick plate tracery windows rising into the Gothic mansard gables, circular turrets and a big broach spire at the angles, and huge ragged chunks of capital and corbel in part hacked into rich naturalistic jungle. The details, if they have sources, are based on early French Gothic, but the effect is entirely original. The same motives can be found used equally successfully in the churches by Burges at Studley Royal and at Lowfield Heath, Surrey (1867), and in Bodley's church at Selsley and his St Michael, Brighton (1859), the last being in brick. Street's brick churches, such as St James-the-Less, Westminster (1860), owe more to Italian Gothic.

Italy was also the inspiration for the high Victorian experiments with colour, led by Butterfield's All Saints, Margaret Street, London (1849–59). His colours are daring, but not, as is sometimes thought, intentionally discordant – although urban soot has often made them so. St Augustine, Penarth (1865), white outside, with an interior [155] of creamy ashlar, pink sandstone, and raw red brick diapered white and black, or the strangely marbled All Saints, Babbacombe, Devon

156. Shadwell Park, clock tower

(1868–74), are his best polychromatic churches. The hard, wiry, restless linear patterning of his architecture sometimes anticipates Expressionist feeling. Alfred Waterhouse, as architect to Prudential Assurance, developed a comparable style in hot red brick and terracotta, although his brownish terracotta Natural History Museum, South Kensington (1873–81), and his soot-black Manchester Town Hall (1869–77) are much more thick and plastic. Equally sharp and linear is Joseph Peacock's black and white St Simon Zelotes, Chelsea (1859). More serious, and softer in shape and colour, are William White's fine churches at Lyndhurst (1858) and Fenny Stratford, Buckinghamshire (1866), and his St Saviour, Aberdeen Park, London (1859), which handle abstract geometric patterning in red, white, and black brick with fascinating invention and subtlety, in diapers, herring-bone, diamonds, and chequers; even the window tracery is often of brick, and Lyndhurst steeple glitters red and yellow to its apex.

The most violent combinations of constructional colour and violent design are in the houses and churches of S. S. Teulon. His detail is flamboyant and coarse, and his minor work is intolerable. But he knew how to produce a climax, throwing together flint and stone, red and yellow brick, buttressing towers with compressed apses, breaking gables with chimneys, juxtaposing plain plate tracery and rich naturalistic ornament. His buildings may be aesthetically indefensible, but the power of his churches of St Stephen, Hampstead (1876) and at Silvertown Docks, London (1861), his houses at Elvetham, Hampshire (1860) and Shadwell Park, Norfolk (1858–60) is furious, indisputable [156].

Bassett Keeling and E. B. Lamb were two other church architects with remarkable personal styles. Lamb, an older man, had started as a designer of very Victorian-looking villas in the early 1830s, and the detailing of his churches was unusually unarcheological even in the 1840s. Built for evangelical congregations, most of them have the added interest of central planning. Aldwark, Yorkshire (1846) is especially original for its date, with an ambulatory round a wide central space, while his mannered notchings, chamferings, and spidery timbers reach a climax in St Martin, Vicars Road, St Pancras (1866).

Of secular buildings, E. W. Godwin's sturdy Congleton Town Hall, Cheshire (1864–7), W. H. Lunn's Chester Town Hall (1865), and Thomas Worthington's brick Sessions Court, Minshull Street, Man-

chester (1868), are noteworthy. All these are Gothic, and there is no doubt that Gothic was the style most readily adapted to high Victorian aims. But there was also a classical variety, in which the regular horizontality of Greek revival colonnades gave way to a more broken grouping, often with detached columns, building up to unprecedented towers and spires. The pioneer here was Alexander Thomson of Glasgow, who broke away from the severity of his classical terraces in the Egyptian Halls, Union Street (1850s) and the outstandingly fine Caledonia Road Free Church (1856–7) [157]. More characteristic examples are Cuthbert Brodrick's Leeds Town Hall (1855–9), Weightman and Robson's Liverpool Municipal Buildings (1866), and Barry's Halifax Town Hall (1860–2); the last [158], in Italian Renaissance detail, is thrown up into an extraordinary thick tower and jagged spike. This final development of Barry's style epitomizes that of Victorian architecture. His taste had changed out of all recognition from the sober respectability of the Reform Club. But he had achieved a new freedom, a new power of expression. This last work of his, although more difficult to appreciate, can convey a unique and moving aesthetic experience. In this it is representative of the best architecture of the age.

157. *Left* Caledonia Road Free Church, Glasgow

158. Halifax Town
Hall

13   Modern Architecture

The contrast between high Victorian and the first modern architecture could hardly be more abrupt. Nevertheless there is a historical connexion. Some of the most important influences in forming the international modern style came from Victorian Britain. The theories of Pugin, Ruskin, and Morris, emphasizing functional planning, honest construction, and frankly used materials, directly influenced two of the leading European pioneers, Henri van der Velde and Walter Gropius. English decorative design, especially the sinuous, seaweedy wallpaper patterns of Walter Crane and A. H. Mackmurdo, was one of the most important sources of Art Nouveau. Through the writings of Hermann Muthesius, the imaginative freedom achieved by mid and late Victorian English house and church architects was made known abroad. Most important of all, at the end of the century two major architects appeared whose work, although historically the climax of late Victorian architectural originality, so strikingly anticipates the modern style that it is more easily seen as the beginning than the end of a period.

The first was Charles Voysey, an architect of the school of Pugin and Ruskin, who created a new version of the vernacular house tradition: slate-roofed, with rendered white walls, windows in long horizontal bands, and crisply battered chimneys. His best and simplest houses, such as Greyfriars, Puttenham, Surrey (1896), Perrycroft, Colwall, Herefordshire (1893), and his own house, The Orchard, Chorleywood, Hertfordshire (1900), have much of the character of Frank Lloyd Wright's early low-roofed horizontal houses. Voysey's utilitarian white brick Sanderson's Wallpaper Factory, Turnham Green, Middlesex (1902), and his tall cubic house at 14 South Parade, Bedford Park (1891) [159], are equally modern in feeling.

Still more remarkable was the work of a Glasgow architect, C. R. Mackintosh. In spite of his use of spare attenuated Art Nouveau decorative detail, some of the austere white interiors which he designed between 1898 and 1912, unified and uncluttered, with fitted cupboards and tall rectilinear furniture, have the spirit of the purest modern design of the 1930s. His work was known and influential in Austria and Germany in the 1900s. These interiors have nearly all

159. No. 14 South Parade, Bedford Park

160. Glasgow School of Art, library wing

161. Glasgow School of Art, library, interior

162. Mary Ward Settlement, Tavistock Place, London

disappeared now, with one important exception: those of his master-piece, the Glasgow School of Art. Here, the main front, with its big metal studio windows, dates from 1896–9, the library wing [160], with tall elongated oriel windows, from 1907–9. The library interior with its insistent vertical posts remains intact [161].

Both Voysey and Mackintosh worked within the theory of the English Gothic revival. Although their work comes as close to a new functional aesthetic as the industrial building of the mid nineteenth century, it equally failed to produce a revolutionary theory. The transformation of Gothic principles though wholly accepting the central importance of the machine in design was a Continental achievement. Thus all that can be seen of the modern style in England in these early years are unconscious anticipations of it: developments of the light late-Victorian free historicism of Shaw and Sedding which parallel those of Voysey and Mackintosh.

The wide eaves, white upper storey over red brick, and long horizontal lines of the Mary Ward Settlement, Tavistock Place, London (1897–8) [162], come still closer to Frank Lloyd Wright than Voysey. It was the first important work of its architects, A. D. Smith and Cecil Brewer, but their promise was not fulfilled, and only Heal's, Tottenham Court Road, London (1916), recaptured something of their early originality. More consistently rewarding is the work in the 1880s and 1890s of A. H. Mackmurdo, including 25 Cadogan

Gardens, Chelsea (1899), with its generous, tall vertical window bands. Mackmurdo probably also designed the remarkably straightforward river front of the Savoy Hotel, London (1889). George Walton, a Glasgow decorator who had worked with Mackintosh, showed the influence of Voysey in his White House, Shiplake, Oxfordshire (1906), while Edgar Wood's rather lumpish brick Upmeads, Stafford (19.0), also has proto-modern mannerisms. The pale brick Gothic church of St Silas, St Pancras, by E. Shearman (1912), has woodwork in the style of Mackintosh, but the only church in which the architecture itself was conceived in a modern spirit was Roker, Durham, by E. S. Prior (1907). Although traditionally built, of rough grey stone, its great clean transverse arches and odd matchstick window tracery could have been as easily designed for concrete. It is significant of the failure of architectural theory in the period that W. R. Lethaby's enchanting thatched church at Brockhampton, Herefordshire (1901), which is actually vaulted in concrete, should be much more Gothic in feeling.

Continental developments were more obviously reflected in a small number of buildings in an English version of the Art Nouveau

163. Royal Arcade, Norwich

style. Edgar Wood's Lindley Clock Tower at Huddersfield (1902) sprouts into a jaunty cap and vegetable plasticity, and C. J. Skipper's Royal Arcade at Norwich (1900) is gaily tiled with characteristic tulip and heart patterns [163]. Similar decorative motifs and plastic originality were used by Harrison Townsend in his Whitechapel Art Gallery, London (1897–8), Horniman Museum, Lewisham (1902), and Great Warley Church, Essex (1904).

Original architecture of this kind was exceptional in early twentieth-century Britain. Generally the period was rather a continuation of the Victorian architectural situation, and its best architecture falls into comparable groups and must be approached in similar terms.

Serious historicism was most obviously continued in church architecture, where there is little distinction between the sensitive, correct English Gothic of the late Victorians and the work of Temple Moore and Ninian Comper. Examples by Moore are St John (1895) and St Mary (1914), Hendon, Middlesex, St Margaret, Leeds (1908), and Pusey House, Oxford (1906); by Comper, St Cyprian, Clarence Gate, London (1903), and St Mary, Wellingborough (1906–30). In Liverpool Cathedral, begun in 1903, Sir Giles Gilbert Scott, grandson of the Sir Gilbert Scott of St Pancras station, handled Gothic with a conviction and on a scale equal to the boldest Victorian work.

In Baroque revival architecture the distinction between historicism and originality is particularly difficult. The wilful vitality of Baroque was best recaptured by the most original buildings of the revival. Norman Shaw's Chesters, Northumberland (1891), one of the earliest examples of the style, with tall blank rusticated walls sweeping round to a recessed portico, and the later Piranesian fantasy of his Piccadilly Hotel (1905–8), a great arcaded rusticated base supporting a giant colonnade against the sky, succeed through sheer boldness. Sir Edwin Lutyens's Heathcote, Ilkley, Yorkshire (1907), has a similar conviction in its bold massing, as has the best work of Sir John Belcher, such as the Institute of Chartered Accountants, off Moorgate (1889), and Mappin and Webb, Oxford Street (1905), London, or Norwich office buildings by C. J. Skipper such as the Norwich Union, Surrey Street (1903–4) [164]. A happy version of Baroque revival, enlivening red brick with heavy stone bands, emphatic quoins and keystones, white cupolas and curved gables, proved popular for public libraries and town halls, especially for the series of libraries given by Carnegie and Passmore Edwards in the 1890s and 1900s. The libraries at West Ham, by Gibson and Russell (1896), and Shoreditch and Hammersmith

164. Norwich Union

(1897 and 1904) by H. T. Hare are characteristic. A more sober but often acceptable Baroque can be found in many branch banks of the early twentieth century.

Although Baroque continued to be favoured for public architecture, good examples are rare after 1910. Successful Baroque revival shared the bold vitality of high Victorian classical originality, and it could not survive in a period much more generally characterized by cautious sensitivity. During the 1900s the imaginative 'Queen Anne' domestic style gave way either to the roughcast simplicity introduced by Voysey or to a reticent neo-Georgian. These reserved tastes tended more and more to reduce public Baroque to lifeless pedantry.

Among the few architects who continued into the 1920s to display a bold creative eclecticism, Sir Edwin Lutyens was dominant. His work was astonishingly varied. He began with romantic vernacular country houses, which culminate in Sonning Deanery, Berkshire, and

Orchards, Godalming, both in warm red brick with ample tile roofs, tall chimneystacks, and a deep entrance-way next to a grand hipped bay window, and Tigbourne Court, Witley [165], rather more mannered, with classical columns and a curved screen wall, but a beautiful texture of local greenish Burgate stone with bands of red tile. All three were built in 1898–9. At the same moment he designed his first classical house. Lutyens proved capable of exceptionally convincing serious neo-Georgian, as at The Salutation, Sandwich (1911), as well as of vigorous Baroque in his house at Ilkley (1907) and his grandiose schemes for New Delhi and for the Liverpool Catholic Cathedral in the 1930s. A pleasant mixture of classicism with his earlier ample vernacular roofs is Gledstone Hall, Yorkshire (1923). His adaptation of Baroque to multi-storey offices by inserting rows of plain windows between a rich ground floor and skyline proved far too popular with less able architects, although in Lutyens's own hands, as at the Midland Bank, Poultry, London (1924), the device could be powerfully used. A happier period adaptation was his Westminster Housing Scheme (1928), in which six storeys of neo-Georgian sash windows are set in a grandly scaled red and white

165. Tigbourne Court

chequer of brick and cement. Lutyens's imaginative originality could also succeed with Gothic, as in his romantic reconstruction of Lindisfarne Castle on Holy Island off the Northumberland coast (1903). His versatility is brilliantly summed up in St Jude's Church, Hampstead Garden Suburb (1910), where classical forms are given the roughness of Romanesque and the upward thrust of Gothic, enfolded by one of his big spreading roofs.

Lutyens is most easily explained as an exceptional survival of the best of the Victorian period. The same is true of early twentieth-century architecture in the functional tradition. There are occasional good industrial buildings, such as Messrs Roberts's factory, Botolph Street, Norwich, by A. F. Scott (1903), but they come no closer to modern architecture than their more numerous mid Victorian equivalents. In housing, the excellent standards set by the London County Council were continued in Old Oak Common, Hammersmith (1912), White Hart Lane Estate, Tottenham (1911–c. 1930), and Watling Estate, Hendon (1926 onwards), the last [166] laid out on garden-city lines with undulating streets and a varied use of red brick, black weatherboarding, and roughcast. These estates are visually quite as attractive as the garden cities themselves at Letchworth and Welwyn in Hertfordshire. At Letchworth, laid out by Barry Parker and Sir Raymond Unwin from 1903, the houses are mainly roughcast; at Welwyn, by Louis de Soissons and A. W. Kenyon from 1919, they are mostly of neo-Georgian brick. Hampstead Garden Suburb, delightfully planned by Parker and Unwin in 1906, with a central group of buildings by Lutyens, is an attractive mixture of red brick and rough cast. But the importance of these garden cities and garden suburbs lies not so much in their architecture, which is less interesting than comparable Victorian housing, as in their triumphant vindication of the planning vision of Ebenezer Howard's *Tomorrow* (1898). Howard gave the Victorian experiments in model industrial settlements and garden suburbs something of the communal idealism which had inspired attempts at cooperative communities, and through this he created the twentieth-century concept of the new town, depending on its own industry, surrounded by open country, and socially self-sufficient.

The garden cities stand out as the one fresh achievement in a period generally lacking in vitality. There was little built after 1905 which can stand comparison with the imaginative vigour of the best mid or late Victorian architecture. Nor did the growing cautiousness of early

166. Watling Estate, Hendon

twentieth-century taste lead, as was once thought, to a general improvement in popular architectural standards. The half-hearted neo-Georgian pastiche and half-timbered roughcast mockery of Voysey which makes up the typical British suburb now seems quite as ugly as its Victorian equivalent, and certainly it was more cheaply and shoddily built.

An effective recovery of architectural standards could only come from a fundamental change in the architectural situation, a change which meant the ousting of creative historicism by an original and functionally appropriate new style, and could lead to cheap building which did not have to be ugly. In spite of its achievements, both original and functionalist, British architecture failed to find this new style, and instead it was evolved on the Continent, reaching Britain as a mature style abruptly, without any transitional stages. 'New Ways', 508 Wellingborough Road, Northampton, first house in the modern style in Britain, was designed in 1925 by Peter Behrens, the great German pioneer, for an engineering industrialist, W. J. Bassett-Lowke, who was also a patron of C. R. Mackintosh. It sits between its commonplace neighbours, as alien and pure in its geometric whiteness as the Renaissance sculpture of Torrigiano within the Gothic screens of Henry VII's tomb at Westminster.

This revolutionary house, and the other pioneering modern buildings which followed it, wholeheartedly adopt the international modern style of the period. As might be expected of a style which stood for a crusade against historicism, it was puritanical, purged of ornament, framed on bare aesthetic geometry. Inevitably some mannerisms creep in which can mar this purism. 'New Ways' has an Expressionist triangular staircase window in the jazzy style which became popular for cinemas in the 1930s. But the awkwardness of motifs of this kind when they appear only emphasizes the reliance of the style upon essentials. The new architecture was in general remarkably consistent. It was characterized by white concrete or rendered walls, flat roofs, thin white projecting balconies with concrete parapet panels, concrete staircase ramps, and strips of horizontal metal windows often carried round a corner. The shapes were always cubic, the façades dependent on rectilinear geometry and the contrast of black and white, of solid and void. It was an abstract, formal architecture, closely related to abstract and Cubist painting.

At the time, it was defended as a thoroughly functional style, but it is easy to see now that it was pushed far beyond the limits of strict functionalism. The principles of functional planning, honest construction, and frankly used materials had in fact been inherited from the Gothic revivalists. The new principle, which allowed the transformation of their meaning, was a wholehearted confidence in the potential beauty of a machine age. Instead of the personal integrity of craftsmanship, the rough beauty of local materials, a new excitement was found in the power and elegance of metal and concrete, the clean repetitive shapes of mass production. It was a discovery of fundamental importance, without which a rational twentieth-century style would have been impossible. But just because it was a pioneering aesthetic, ruthlessly insistent, much of the early modern architecture must be appreciated for its aesthetic rather than its functional qualities, just like the historicist architecture so scorned by the pioneers. Not much use was made of the new freedom in planning which came from flat roofs. Concrete was preferred to brick although it was more expensive both in building and maintenance and rarely recaptured the gleaming purity of its effect under the Mediterranean sun. Moreover, the mechanical shapes in which concrete was used were deceptive, for it was usually constructed by unskilled labour on the site rather than precast – or it might be simply brick, rendered to look like concrete.

The international character of the new style in these early years was emphasized by the part played in its British development in the 1930s by three Russians, Serge Chermayeff, Bertholdt Lubetkin, and A. V. Pilichowski, and, during their temporary sojourn in England in 1933–7, by three German leaders of the movement: Walter Gropius, Erich Mendelsohn, and Marcel Breuer. Gropius for a period worked in partnership with Maxwell Fry, Breuer with F. R. S. Yorke, while Lubetkin was the leading spirit of the Tecton group. There is no distinction between their work and that of British architects: Wells Coates, Joseph Emberton, Owen Williams, the firms of Connell, Ward, and Lucas and Sir John Burnet, Tait, and Lorne, or Frederick Etchells, the English translator of Le Corbusier's *Vers une architecture*.

It was significant of its position as the cause of a minority whose attacks on official architectural pomp were most easily answered by official indifference, that the largest group of buildings in the first fifteen years of the style was of private houses. The *Architectural Review*, the principal press supporter of modern architecture, had published illustrations of some sixty by 1939. They were all south of a line between the Bristol Channel and the Wash, and half were in London, Surrey, and Buckinghamshire. Among the best examples which can easily be seen are the very early group of houses by Burnet, Tait, and Lorne at Silver End [167], Essex (1926), and 'High and Over' and four other houses of 1929–34 above Station Road, Amersham, by A. D. Connell and Basil Ward respectively. In London there are: 'Six Pillars', Crescent Wood Road, Dulwich, by Harding and Tecton (1935), 32 Newton Road, Paddington, by Denys Lasdun (1938), and two striking groups: in Old Church Street, Chelsea, Nos. 64 and 66 (both 1936), by Mendelsohn and Chermayeff and by Gropius and Fry respectively; and in Frognal and Frognal Way, Hampstead, Sun House by Maxwell Fry (1935), No. 66 by Connell, Ward, and Lucas (1937), and a close of houses by E. L. Freud (1937).

These last houses by E. L. Freud were in brick, which makes the boxy cubic mannerisms of the period especially obvious. The brick

311

167. House at Silver End

pithead baths built in the Midlands, Wales, and the north by the Miners' Welfare Committee from 1932, which introduced the modern style to these parts of the country, are similar in character, but benefit from their larger scale [168]. They show the influence of the brick building of Dudok in Holland, and make an interesting contrast with the only other important modern brick buildings in Britain in the period, the London underground stations designed by Charles Holden. If the stations now seem rather less mannered, it is perhaps because they rely on a detailed sensitivity which owes more to Scandinavian tradition.

Towards the end of the 1930s a more general sensitivity and lightness began to appear. It can be seen in the latest of the houses mentioned. Elegant white rails replaced concrete parapets, and the windows, from being horizontal strips alternating with concrete, become fuller, even dominant. The stylistic change was anticipated in seaside architecture, and especially by Joseph Emberton's Royal Corinthian Yacht Club, Burnham-on-Crouch (1931). It indicated an easier confidence in the modern style, a less pressing need to be coldly serious, to shock the unconverted.

The change can be seen particularly well in school architecture. The school boarding house at Dartington Hall, Devon, by Howe and Lescaze (1934), is in the same uncompromising white and black cubic style as the masters' houses which they also built there. A. V. Pilichowski's work at Whittinghame College, Brighton (1936), is only a little more relaxed. But by 1938–9 a remarkably mature school style had been evolved. Impington Village College, Cambridgeshire [169], by Gropius and Fry, loosely shaped with the splayed walls and sloping roof of its hall set against more formal, plainer rear wings, is built of varied red and yellow brick with gaily coloured tiling and ironwork. Less well known, but clearly showing the same freedom, is Whitwood Mere Infants School, Yorkshire, by Oliver Hill, single-storeyed, with a long, delicately curving canopy, and a kindergarten at Northwich, Cheshire, by Leslie Martin and S. Speight, a prophetic

168. Blackhall pithead baths, Durham

experiment in light timber construction.

By 1939 the modern style had been successfully applied to other building types. Its clean forms and hygienic whiteness were naturally suited to hospitals. The best of a good series by Burnet, Tait, and Lorne was St Dunstan's Home for the Blind, Rottingdean, Sussex (1939). The Peckham Health Centre by Sir Owen Williams (1935) was both architecturally and socially more original, a combination of club and consultation rooms for regular medical checks, constructed of concrete pillars so that cafés, kindergarten, and gymnasium opened out from the central swimming pool.

Williams also designed the Boots Factory at Nottingham (1932), which, with Dunston Power Station, County Durham, by Merz and McLellan (1933), ironically remained the only important industrial building in the style. These two represented an important variation on the characteristic white cube, for both were almost entirely encased in glass window-walls standing free of the internal structure. This striking curtain-walling, later to become typical of office building rather than factories, was only paralleled by the gleaming window-

169. Impington Village College

170. Lawn Road flats, Hampstead

and-black-glass wall of the *Daily Express* offices in Fleet Street, by
Herbert Ellis and Clarke (1932), and later by the first large modern
shops, Peter Jones, Sloane Square, by William Crabtree and others
(1936), and St Cuthbert's Co-operative, Broad Street, Edinburgh, by
Thomas Marwick and Son (1937).

The plastic possibilities of concrete, which were to be equally
influential in the future, were developed in other building types. As
applied to blocks of flats, with long horizontal balconies, solid
staircase ramps, and tall blank end walls, concrete could have the
forbidding impressiveness of a fortress. The flats in Lawn Road,
Hampstead, by Wells Coates (1934) are an extreme example [170], and
if those at Ladbroke Grove by Maxwell Fry (1936) and Quarry Hill,
Leeds, by R. A. H. Livett (1935) are a little lighter, it is easy to see
how their emphatic shapes could lead to the treatment of concrete
as a coarse roughly-shuttered surface rather than as clean whiteness.

315

In complete contrast, the zoo buildings by Tecton at London and Dudley, especially the London Penguin Pool (1934), exploited the thin curves of concrete with daring imagination. Here concrete was given a quite different character, an elegance inducing fantasy.

These early examples of modern architecture in Britain were more important in preparing the way for the wider post-war acceptance of the style than for their intrinsic quality. It is true that when compared with the common architecture of the inter-war years they represent an undeniable improvement, but it cannot be said that by 1939 British architecture had recovered from the nadir to which it had fallen after 1910. Not only were buildings in the modern style still rare, but very few of them were of lasting architectural importance. While the best British buildings of the nineteenth century are of international significance, this is not true of those of this period. None of them is of sufficient originality or quality to appear in international histories of modern architecture. At best they are but sound examples of styles centred upon Germany, France, and America.

How far is this still true of British architecture? Direct comparison with the inter-war years is difficult for two reasons: changing patronage and changing style.

In the first post-war years the conversion of public authorities to the modern style – a reflection of the prevalent reforming atmosphere – together with the restriction of private building, meant that important architecture was no longer in private houses, private schools, shops, and luxury flats, but in local authority schools and housing. Tecton, Drake, and Lasdun, for example, were now to be found at work on the Hallfield Estate, Paddington, while Powell and Moya made their name with Churchill Gardens, Westminster. Both estates were begun in 1946, and in sheer scale their rows of balconied slabs quite overshadowed any pre-war modern work.

The climax of public patronage was the Festival of Britain in 1951, which was probably a decisive influence in converting popular taste to the modern style. Brilliantly laid out on the south bank of the Thames by Sir Hugh Casson, it was a series of varied pedestrian spaces between gay glass-walled pavilions and more ambitious structures like the wide Dome of Discovery and the Royal Festival Hall. This splendid concert hall, commissioned by the London County Council and designed by Leslie Martin and Robert Matthew, remains as evidence of the achievement of the Festival. With its auditorium raised above a great glass-walled concourse on varied levels, and

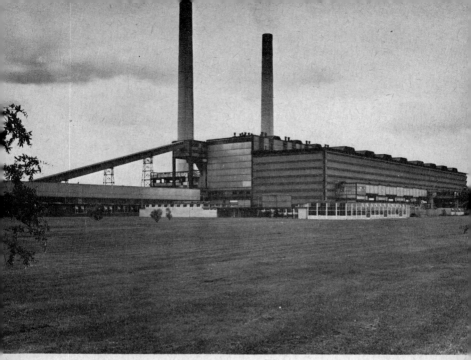

171. Power station, Marchwood

staircases rising into free-flowing space it is still the most impressive modern interior in Britain.

After the Festival, with the recovery of private building in the 1950s, there has been a revival of private patronage. In London especially an extraordinary spate of office building has transformed the landscape, sometimes intruding fatally on pleasant scenes, but elsewhere bringing exciting new contrasts of scale. Upstream from Westminster, a great wall of offices lines the south bank of the Thames, and on the other side the curved and counter-curved glass walls of the Vickers tower, by Ronald Ward (1963), rise to 387 feet, a height exceeded in England only by Salisbury spire. In the City and inner West End other curtain-walled slabs, like Basil Spence's Thorn House, St Martin's Lane (1959), or Trehearne and Norman Preston and Partners' State House, High Holborn (1961), with bold external grey ribs, dominate the narrow old brick streets around them.

At the same time the building of private housing has revived, and a number of houses of high quality have been built. Especially interesting are the estate village of low white houses at Rushbrooke, Suffolk, by Richard Llewelyn Davies, and the big-windowed, elegant, luxury flats in St James's Place by Denys Lasdun (1961).

In spite of this, public commissions still dominate the architectural scene. Office building has been more remarkable for quantity than quality, and has usually been little more than a crude effort to force as much floorspace into a confined site as the planning and day-lighting laws permit. Shops have been disappointing; Lasdun's Peter Robinson in the Strand (1958) is a rare exception. There are still very few private factories worth noticing. The best are perhaps the low-domed Brynmawr Rubber Factory, by Architects' Co-Partnership (1951), and the flint and concrete Bowater Paper Mill, Northfleet, by Farmer and Dark. These are balanced by consistent public work in power stations, collieries, and public transport. Farmer and Dark's power stations at Marchwood, Hampshire [171], and Belvedere, Kent, have the directness and scale of the best industrial architecture, while the light, plain airport buildings at Gatwick by Yorke, Rosenberg, and Mardall (1958) convey something of the urgency of flight. In housing and education, most of the best work is still built for local authorities; in addition, the universities have become an important source of new patronage in the last few years. Finally, a number of churches are now being built in the modern style, and one of these, St Paul, Bow Common, London, by Robert Maguire (1960) is of high architectural quality, simply designed around a central altar under a glazed lantern. It is unfortunate that far too much attention has been given to Sir Basil Spence's Coventry Cathedral (1951–63), which is essentially a Gothic revival structure with Baroque tricks and modernistic detail, no more than superficially representative of the modern movement.

The second difficulty in any comparison is that since the war the modern style has developed startlingly in divergent directions. Most of the buildings so far mentioned are straightforward developments of the architectural manner of 1938–9. Their quality is undeniable, and had they been built earlier they would have been of outstanding importance. But in a way that is typically, even sometimes fortunately British, they do not touch the extremes of style reached abroad in these years. Thus, in office building, the development of the curtain wall into towers and slabs of glacial refinement by Mies van der Rohe

172. Castrol House, London

is but moderately echoed in comparable British offices such as Castrol House, Marylebone Road [172], by Gollins, Melvin, and Ward (1960) or New Zealand House by Robert Matthew and Johnson-Marshall (1963).

Equally, the new developments with concrete, the thin rococo curves of parabolic shell vaulting on the one hand and the thick rough plastic peasant style achieved with crude in situ shuttering by Corbusier on the other, until recently had very little influence. Concrete was no longer painted white, but maintenance difficulties would have led to this anyway. There have been no startling shell domes in Britain. The curious curved concrete Wolfson Building at St Anne's College, Oxford, by Howell, Killick, and Partridge (1964), with windows jutting out as from a curved egg-box, is perhaps the nearest native parallel to Corbusier. Again, there have been few emulations of the strange clusters of brick tower shafts built in America by Louis Kahn, although a library in this style is planned by Glasgow University, and something of his influence may be seen in the very striking Engineering Block at Leicester University [173] by Stirling and Gowan (1963), a glass tower jacked up on a brick lecture box, with crisply tailored triangular corners creating a series of diagonal lines which focus on an entrance ramp.

These remarkable buildings owe much of their success to aesthetic originality; and, widely repeated by less sure hands, their mannerisms would be intolerable. Like those early modern houses in which the brick was rendered to look like concrete, they use the style of the present in the spirit of the past. Although a functional justification is usually made out for their shapes, the very fact that they are unique solutions not intended for repetition makes them expensive buildings in a machine age. When the pressure of university expansion forces the use of industrialized building as in schools, it is doubtful whether there will be many more buildings of this type. But for the moment university patronage appears to be unusually free of financial stringency, and it is also providing the leading examples of another architectural development which is overtly retrospective.

Immediately after the war shortages of materials ended the ubiquitous use of concrete in modern architecture, and experiments were made in weatherboarding, brick, and tile-hanging, which brought the modern style much closer to traditional British domestic architecture. A new modern vernacular was created, which has been attractively used in schools such as those in Nottinghamshire and in

173. University of Leicester, Engineering Block

174. University of Sussex

much public and private housing. It has helped to raise the general architectural standards of speculative building, and in the best private housing schemes, such as the Span estates by Eric Lyons at Blackheath, London (1957) and Ham Common, Surrey (1954) it has produced delightful results. But the return to tradition is now being pushed further towards historicism. At Brighton, the University of Sussex [174], by Sir Basil Spence (1963), deliberately echoes the ruined Roman Colosseum with its rhythmic concrete vaults and its great girders stretched across empty spaces, revealing glimpses of the grandly wooded park beyond. Still more remarkable in style is a library group at Manor Road, Oxford [175], by Sir Leslie Martin (1961–4), a series of dusty yellow brick slabs, overlapping at different levels, arranged around a long broad external flight of steps which runs almost to the top of the building, creating an unmistakably Egyptian air of dynastic terror.

Perhaps this architecture marks the beginning of another phase of aesthetic violence comparable to the high Victorian period. Perhaps it will remain an eccentric by-way. The outcome will almost certainly depend upon the social development of Britain during the coming decades. With a widening gap between rich and poor, too much money for a few commissions and too little for most, we shall come closer to the Victorian situation, with strange originality standing out in a mass of cheapness. If on the other hand we move towards equality, we shall probably make an increasing use of well-designed machine-produced building to satisfy social needs, and aesthetics will be disciplined by the simple economic shapes of machine production. If the post-war history of British architecture is any guide, there should be confidence in the outcome of development in this second direction, for there is little doubt that the really significant British contributions to architecture since 1945 have been in building for the community, in schools and in housing. Moreover, this is not just because of the high standard of design: it is the approach, fundamentally the humanity of approach, which has counted most.

175. Faculty libraries, Oxford

176. Roehampton Estate, London

In housing, the key to success has been in layout, and especially in the interest in community planning. The most striking examples have been the new towns, an attempt to realize the garden-city vision of vital urban communities set in the healthy air and natural beauty of the countryside. The most interesting of the first group of new towns begun in the 1940s are Harlow, planned by Frederick Gibberd, with very varied housing including some by Maxwell Fry and by F. S. R. Yorke separated by strips of rolling parkland, and Stevenage, where the attractive central shopping precinct was designed by L. G. Vincent. Comparable intentions on a smaller scale, but architecturally more impressive are new versions of the garden suburb like Tile Hill, tall yellow blocks in a birch wood outside Coventry, by Arthur Ling (1958), and Roehampton, London [176], by the L.C.C. Architect's Department (1952–9), a brilliant mixture of concrete slabs and towers and neat brick terraces set in mature undulating parkland.

324

Equally attractive, but more urban, are Camberwell Borough Council's Sceaux Gardens (1960), where tall curtain-walled slabs and low little terraces of old people's houses make delightful use of the former gardens of houses in Peckham Road, and the near-by L.C.C. Brandon Estate, Kennington (1961), with varied red and yellow terraces and tall concrete-boned towers grouped around a little shopping square.

There has been recently a tendency towards more close-knit housing, partly due to its greater aesthetic interest, but also because of the need to separate pedestrians and motor traffic, the danger of dispersed layouts to communal cohesion, and the shortage of land. The most interesting examples of this are the great twisting wall of elevated street-decks at Park Hill, Sheffield, by J. L. Womersley, and the grey slate-roofed terraces at Cumbernauld New Town [177], by Hugh Wilson, both begun in 1956. Cumbernauld is the first town to have a completely separated network of footpaths and motor roads. Undoubtedly there are dangers that the aesthetics of this denser housing, in which some of the visual drama of old working-class slums can be recaptured, will be more successfully exploited than its

177. Cumbernauld New Town

178. Primary School, Pentley Park, Welwyn Garden City

social possibilities. For example, Denys Lasdun's well-known 'cluster block' at Bethnal Green (1960), with its coarse concrete columns, strange criss-cross balconies, slatted wooden drying-spaces and exposed piping, certainly uses the visual atmosphere of a slum tenement with Piranesian drama, but at the expense of the humane quality of environment which has been the real distinction of recent English housing.

In schools, there has been a particularly important distinction between architecture of purely visual success and that of real significance. There have been many attractive schools commissioned by local authorities from private architects, but the most important advances have come from the local authorities themselves, and from the Ministry of Education.

Immediately after the war, Hertfordshire was faced by an acute immediate shortage of school places and by the need to prepare for the building of the New Towns and the growth of population in outer London, at a moment when traditional building materials and craftsmen were in short supply. To meet this situation the county architects evolved a new type of flexible prefabrication [178].

It was a building system based on a standard set of prefabricated parts – windows, roofing, walls and other components – which could be arranged in different ways on a repeating planning grid, manufactured in light engineering factories, and assembled on the site with a minimum of skilled labour. The new system not only allowed the economic benefit of programmed mass production but, because of its flexibility, enabled continual experiment in the educational planning of the schools. In 1948 the Ministry of Education set up a development group led by three architects from Hertfordshire, Stirrat Johnson-Marshall, David Medd, and Mary Crowley, which built a series of experimental schools, applying the Hertfordshire method to different materials and types of school. Of these, a secondary modern school at Wokingham, a primary school at Mitchell Walk, Amersham, and a village school at Finmere, Oxfordshire, were especially important. Meanwhile, in 1957, seven

179. Henry Hartland Grammar School, Worksop

authorities, led by Nottinghamshire, set up a consortium for school-building in mining areas, where subsidence created special problems. A typical primary school produced by this consortium, which is known as CLASP, was awarded the top medal at the Milan Triennale International School-Building Congress in 1960, and as a result Italy and West Germany have made long-term agreements by which they receive CLASP working drawings and architectural advice. A second British consortium, SCOLA, was formed in 1962. It would be impossible to mention even a selection of the schools built under these systems, but in addition to the continual good work by Hertfordshire and Nottinghamshire [179], the comprehensive schools built by Coventry in the CLASP system deserve special notice. A number of experiments with system-building are now being made with housing, and a War Office group which began by using the CLASP system has developed the NENK method, starting with a new barracks at Maidstone in 1963.

The key to the success of these industrialized systems pioneered in schools is not, as is often thought, simply in the techniques of mass production which they use. From the beginning their architects realized that buildings help to determine the quality of education, and over the years the details and planning have been continually refined to suit the needs of teachers and children. The architects have read and discussed educational theory, spent hours at both traditional and progressive schools watching teachers and children at work, noting the oversize furniture, the window that the child could not open, the lack of space for pinning up drawings or shelves for books, the cramped classrooms and the wasted corridor space. In the light of this intensive observation, they have been able to replan the schools so that corridors are almost eliminated and the space gained is thrown into classrooms, and these classrooms are shaped around the furniture and varied movement and activity within them. At the same time all the fittings and furniture have been redesigned. These schools are easily missed, for outside – although often attractive – they rarely seek to impress. But go inside, see the complex and delightful environment that has resulted: the study spaces with bookshelves and tables, the miniature kitchen, the tough floors and benching for carpentry, the greenhouse and the fishponds, the space for acting and music – see the school at work, and you realize that these buildings represent a fundamental architectural discovery.

Functionalism, as understood by modern architects, had been the aesthetic expression, above all externally, of the building's purpose, its materials, and its method of construction. In these schools it has been transformed to mean the design of the building from the inside outwards, taking its shape from the human activity within, which is itself understood by social observation. The very fact that they are mass produced has meant that far more thought has been given to the refinement of planning and detail than is possible in a conventional building. In the evolution of the modern style a crucial stage was the rejection of the English belief in the central importance of craftsmanship, of pleasure in skilled handwork. The problem of work, so fundamental to the Victorians, to Ruskin and Morris, has been neglected rather than solved by the twentieth century; but it is probably no accident that this transformation of functionalism, which makes ordinary people once more the centre of architectural design, should come from Britain.

Bibliography

There is a very considerable literature on English architecture, and perhaps the most important books are those published by or on behalf of the architects themselves and intended as more or less genteel self-advertisements. These include such important source-books as Colen Campbell's *Vitruvius Britannicus*, and the *Works in Architecture* of Robert Adam and his brothers, but they are not always easy to get hold of, nor are they very useful to the general reader. The following books are nearly all modern, authoritative, and fairly easy to come by: all of them ought to be in every Public Library of any size. For all three parts of the book volumes in *The Buildings of England* series by Nikolaus Pevsner (Penguin Books) will be useful.

PART I

T. S. R. BOASE, *Oxford History of English Art*, vol. 3, 1100–1216, Oxford University Press, 1953.

P. BRIEGER, *Oxford History of English Art*, vol. 4, 1215–1307, Oxford University Press, 1957.

A. W. CLAPHAM, *English Romanesque Architecture before the Conquest*, Oxford University Press, 1930; *English Romanesque Architecture after the Conquest*, Oxford University Press, 1934.

JOAN EVANS, *Oxford History of English Art*, vol. 5, 1307–1461, Oxford University Press, 1949.

JOHN HARVEY, *Gothic England*, Batsford, 1948; *Henry Yevele*, Batsford, 1946.

T. RICKMAN, *An Attempt to Discriminate Styles of English Architecture*, J. H. Parker, 5th ed., 1848.

L. F. SALZMAN, *A Documentary History of Medieval Buildings*, Oxford University Press, 1952.

A. HAMILTON THOMPSON, *Military Architecture in England*, Oxford Unisity Press, 1912.

G. F. WEBB, *Architecture in Britain: The Middle Ages*, Penguin Books, 1956.

PART II

H. M. COLVIN, *A Biographical Dictionary of English Architects, 1660–1840*, John Murray, 1954 (not a history but with very full details of the lives and works of every British architect of the period).

SIR J. SUMMERSON, *Architecture in Britain, 1530–1830*, Penguin Books, 4th ed., 1963 (the most complete and up-to-date historical survey of the whole field).

Three volumes in *The Oxford History of English Art* have so far appeared, dealing with the period since 1550:

E. MERCER, *English Art, 1553–1625*, Oxford University Press, 1962.

M. WHINNEY and O. MILLAR, *English Art, 1625–1714*, Oxford University Press, 1957.

T. S. R. BOASE, *English Art, 1800–70*, Oxford University Press, 1959.

The intervening period has been covered by three volumes by:

CHRISTOPHER HUSSEY, *English Country Houses*: (i) *Early Georgian, 1715–60*, (ii) *Mid Georgian, 1760–1800*, (iii) *Late Georgian, 1800–40*, Country Life Ltd, 1955–8.

PART III

BASIL CLARKE, *Church Builders of the Nineteenth Century*, S.P.C.K., 1938.

PETER FERRIDAY, *Victorian Architecture*, Jonathan Cape, 1963.

H. S. GOODHART-RENDEL, *English Architecture since the Regency*, Constable, 1953.

H. R. HITCHCOCK, *Architecture: Nineteenth and Twentieth Centuries*, Penguin Books, 1958; *Early Victorian Architecture in Britain*, Architectural Press, 1955.

N. PEVSNER, *Pioneers of Modern Design*, Penguin Books, 1960.

J. M. RICHARDS, *The Functional Tradition in Early Industrial Buildings*, Architectural Press, 1958.

Biographies:

G. F. CHADWICK, *The Works of Sir Joseph Paxton*, Architectural Press, 1961.

THOMAS HOWARTH, *Charles Rennie Mackintosh and the Modern Movement*, Routledge & Kegan Paul, 1952.

CHRISTOPHER HUSSEY, *The Life of Sir Edwin Lutyens*, Country Life Ltd, 1953.

W. R. LETHABY, *Philip Webb and his Work*, Oxford University Press, 1935.

Guide books:

QUENTIN HUGHES, *Seaport*, Lund Humphries, 1964.

SAM LAMBERT, *New Architecture of London*, British Travel and Holidays Association, 1963.

IAN NAIRN, *Modern Buildings in London*, London Transport, 1964.

NICHOLAS TAYLOR, *Cambridge New Architecture*, Trinity Hall, Cambridge, 1964.

Glossary

ACANTHUS: plant with thick fleshy and scalloped leaves used as part of the decoration of a Corinthian capital (*q.v.*) and in some types of leaf carving.

AISLE: lateral division of a church, generally parallel to and divided by pillars from the nave, choir, or transept.

AMBULATORY: semi-circular or polygonal aisle enclosing an apse (*q.v.*).

APSE: vaulted semicircular or polygonal end of a chancel or a chapel.

ARCHITRAVE: lowest of the three main parts of the entablature (*q.v.*) of an order (*q.v.*).

ART NOUVEAU: decorative style popular in the 1890s and 1900s, characterized by sinuous asymmetry.

ASHLAR: masonry of large blocks and smooth surface.

BARGEBOARDS: decorative boards placed along the inclined edges of a gable.

BATTER: sloping face of an upwardly narrowing wall.

BAYS: internal compartments of a building; each divided from the other not by solid walls but by divisions only marked in the side walls (columns, pilasters, etc.) or the ceiling (beams, etc.). Also external divisions of a building by fenestration.

BILLET MOULDING: ornamental motif made up of short rolls or cubes placed within a hollow moulding (Fig. 1).

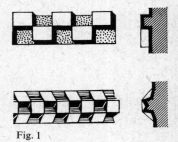

Fig. 1

BLOCK CAPITAL: Romanesque capital cut from a cube by having the lower angles rounded off to the circular shaft below (Fig. 2). Also called cushion capital.

Fig. 2

BOSS: knob or projection usually placed to cover the intersection of ribs in a vault.

BROACH SPIRE: spire, which is generally octagonal in plan, rising from the top or parapet of a square tower.

334

A small pyramidal piece of masonry covers the vacant triangular space at each of the four angles of the square and is carried up to a point along the diagonal sides of the octagon.

BUTTRESS: mass of brickwork or masonry projecting from or built against a wall to give additional strength. *Flying Buttress:* arch or half arch transmitting the thrust of a vault or roof from the upper part of a wall to an outer support or buttress.

CANTILEVER: bracket of lengthy projection.

CAPITAL: head or top part of a column.

CHAMFER: surface cut across a square corner at an angle of 45° to the other two surfaces.

CHANCEL: part of the east end of a church, usually applied to the whole continuation of the nave east of the crossing.

CHANCEL ARCH: arch at the west end of the chancel.

CHEVET: French term for the east end of a church (chancel, ambulatory, and radiating chapels).

CHEVRON: Norman moulding forming a zigzag.

CHOIR: that part of the church where divine service is sung.

CLERESTORY: upper storey of the nave walls of a church, pierced by windows.

COFFERING: decorating a ceiling with sunk square or polygonal ornamental panels.

CORBEL: block of stone projecting from a wall, supporting some horizontal feature.

CORINTHIAN: *see* Order.

CORNICE: in classical architecture, the top section of the entablature (*q.v.*). Also a projecting decorative

feature along the top of a wall, arch, etc.

CRENELLATION: battlement, that is, indented parapet.

CROCKET: Gothic leaf ornament placed on the sloping sides of spires, pinnacles, gables, etc.

CURTAIN WALL: wall acting as a screen and not as part of the structure of a building, as the connecting wall between the towers of a castle, or the external wall of a building constructed on an internal steel or concrete frame.

CUSHION CAPITAL: *see* Block capital.

DADO: decorative covering of the lower part of a wall.

DAGGER: tracery motif of the Decorated style (Fig. 3).

Fig. 3

DIAPER WORK: surface decoration composed of square or lozenge shapes.

DORIC: *see* Order.

DRUM: circular or polygonal vertical wall of a dome or cupola.

ENGAGED COLUMNS: columns attached to, or partly sunk into, a wall.

ENTABLATURE: in classical architecture the whole of the horizontal members above a column (that is architrave, frieze, and cornice).

FAN VAULT: *see* Vault.

FLUTING: vertical channelling in the shaft of a column.

FLYING BUTTRESS: *see* Buttress.

FRIEZE: middle division of a classical entablature (*q.v.*).

GALLERY: in church architecture, upper storey above an aisle, opened in arches to the nave.

GAZEBO: look-out tower or raised summer house in a picturesque garden.

'GIBBS SURROUND': of a doorway or window. An eighteenth-century motif consisting of a surround with alternating larger and smaller blocks of stone, quoin-wise, or intermittent large blocks, sometimes with a narrow raised band connecting them up the verticals and along the face of the arch.

GROIN: sharp edge at the meeting of two cells of a cross vault.

GROIN VAULT: see Vault.

HEXASTYLE: having six detached columns.

HIPPED ROOF OR GABLE: roof or gable with the upper part of the gable end sloped backwards.

IONIC: see Order.

LANCET WINDOW: slender pointed-arched window.

LANTERN: in architecture, a small circular or polygonal turret with windows all round crowning a roof or a dome.

LIERNE: see Vault.

LINENFOLD:. Tudor panelling ornamented with a conventional representation of a piece of linen laid in vertical folds. The piece is repeated in each panel.

MANSARD ROOF: roof with a double slope, the lower slope larger and steeper than the upper.

MASTIC INFILL: coloured cement used in grooves cut in stone.

MULLION: vertical post or upright dividing a window into two or more 'lights'.

ORDER: in classical architecture: column with base, shaft, capital, and entablature (q.v.) according to one of the following styles: Greek Doric, Roman Doric, Tuscan Doric, Ionic, Corinthian, Composite (Fig. 4). The established details are very elaborate, and some specialist architectural work should be consulted for further guidance.

PALLADIAN: architecture, following the ideas and principles of Andrea Palladio, 1508–80.

PANTILE: tile of curved S-shaped section.

PARABOLIC SHELL VAULTING: modern method of vaulting in thin domes of reinforced concrete or layers of wood, shaped in parabolic curves calculated to withstand stress; hyperbolic forms are also used.

PEDIMENT: low-pitched gable used in classical, Renaissance, and neo-classical architecture above a portico and above doors, windows, etc. It may be straight-sided or curved segmentally. *Broken Pediment:* one where the centre portion of the sloping sides is left out.

PIANO NOBILE: principal storey of a house with the reception rooms; usually the first floor.

PIER: strong, solid support, frequently square in section or of composite section (compound pier).

PILASTER: shallow pier attached to a wall.

PORTICO: centre-piece of a house or a church with classical detached or attached columns and a pediment.

PRESBYTERY: the part of the church lying east of the choir. It is the part where the altar is placed.

QUOINS: dressed stones at the angles of a building. Sometimes all the stones are of the same size; more often they are alternately large and small.

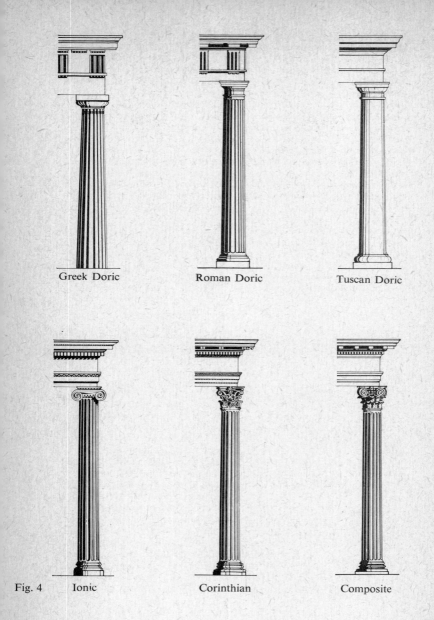

Greek Doric   Roman Doric   Tuscan Doric

Fig. 4   Ionic   Corinthian   Composite

RADIATING CHAPELS: chapels projecting radially from an ambulatory or an apse.

RENDERING: plastering of an outer wall.

RETROCHOIR: part of church behind the high altar.

ROLL MOULDING: moulding of semi-circular or more than semicircular section.

ROSE WINDOW: circular window with patterned tracery arranged to radiate from the centre.

ROTUNDA: building circular in plan.

ROUGHCAST: plaster of lime and gravel for outer walls.

RUSTICATION: work with large blocks of ashlar stone: *rock-faced* if the surfaces of the blocks are left rough like rock; *smooth* if the blocks are smooth and separated by V-joints; *banded* if the separation by V-joints applies only to the horizontals.

SANCTUARY: area around the main altar of a church (*see* Presbytery).

STIFF-LEAF: Early English type of foliage of many-lobed shapes (Fig. 5).

Fig. 5

STUCCO: plaster work.

SWAG: festoon formed by a carved piece of cloth suspended from both ends.

TRACERY: intersecting ribwork in the upper part of a window, or used decoratively in blank arches, on vaults, etc.

TRANSEPT: transverse portion of a cross-shaped church.

TRIFORIUM: arcaded wall passage or blank arcading facing the nave at the height of the aisle roof and below the clerestory (*q.v.*) windows (*see* Gallery).

VAULT: Barrel vault: vault of semi-circular or pointed section. Chiefly Norman and Renaissance. Also called tunnel vault. Cross vault: *see* Groin vault. Domical vault:

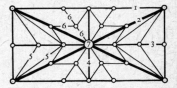

1. transverse rib
2. diagonal rib
3. transverse ridge rib
4. longitudinal ridge rib
5. tiercerons
6. liernes
7. boss

Fig. 6

square or polygonal dome rising direct on a square or polygonal bay, the curved surfaces separated by groins (*q.v.*). Fan vault: late medieval vault where all ribs springing from one springer are of the same length, the same distance from the next, and the same curvature. Groin vault or Cross vault: vault of two barrel vaults of identical shape intersecting each other at right angles. Chiefly Norman and Renaissance. Lierne: tertiary rib, that is, rib which does not spring either from one of the main springers or

338

from the central boss. Introduced in the fourteenth century, continues to the sixteenth century. Quadripartite vault: one wherein one bay of vaulting is divided into four parts. Rib vault: vault with diagonal ribs projecting along the groins. Ridge rib: rib along the longitudinal or transverse ridge of a vault. Introduced in the early thirteenth century. Sexpartite vault: one wherein one bay of quadripartite vaulting is divided into two parts transversely so that each bay of vaulting has six parts. Tierceron: secondary rib, that is, rib which issues from one of the main springers or the central boss and leads to a place on a ridge rib.

Introduced in the early thirteenth century. Transverse arch: arch separating one bay of a vault from the next. *See* Fig. 6; for tunnel vault, *see* Barrel vault.

WAGON ROOF: roof in which by closely set rafters with arched braces the appearance of the inside of a canvas tilt over a wagon is achieved. Wagon roofs can be panelled or plastered (ceiled) or left uncovered.

WEATHERBOARDING: overlapping horizontal boards covering an outer wall.

Index

Note: Page numbers in bold indicate illustrations

Palladio, Andrea, 172–3, 178, 213, 220, 224, 225, 226, 230
Pantheon, *see* London
pantile, 336
Papworth, J. B., 264
parabolic shell vaulting, 336
Parker, Barry, 308
Park Town, *see* Oxford
Parliament, Houses of, *see* London
Paul of Caen, 35
Paxton, Sir Joseph, 273, 279, 288
Peacock, Joseph, 295
Pearson, J. L. 289
Peckforton, Gothic castle at, 289
pediment, 336
Penarth, St Augustine, **293**, 294
pendants, 137–8, 143
Penrhyn Castle, 289
Penshurst Place, 156, **156**
Perpendicular style, 106, 108, 114, 118 ff., 140–1, 146–51
Pershore Abbey, 27, 108
Peterborough Cathedral, 26, 27, 31, 34, 35, 41–2, 47, 48
Peter of Rome, 93
Peter of Spain, 93
Pevsner, N., *Pioneers of Modern Design*, 332
piano nobile, 336
pier, 336
Pietro da Cortona, 201
pilaster, 336
Pilichowski, A. V., 311, 313
Pilkington, F. T. 293
Piranesi, Giambattista, 253
Pitzhanger Manor, *see* London
Playfair, W. H., 287
Pollington, 284, 286
Poore, Bishop, 87–8
portico, 336
porticus, first appearance of, 18
power stations, 318
Pratt, Sir Roger, 183, 185, 191
prefabrication, 327
presbytery, 336
Prior, E. S., 304
Prosser, Thomas, 279
Pudsey, Bishop, 145
Pugin, A. W. N., 272, 289, 299

Purbeck marble, 75, 80
Puttenham, 299

Queen's Chapel, *see* London
Queen's House, Greenwich, 175, **177**, 178–9, **178**, 207
quoins, 336

Radcliffe Camera, *see* Oxford
radiating chapels, 338
railway stations, 279, 281
Ramsey, monastery founded at, 27, 29
Ramsey, William, 117
Ravenna, polygonal-apse form at, 18
Reading Abbey, 60
Reculver, church at, 17, **17**, 19
Reform Club, *see* London
Regent Street, *see* London
Reims Cathedral, 94, 96
Rendering, 338
Repton, crypt at, 29, **30**
Repton, Humphrey, 259, 262, 264
retrochoir, 70, 110–13, **111**, 338
Revett, Nicholas, 250
Reynolds, Sir Joshua, 233–4
Richard of Paris, 93
Richard II, 150
Richards, J. M., *The Functional Tradition in Early Industrial Buildings*, 275 n., 332
Richmond Castle, 145
Rickman, T., *An Attempt to Discriminate Styles of English Architecture*, 331
Rievaulx Abbey, 64, 66, 71
Ripon Cathedral, 22, 70–1, **70**, 103
Roberts, Henry, 283
Robson, E. R., 286
Roche Abbey, 67–9, **67**, 70
Rochester:
    Castle, 144
    Cathedral, 17
Roger of Pont l'Évêque, 70
Roker Church, Durham, 304
roll moulding, 338
Rome, 31
    old St Peter's, 16
Romsey Abbey, 57, **57**, 61
rose window, 96, 126, 338

349